Public Expressions of Religion in America

CONRAD CHERRY,
Series Editor

*Published in cooperation with the Center for the Study of
Religion and American Culture
Indiana University-Purdue University at Indianapolis*

BOOKS IN THE SERIES

Producing the Sacred: An Essay on Public Religion
ROBERT WUTHNOW

Unsecular Media: Making News of Religion in America
MARK SILK

Uncivil Rites: American Fiction, Religion, and the Public Sphere
ROBERT DETWEILER

Houses of God: Region, Religion, and Architecture in the United States
PETER W. WILLIAMS

Private Needs, Public Selves: Talk about Religion in America
JOHN K. ROTH

PRIVATE NEEDS, PUBLIC SELVES

PRIVATE NEEDS, PUBLIC SELVES

Talk about Religion in America

JOHN K. ROTH

UNIVERSITY OF ILLINOIS PRESS
Urbana and Chicago

1 2 3 4 5 C P 5 4 3 2 1

This book is printed on acid-free paper.

Library of Congress Cataloging-in-Publication Data

Roth, John K.
    Private needs, public selves : talk about religion in
America / John K. Roth.
        p.   cm. — (Public expressions of religion in America)
        Includes bibliographical references and index.
        ISBN 0-252-01933-4 (alk. paper). — ISBN 0-252-06651-0
(pbk. : alk. paper)
        1. United States—Religion—20th century.   2. United
States—Religion.   I. Title.   II. Series.
BL2525.R68   1997
200'.973—dc21   97-4613
200'.973—dc21   97-4613
                                                       CIP

To
Conrad and Tony
Jan and Jim
Amanda and Anne
Bill and Hugh
Ed and Terry

Although I have much to write to you, I would rather not use paper and ink; instead I hope to come to you and talk with you face to face, so that our joy may be complete.

— 2 JOHN 12

Lift up your eyes
Upon this day breaking for you.
Give birth again
To the dream.
Women, children, men,
Take it into the palms of your hands,
Mold it into the shape of your most
Private need. Sculpt it into
The image of your most public self.

— MAYA ANGELOU,
"On the Pulse of Morning"

CONTENTS

Preface *xiii*

Introduction: Defining Talk about Religion *1*

ONE Mapping America *19*

TWO How Much? What Kind? American Needs for
Religious Discourse *44*

THREE Virtue and Religion *68*

FOUR American Beliefs: Popular Opinions and
Religious Inclinations *90*

FIVE Religion Matters *121*

SIX Getting Along in America: How Talk about
Religion Can Help *142*

SEVEN Things Unspoken: Religion and Human Rights *166*

EIGHT The Shadow of Birkenau: How to Talk about
Religion in Public *195*

Epilogue: Deepening Talk about Religion *219*

Select Bibliography *243*

Index *251*

More than a decade ago, I learned about a series of symposia and seminars on American religion that would be sponsored by the Department of Religious Studies and the Center for American Studies at Indiana University–Purdue University in Indianapolis, Indiana. Although I did not know the leaders of that initiative, their agenda attracted me. I felt a need to get involved.

Little did I know how much that private need would affect me, but those ongoing sessions of study and reflection at IUPUI changed my public roles by leading me to work in new and different ways. Especially by bringing me into close and sustained contact with adventurous scholars from many regions of the country who study American culture and in particular the multiple ways in which it is infused by religious expression, involvement in those symposia and seminars expanded my philosophical and religious horizons.

Pioneered by Tony Sherrill, Jan Shipps, Jim Smurl, and others, the work on American religion flourished at IUPUI and found more secure institutional form with the establishment of the Center for the Study of Religion and American Culture, which has been under the sure direction of Conrad Cherry since 1988. The Center has attained national prominence because it fulfills with distinction its mission to improve the public understanding of American religion and to reveal the continuing influence of religion in American life as a whole.

From 1992 to 1994, the Center's work included four major conferences that addressed "Public Expressions of Religion in America." Funded by the Lilly Endowment, this series explored major, but often unconventional, ways in which religion "goes public" in the United States. Beyond sponsoring scholarly papers and creative expressions in the arts, the project commissioned books. One of the invitations to write on this theme came to me.

As I realized at once and would continue to discover, the acceptance of that invitation was not to be taken lightly. It meant that I needed to write a book that focused on public expressions of religion in the United States, a topic as ambiguous as it is vast. In addition, the writing had to be readable, interesting, and informed by sound scholarship but directed to an audience wider than that of the professional scholars in religious studies. In keeping with the tone and substance of the IUPUI symposia out of which it was commissioned, the book also needed to identify public expressions of religion that were not confined to obvious religious institutions or conventional scholarly studies of religion. The IUPUI series had pointed the perspectives on public expressions of religion in the United States in new and different directions. My book had to take the risk of advancing those investigations. Part of that risk would include facing the criticism that I had talked about too many things and had not narrowed the discussion enough.

This book does concentrate on diverse experiences and events. The reason is not because religion exists anywhere and everywhere. It does not. But religion does involve many different things, and many different things do involve religion. To show those connections empirically is risky business. It requires methods that are unorthodox, scope that breaks conventional standards of precision, and inquiry that crosses disciplinary lines between the field of religious studies and other scholarly areas, and at times crosses disciplinary lines within the field of religious studies itself.

For example, this book's contributions to the study of religion in America include bridge-building over a divide that separates two theoretical camps. On one side of this divide are interpreters who concentrate on the civic roles of religion and whose perspectives emphasize critical appraisals and recommendations about religion's proper place within the American sociopolitical scene. On the other side are interpreters who concentrate on popular culture and whose perspectives emphasize description of the ways in which religion flavors and is flavored by it. Typically, the first outlook dwells on the sociological, political, and ethical dimensions of religious life, but without paying sufficient attention to the personal and broadly cultural needs that religion expresses and fills. The second outlook analyses the latter elements more completely, but without paying sufficient attention to sociological, political, and ethical dimensions of religious life. Divided by emphasis and approach, the interpreters in these two camps eye each other uneasily. Those in the popular culture camp are likely to see the other side as "elitist." Those who criticize and advocate particular roles for religion in American life are likely to see the popular culturalists as lacking analytical and philosophical depth. It would be good for all concerned if these two camps communicated less pejoratively and more openly with each other than they typically do. Such communication would show that their most important perspectives all have a place and that the customary quarrels among them are as unnecessary as they are dissatisfying. This book tries to give both popular culture and philosophical analysis their due. Doing so, it starts to bridge a divide that needlessly hinders the study of religion in America.

The challenges to speak publicly on the book's commissioned topic and to speak in the ways that the topic required created many private needs for me. How would I write this book? What questions, themes, data, experiences, and theories would I discuss? How would I organize the inquiry's findings? Such issues were mine to resolve, but the fact that they ultimately belonged to me did not make them mine alone. Critics read what I drafted and criticized it—insistently. So did editors. Audiences listened to lectures that emerged from my thinking and responded with insight. Friends offered much-needed encouragement. Each and all, they helped me to write what I wanted to say but could never have said by myself. The private needs that I wanted to fill could only be met by my "going public," by embracing and evaluating the relationships with others that do so much to identify who I am as an individual and what is personally mine.

Without social relationships, personal life has no content. Without the particularity of experiences that are mine or yours alone—but still in relationship with the lives of others—public life remains an abstraction, which it definitely is not. Working on this book convinced me anew that we have private needs because we are public selves. That relationship works the other way as well. We are public selves because, unavoidably, our private needs entail social relationships.

The realms of the private and the public are intertwined so as to be inseparable. The distinction between private and public identifies and describes dimensions or aspects of life that are particular to each one of us, but even the features of experience that we regard as the most personal cannot be comprehended apart from their location in a context, a world, that is a social reality. Individuals cannot describe themselves without reference to persons and places, feelings, thoughts, memories, and experiences that are social. Each person is individual, but the social qualities of our lives go all the way down—a person is relational, and without relations no individuals exist. In eloquent, down-to-earth terms, a moving reflection on human hands by the sociologist James Stockinger expresses key meanings of those philosophical claims:

It is not at first with our own hands that we pick the acorns and apples from the commonwealth of nature to nourish our own bodies. It is the hands of other people that supply the needs of our bodies, both in our infancy and beyond.

For each of us lives in and through an immense movement of the hands of other people. The hands of other people lift us from the womb. The hands of other people grow the food we eat, weave the clothes we wear and build the shelters we inhabit. The hands of other people give pleasure to our bodies in moments of passion and aid and comfort in times of affliction and distress. It is in and through the hands of other people that the commonwealth of nature is appropriated and accommodated to the needs and pleasures of our separate, individual lives, and, at the end, it is the hands of other people that lower us into the earth.[1]

While revising these prefatory words, I listened to music by Aaron Copland, that well-loved American composer who died at the age of ninety in 1990. The son of Russian-Jewish immigrants who fled antisemitism and pogroms, Copland took musical training in France, but it was American song and story that inspired him best and made him a major contributor, in his own way, to the public expression of religion in the United States. His well-known *Fanfare* was for the Common Man. His *Appalachian Spring*, perhaps the quintessence of American classical music, was drawn from folk songs and the lovely Shaker hymn, "Simple Gifts." Those tunes and words, the memories and hopes they contain, keep moving people all the more because of Copland's distinctive ways of evoking them.

Less familiar than those two pieces is another by Copland that I love. It is his 1942 *Lincoln Portrait*. Among its rich echoes of Stephen Foster melodies and American life are some of Abraham Lincoln's words themselves. Copland's text takes many of its quotations from Lincoln's Second Annual Message to Congress, which was delivered on December 1, 1862, just a month before his Emancipation Proclamation would declare freedom for all slaves in the areas still in rebellion to federal authority. Aptly, Lincoln has been called "the spiritual center of American history."[2] Copland's *Portrait* paints him as a "quiet and melancholy man." It also stresses that "*this* is what Abe Lincoln said":

The dogmas of the quiet past are inadequate to the stormy present. The occasion is piled high with difficulty, and we must rise with the occasion. As our case is new, so we must think anew, and act anew. We must disenthrall our selves, and then we shall save our country.

Fellow-citizens, *we* cannot escape history. We of this Congress and this administration will be remembered in spite of ourselves. No personal significance, or insignificance, can spare one or another of us. The fiery trial through which we pass will light us down, in honor or dishonor, to the latest generation. . . . We—even *we here*—hold the power, and bear the responsibility. In *giving* freedom to the *slave,* we *assure* freedom to the *free*—honorable alike in what we give, and what we preserve. We shall nobly save, or meanly lose, the last best hope of earth.[3]

Lincoln's words fit the United States almost as well in the late 1990s as they did in 1862 or in 1942, when Copland set them to music. Ours is a stormy present. Brewed in history, the storms we face have much to do with its legacies. True, as the twenty-first century approaches, our national life is so internationally related that Americans alone do not possess all the power needed to save it. But the United States does need saving from domestic strife that needlessly wastes hopeful dreams.

In a 1995 book, *Values Matter Most,* Ben J. Wattenberg writes that values are the nation's "most potent *political* issue" and its "most important *real* issue."[4] In agreement, I would add that both dimensions of that issue invite, indeed require, talk about religion in America. Never isolated from the people who embody them and the powers that inspire them, values do matter immensely, and because they do, religion matters, too. Rarely, if ever, are values unrelated to religion. Without public discourse about religion, our understanding of which values matter most will be impoverished and shallow. So this book is about Americans, our values, how religion affects —and is affected by—them and us, and how a sound understanding of what matters most depends on the right kinds of talk about religion in public.

Although the book's relevance extends to anyone who is interested in and affected by what goes on within the United States, I have written primarily to and for American citizens old and new. The pronouns *we, us,* and *our* should be understood that way in the chapters that lie ahead. In the 1990s, American identity has been ambiguous and contested. With the increasing diversity of our people, how could it not be? As this book reconsiders what American identity can mean at the end of the twentieth century and the beginning of the twenty-first, it underscores how we Americans are responsible for our country's well-being and what is at stake in the work of nurturing it. Thus, it is important to notice one more aspect of Lincoln's rhetoric, an aspect also discernible in James Stockinger's previously quoted passage about human hands.

Their themes point to experiences and suggest concerns that are more than political and economic. As he called attention to basic differences between right and wrong, to commendable senses of purpose and destiny, to causes that are—and are not—worth dying for, Lincoln spoke about memory, meaning, and hope that extend beyond the life of individual persons or the existence of particular groups or generations. As it calls attention to the particularity of birth and death and the relationships on which the filling of our specific personal needs depend, Stockinger also alludes to horizons of memory, meaning, and hope that transcend the limits of our particular times and places.

Where such qualities are discussed, religion is never far behind. As I hear Aaron Copland's *Lincoln Portrait* and meditate on Stockinger's picture of human hands, my ears and eyes interpret their explorations as religious—at least in part, and implicitly if not explicitly. Through illustration and analysis, this book unfolds and maps the meanings that such a claim contains. It shows how a religiously attuned interpretation of words like Lincoln's and Stockinger's fits a rich variety of American talk.

The book does not claim that all American talk can be interpreted aptly in that way. Much of it cannot. Nor does the book hold that talk that can be so interpreted is necessarily good. Much of it is not. Instead, the book's chapters explore how American talk about religion—implicit and explicit alike—is at once more varied, widespread, and public than we may think and more restrictive, limited, and private than we should wish.

Suggesting how American talk about religion should be interpreted and understood, appreciated and criticized, limited and amplified, the book's arguments, illustrations, and explorations accent how our private needs and public selves interact. That interaction creates the context where the yearnings of memory, meaning, and hope that define religion find expression and make sense. The quality of that interaction decisively affects how we Americans will bear or shirk our responsibilities to think, speak, and act anew about what matters most.

Acknowledgments

Inescapably we are public selves, because we live and move and have our being with others. In the case of this particular project, that fact has been a blessing, because the support and encouragement of many people at home and abroad have helped to make the book possible. Special thanks go to Conrad Cherry. Without his careful criticism and patient editing, the project would never have been completed. Madeleine Adams, Theresa Sears, and especially Liz Dulany, my editors at the University of Illinois

Press, provided encouragement that sustained my energy and expertise that improved my work all along the way. A gifted graduate of Claremont McKenna College, Irina Khersonsky, spent her senior year assisting me, saving me from pitfalls, and enhancing the book's clarity. I am grateful, too, for opportunities to present early versions of some of the book's chapters at Brigham Young University, Indiana State University, the Highlands Institute for American Religious Thought in Highlands, North Carolina, the Institute for the Humanities at Salado, Texas, and at the Gould Center for the Humanities, Claremont McKenna College, which helped to sponsor my research. Good friends such as Terry Warner, E. J. Tarbox, Creighton Peden, Harry Wilmer, and Ricardo Quinones made those occasions possible. I also got special help from the members of a seminar group that Conrad Cherry convened regularly at IUPUI. It included Catherine Albanese, Randall Balmer, Bill Dean, Robert Detweiler, Ted Estess, Yvonne Haddad, Hugh Laughlin, Ed Linenthal, Stephen Marini, Jay Moseley, Peter Paris, Amanda Porterfield, Tony Sherrill, Jan Shipps, Mark Silk, Jim Smurl, James Wall, and Peter Williams. An adult study group at the Claremont Presbyterian Church, my home congregation in Claremont, California, provided another place where I could test my ideas. My pastors, John Najarian and Sandra Tice, have been supportive, too, through the meaningful public expressions of religion that their leadership promotes.

Substantial revision and final editing of the manuscript took place in Oslo, Norway, where I spent my 1995–96 sabbatical as a roving Fulbright scholar in American Studies. This position attached me to the Royal Norwegian Ministry of Education, Research, and Church Affairs. As I interpreted American experience during my Fulbright year, discussion with teachers and students in Norway's upper secondary schools deepened my understanding of religion and American culture. In addition, I am especially indebted to Barbara Lysholt Petersen, who retired in 1996 after thirty years as the executive director of the U.S.-Norway Fulbright Foundation for Educational Exchange, to her staff, and also to Donald MacCulloch at the Ministry of Education. They all gave me invaluable help and counsel.

Finally, nothing of value that I could say concerning talk about religion—in public or in private—would have been possible without the love of my wife, Lyn, and my children, Andy and Sarah, or without the nurture of my father, Josiah, and my mother, Doris, who died as this book neared completion. This book is about talk, but words can express only in part my gratitude to the five of them, who show me what most deserves respect and loyalty.

NOTES

1. The statement is from Stockinger's Ph.D. dissertation, "Locke and Rousseau: Human Nature, Human Citizenship, and Human Work," which he wrote in the Department of Sociology at the University of California, Berkeley. The passage is cited from Robert N. Bellah, Richard Madsen, William M. Sullivan, Ann Swidler, and Steven M. Tipton, *The Good Society* (New York: Alfred A. Knopf, 1991), 104.

2. Sidney E. Mead, *The Lively Experiment* (New York: Harper and Row, 1963), 73.

3. See Richard N. Current, ed., *The Political Thought of Abraham Lincoln* (Indianapolis: Bobbs-Merrill, 1967), 234.

4. Ben J. Wattenberg, *Values Matter Most: How Republicans or Democrats or a Third Party Can Win and Renew the American Way of Life* (New York: Free Press, 1995), 10.

PRIVATE NEEDS, PUBLIC SELVES

Defining Talk about Religion

Orel, I'm afraid this is very serious.
—DR. FRANK JOBE TO OREL HERSHISER

When I speak of "talk about religion in America," the word *religion* signifies a broad category. It refers to multiple dimensions and expressions—personal and public—of the nation's *spiritual culture*. Following William Dean, I interpret this culture to be constituted by and expressed through "myths, rituals, narratives, traditions, and theories," as well as through institutions and communities, all of which inform and mold a society's deepest beliefs and meanings, yearnings and purposes.[1] Following Dean again, I take those *deepest beliefs and meanings, yearnings and purposes* to refer to "a person's or a people's 'sense of the whole,'" to "whatever is ultimately important within 'the whole'" as a person or a people understands it, and thus to what is sacred or thought to be sacred.[2]

Sensing the Whole

As I use the phrase, a "sense of the whole" emerges from a basic human awareness, which is widely if not universally shared: we are small but perhaps not insignificant beings within a vast reality. Although reality may not be restricted to history and nature, it at least includes all the powers and processes, individual things and particular persons that history and nature contain. So the awareness of which I speak entails plurality, "manyness," the sense that reality is full of great variety and particularity. Within that variety and particularity there may be plenty of disconnections and discontinuities, too. Nevertheless, the awareness of which I speak also involves relationships, order, and coherence; it senses that reality hangs together more or less.

In addition, these varied dimensions of our experience are rich with meanings, purposes, aims, and goals, which human freedom helps to initiate and actualize. These elements increase reality's diversity. They also make us wonder how all of these ingredients fit together—to the extent that they do. A sense of the whole reflects, expresses, builds upon, and interrogates that wondering. Thus, a sense of the whole is not complete but in process, for reality eludes our full comprehension. We experience horizons that can be approached but never reached; they keep receding as experience unfolds. As we have these experiences, our sense of the whole expands accordingly. Finite though we are, we can and often do produce a sense of the whole, infinite though the whole may be. And although the infinite whole we experience may ultimately be one, the particular sense of the whole that each of us produces, finite as we are, may vary over time and differ from the sense of the whole produced by other individuals and groups. Thus, in this book I sometimes speak of "senses of the whole" to emphasize that mutability and plurality. By indicating that there can rightly be "senses of the whole," I also underscore that no individual's, community's, or nation's sense of the whole can reasonably claim finality or completeness. On the contrary, as I refer to a sense or senses of the whole, both concepts entail rejections of and warnings against every form of totalitarian or exclusively absolutist tendencies.

To be more specific, five movements are necessary to produce a sense of the whole that includes perspectives about what is thought to be ultimately important and sacred: (1) discerning to what extent and how the many features of reality fit together; (2) clarifying what is most important about those relationships; (3) focusing the wisdom that such discernment and clarification bring; (4) intensifying the hopes and encouraging the actions that such wisdom enjoins; and (5) putting into practice what has been discerned, clarified, focused, intensified, and encouraged. Although it often distracts us from such understanding, American life can put us in touch with those depths.

To begin considering how that contact can happen, notice that although human consciousness can conceive a sense of the whole, nobody is born in possession of any definite understanding of that kind. To speak of a sense of the whole, then, is to refer neither to an innate idea nor to one unrelated to the particularities of experience. In fact, a sense of the whole depends on sensing something. To sense something means to perceive, grasp, or comprehend it. Expanding the activity of sensing further, to sense something might also mean to interpret it, even to invest it with meaning or to bestow meaning upon it. Out of such activities, insight can emerge. An understanding that focuses on fundamental relationships, insight grows from and develops through the particularities of experience. Through the interaction and interdependence of feeling, imagination, tradition, and reasoning, insight brings a sense of the whole to life.

A sense of the whole begins with and, in turn, informs the particularities of experience. Its primary sources and impacts include the loyalties that govern our lives. Those loyalties are not abstractions. They are definite and vital connections that consist of real persons and places, commitments and causes, values and virtues. Even more specifically, the loyalties that connect with life's profoundest depths are those that transcend the finitude of our individual lives, which is to say that these loyalties are not ones that ever get completely fulfilled and finished.

Loyalty to one's family, to a political cause such as liberty or justice, to one's country or specific religious faith may be like that. Such loyalties can appeal so strongly to us as individuals, as members of a community or a tradition, as citizens of the United States, that we become willing and even compelled to spend our lives, indeed to give up our lives, in their service. Human judgment, of course, can be blind, illusory, or deceived about these matters. A feeling or belief that something is worth dying for is not sufficient to make it so. Nevertheless, such loyalties can both lead and respond to senses of the whole. More specifically, such loyalties can both lead and respond to senses of the sacred within the whole.

To speak of the sacred is to identify what remains as most important, valuable, precious, meaningful, and good after critical reflection peels away error and dross. Here, too, human judgment is limited and imperfect. Ongoing evaluation is crucial. As that evaluation takes place, clarity about a central truth emerges. Much does not deserve to be called sacred in these senses, but much that does deserve such identification—take justice, for example, or liberty and life itself—is also fragile, vulnerable, irreplaceable, and often tragically targeted for violent destruction. Thus, our American senses of the sacred reflect and intensify loyalties, which, in turn, raise questions and responses pertaining to senses of the whole. How do the things we Americans care about most deeply fit together, if they do? Especially in a world with the awesome mixtures of beauty and banality, pleasure and pain, happiness and sorrow, virtue and vice, good and evil that ours contains, how are we to cope and live well—individually and as members of communities? What lasts beyond the finitude of our private needs and public selves? What is the significance of that reality? What about that reality might be of ultimate importance? How could we relate to that ultimate importance? How should we?

The things we Americans care about most as individuals and as members of communities reach beyond the boundaries of our finite lives. Our loyalties make us wonder what will happen next—when our energy is spent or replenished, when our causes are lost or won, when we recognize that history is not ours to control completely and that death awaits us. Only through the particular embodiments and expressions of our lives can loyalty exist, but when it is most profound, loyalty shows that, within history and beyond, so much eludes its particular embodiments and expressions.

More than any other aspect of human experience, religion involves those recognitions and responses to them. Indeed, religion is defined by their presence. Often that presence is obvious, explicit, and articulated directly. Probably even more often, such recognitions and responses are less than obvious and indirectly expressed, if they are articulated verbally at all, but they do exist, latent and implicit though they may be. Not every experience has religious qualities, overt or latent, any more than every expression of religion is beneficial, but one advantage of my interpretation of "religion" is that it enables us to define talk about religion broadly.

What Talk about Religion Involves

Not all expressions of religion involve words and talk. Symbol, ritual, art, music, dance, meditation, silence—all have their place in religion. Words can even obscure and distort the meanings that those forms communicate, but without speaking and writing to contextualize and interpret them, the meanings those forms convey have limited power to communicate. Without talk—talk in public—to situate these expressions, their impact is likely to be diminished.

As I use the term, then, talk about religion consists of conversation, discussion, debate—any communication involving language, spoken but also written—that concerns itself implicitly as well as explicitly with senses of the whole and with what is or is thought to be sacred. Like all communication, talk about religion is always social, even when it involves our most deeply personal feelings and experiences. Still, social though it is, not all talk about religion is public. Often appropriately, much talk about religion remains a more private, narrowly shared expression. Because talk is always social, however, its private and public aspects cannot be sharply separated. As the private and the public dimensions of experience always are, talk that is private and talk that is public are relative to one another, shaded in ways that experience acknowledges.

The key difference is that talk shades toward public expression to the extent that it is intended for and accessible to anyone who will or should take interest in it. Talk that involves neither intention nor accessibility of that kind shades toward private expression. Talk about religion in public, then, can be defined as discourse that is intended to be widely accessible and whose content involves — explicitly or implicitly, manifestly or latently — senses of the whole and of what is or is thought to be sacred.

Further aspects of these definitions will be amplified shortly, especially as they apply to public expressions of religion in the United States, but for now notice that they have the advantage of facilitating detection of diverse dimensions of spiritual culture — the latent as well as the manifest, the nontraditional as well as the traditional. This detection process can even help us to interpret nonverbal and symbolic forms of expression that have religious content. Another advantage is that leverage for *evaluating* talk about religion is gained by interpreting religion as essentially connected to senses of the whole and of what is ultimately important within the whole.

No sense of the whole, no identification of the sacred, can be sound if it fails to do justice to the diversity or the commonality of human experience. More specifically, senses of the whole and identifications of the sacred cannot be sound if they distort the varieties or the shared dimensions of religious expression. Especially crucial for this study, no sense of the whole or identification of the sacred can be sufficient unless it attends not exclusively to the well-being of particular persons or communities but inclusively to the public interest and the common good. Some talk about religion is better, other talk is worse, where understandings of the whole and of the sacred are concerned.

Having identified religion, and talk about it, in ways that can help us detect and evaluate its latent and nontraditional expressions, I want to underscore one of this book's major claims: If we watch for it, talk about religion in public happens in America more than we may think. It is out there — often in the expected places, but probably just as often in places we do not expect. Yet it is also true that we Americans do not talk about religion in public as much or as well as we should. One thing to notice about this claim is that it appears paradoxical: There is more public talk about religion in America than we might think at first glance, and yet we do not talk sufficiently or well enough about religion. This book's analysis will show that the paradox is more apparent than real.

An illustration can anticipate what I mean. As the book shows, there are plenty of expert voices—they range from public moralists, ideologues, and theologians to pollsters, reporters, psychologists, sociologists, and other scholars—talking about religion in public. One could even argue that there has been a proliferation of specialized ways of talking about religion in public. Yet an issue remains, and perhaps it is even intensified by the "experts'" public talk about religion: The American people, not just experts of one kind or another, need to speak more openly and more often about religion—about the things that matter most—and to do so successfully, we Americans have to think about and discuss how to carry on such conversations well. Left to "experts," such conversations are sure to fail because they will not involve the widespread participation that is essential for their success. So, where public discourse about religion is concerned, we need to reconsider what expertise does and does not involve. We need to be more democratic but not less thoughtful, more willing to share with each other but not less critical, more oriented toward shared values and respect for our diversity and less driven apart by our differences. In those senses we Americans need more and better talk about religion in public even—indeed especially—in times when there are so many "experts" talking about religion in public. Hence, although this book deals with the issue of talking *about* religion and with the challenge of forging a new civil discourse about religion in America, its central intentions also concentrate on identifying and promoting good ways of talking religiously.

Unexpected Talk about Religion

Talk about religion in America often takes place in unexpected times and ways. Because they are unexpected, one has to watch for these expressions of religion, lest they be missed and not discussed, which too often is the case. If those expressions of religion are missed and not discussed, important insights about our private needs and public selves get obscured or lost. To illustrate those points, to set the scene for others that follow from them, and to explain how the chapters of this inquiry are organized, an example from major league baseball, a profoundly American domain, can advance the inquiry.

Orel Hershiser has won more than 175 games as a major league baseball pitcher. Until he signed a 1995 contract that took him to the Cleveland Indians, this gritty right-hander had long been a mainstay of the Los Angeles Dodgers. In the twilight of his distinguished career, he won the most valuable player award in the 1995 American League Championship Series. His sixteen victories helped to take Cleveland to its first World Series since 1948. The Atlanta Braves won that series, four games to two, but Hershiser's winning accomplishments in 1995 and again in 1996 and 1997 continued a remarkable athletic comeback story.

Like many athletes, Hershiser observes certain rituals as he prepares for a game. Just before he throws his first pitch, for example, he turns away from home plate, steps off the mound toward second base, and apparently checks the outfield. This routine was curtailed on April 25, 1990. On that Wednesday night, Hershiser and his Dodger teammates had taken an early-season beating from the St. Louis Cardinals. The first six innings had gone well enough, but in the seventh Hershiser knew he had nothing left. Badly worn from 195 consecutive starts, the shoulder of his pitching arm had been hurting for some time. The St. Louis loss confirmed his need for medical help.

The next morning Hershiser took a magnetic resonance imaging (MRI) test. The Dodger team physician, Dr. Frank Jobe, a brilliant sports medicine surgeon, examined the results. He did not like what he saw. "Orel," he said, "I'm afraid this is very serious." The injury to Hershiser's shoulder was career-threatening. If he was going to pitch effectively in the major leagues again, a prospect the MRI report made doubtful, his shoulder would have to be completely rebuilt. To complicate matters, the reconstructive surgery he needed had never been performed on a major league pitcher, so nobody knew for sure how to handle the rehabilitation program, either.

On Friday of that same week, Dr. Jobe operated successfully on Hershiser's shoulder. Soon a recovery program was under way. Tenaciously — his Dodger teammates aptly called him "Bulldog" — Hershiser endured the long, painful, and anxious rehabilitation period. Thirteen months after his operation, he was again scheduled to take the mound at Dodger Stadium.

Thanks to an invitation from our friend Nancy Thum, my wife, Lyn, and I would get to see that game on Wednesday night, May 29, 1991. So I read with special interest the morning sports page in that day's *Los Angeles Times*. Coauthored by Hershiser, a man with deep Christian convictions, its feature story began this way: "Maybe people don't know this," Hershiser had told *Times* staff writer Bill Plaschke a week before, "but I always say a prayer before I start a game—that's what I'm doing when my back is turned to home plate. When I make my first start, I am going to be praying so hard, I'm worried that I am going to break down and cry right there on the field. I'm worried they'll have to delay the game to calm me down. I just hope everyone understands. What they are seeing, and what I am living, is a miracle." [3]

As his name was announced and Hershiser took the field that night against the Houston Astros, the crowd of 39,127 welcomed him back with a two-minute standing ovation. Then, just before his first pitch, the stadium grew quiet. Evidently many of the fans that night had seen the same article I had read earlier in the day. For as Hershiser paused, stepped off the mound and looked up into the sky above center field, the stadium's silence suggested that the fans knew he was not checking center fielder Brett Butler's position. Instead, most of them understood, he was praying—no doubt giving thanks.

The headline for sportswriter Bill Plaschke's game report the next morning said, "No Ecstasy, No Agony Either." Houston had beaten the Dodgers, 8-2, but that was not the story. Orel Hershiser had lasted four innings and given up four runs on eight hits in the eighty-six pitches he threw. He had gotten a hit of his own in his first at-bat. But those statistics were not really the story either, at least not by themselves. It was a larger picture that held people's attention. Hershiser had made a successful comeback from adversity. The chance to do what he loved so much had almost been denied him, but he had battled back against tough odds, a story that extended well into the 1990s as Hershiser continued to be an effective major league pitcher.

That story contains several features that are keys to this book. First, it illustrates how private needs and public selves are interrelated. Hershiser had his own personal needs—some of them athletic, others religious, to mention just two dimensions of his life. Those needs existed in their particular ways because Hershiser's identity, like every person's, is social. Like all of us, he has a private life but he lives in the public domain.

Although Hershiser has enjoyed public acclaim because of his athletic accomplishments, he is not essentially different from the rest of us Americans. All of us have public and private dimensions in our lives; they tug and pull at each other continually, even in ways that are analogous to Hershiser's specific example. He had the private need to make a comeback because his identity entails the public role of being a major league pitcher.

That identity, in turn, has had much to do with his particular and private way of praying before making his first pitch in a game. Thanks to another person's inquiry—notably, in this case a newspaper reporter's—Hershiser had and took the opportunity to speak publicly about his religious experience. The result was a shared, public experience at Dodger Stadium when he stepped off the mound that night, looked toward center field, and "spoke" again—this time silently but understandably to a crowd of thousands. As that prayer on the occasion of his comeback exemplified, private needs often express themselves publicly, and public occasions can reveal the particularities of our private needs with moving impact. As Hershiser's example also shows, both the fully public expression of his private need and the public impact of that expression were made possible by Hershiser's speaking openly in the press about his religious experience.

Because it involved baseball, a pastime that has a way of bringing Americans together every summer, Hershiser's comeback was all the more interesting.[4] But what gave the story extra appeal was religion's role in it. In his particular and private way, Orel Hershiser had talked about religion in public.[5] By connecting the personal and private dimensions of experience with those that are public and social, he nourished and enriched them all. For if only momentarily, and probably without his intending it completely, those connections played an unmistakable part in the anticipation and joy of those who were brought together by his private needs and his public life.

That May night in 1991 when Orel Hershiser returned to Dodger Stadium was a special one. Writing this book has made me think about it often. I have long recognized that, at least in contrast to other major democracies in the West, the American people are now, and always have been, unusually religious. That night at Dodger Stadium made me realize all the more that public expressions of religion, grounded in experience that always combines personal and social dimensions, can turn up almost anytime and anywhere. Indeed, they often happen when and where one least expects them.

Prayer at Dodger Stadium, offered by a player quietly and privately but in ways that involved public sharing nonetheless, or descriptions of intensely personal religious experience published in a forum as distinctively public as the sports page of the *Los Angeles Times*—such expressions suggest how the private and public dimensions of our lives are dialectically intertwined. Those connections are not infrequent or strange. Nor are they confined to the athletic world, although in the United States sports and religion have a history that has long been interconnected.

Anyone who watches sports regularly will have seen athletes cross themselves as they approach a basketball free throw line, a baseball batter's box, or the starting line of a race. Football end zones are commonly places of prayerful thanksgiving when a touchdown has been scored. As one of the characters in the baseball movie *Bull Durham* puts it, she worships at the church of baseball. Nevertheless, the public spaces of athletic stadiums and sports pages are not the venues most obviously associated with expressions of religion, public or private. Temples, mosques, synagogues, churches, and other overtly religious institutions are the ones people typically think, of first in that regard. A May night in Dodger Stadium, however, helped me to see that American life can look and be quite different from what we typically think if people do a better job of watching for talk about religion in public.

The Varieties of Talk about Religion

Notice, next, that phrases such as "talk about religion in America" or "talk about religion in public"—I will use them interchangeably—can mean either (1) public talk about religion, or (2) talk about the place of religion in public life. More restricted, the second category is a subtopic of the first. Public talk about religion can center on the place of religion in public life, but it may range beyond that issue as well. My aim is to be radically empirical by concentrating on the broader of those two categories. Thus, I will speak not only about the place of religion in public life but also about a variety of experiences and questions that the narrower topic alone would leave unexamined.

Although admittedly harder to anchor, the broader topic allows actual talk about religion in America to be construed more widely and effectively. For not only is discussion of the place of religion in American culture but one dimension of such talk, even that specific dimension rarely exists in isolation. Typically it mixes and mingles with private and public expressions of religious experience and conviction—or with the lack of them, which can also be important to explore when understanding of the nation's spiritual culture is the goal.

Therefore, to clarify the book's intentions further, it will help to keep three additional themes in mind. Orel Hershiser's comeback story illuminates each one.

First, as I use the term, public talk about religion depends on *sharing*. The kind of sharing—talking and listening, giving and receiving—that concerns us here takes place to the extent that people intend to communicate openly and widely and when the communication is about matters of such great concern to them that senses of the whole and of the sacred are involved either explicitly or implicitly. From this perspective, the emphasis falls on talk about *religion* in America and, in particular, on ways of talking religiously. When Hershiser's distinctively American story appeared in the *Los Angeles Times,* it provided an arresting example of such sharing.

Second, public talk about religion involves *understanding.* The kind of understanding that concerns us here takes place as people explore — openly and widely, critically as well as sympathetically — religion's place in American life. From this perspective, the emphasis falls on talk about religion in *America.* Hershiser's captivating story is one that invites inquiry of that kind.

Sharing and understanding are not identical experiences, but, like the private and public dimensions of our experience, the two are inseparable. We cannot understand one another unless we share with each other; we cannot share very well unless some mutual understanding exists. Sharing and understanding build on each other. So, third, public talk about religion involves *searching* widely and openly for the best ways to share and understand together the variety of religious themes and expressions, issues and questions, that give American life its distinctive moods, flavors, tensions, and prospects. From this perspective, the broad and overlapping emphasis is on *talk about religion in America.* Again, Orel Hershiser's story illustrates the point. The religious character of his experience makes his life very different from that of many Americans. Yet the religious character of his experience makes his life American, too. How can we Americans share the varieties of our religious experience — pro, con, and in between — and understand them so that the quality of our life together is enhanced? As Hershiser shared his story, others interpreted it, and enhancement of those kinds occurred, that question was implied. This book explores it explicitly.

Those explorations underscore that when religious expression is set only within the context of private needs, it runs the risk of parochialism and even solipsism, but when it attends only to the political or social orders, religion becomes abstract and impersonal. Promoting the dialectical relation between these private and public dimensions, however, entails more than saying that religious discourse is both private and public. The point is to detect the connections between and the interdependence of these dimensions of experience and to build on them so that our lives — individually and collectively — hold together better than they now tend to do.

This three-dimensional approach to talk about religion emphasizes description, cultural criticism, and ethical appraisal. These dimensions are not discrete and neatly separable. To the contrary, they supplement one another and should be seen as related aspects of experience, which is bigger than any single perspective alone can comprehend. In ways that should be clear as the book progresses, however, sometimes one of those dimensions will come to the fore, sometimes another will do so. In the process, each dimension will help to open up the others.

Methods and Themes

What will this book show, and how will it do so? I have written "show" advisedly, because I do not desire, even if it were possible, to say by any series of arguments alone what needs saying here. Arguments do lie ahead, but their reasoning has more to do with persons, places, problems, prospects, projects—the kinds of things that people actually talk about every day—than with complicated scholarly concepts and intricately abstract theories.

My methods are steeped in perspectives that run through American philosophy from Jonathan Edwards and William James to Josiah Royce, John Dewey, and beyond. They are nondualistic, radically empirical, and governed by emphases on relationship and community. They lead me to believe that what may be called the affective and organic texture of experience is as important as the linear thinking and distinction-driven analysis that characterizes much academic writing.

Thus, I have not tried to write a conventional "scholarly" book as much as one that will make a broader appeal and impact because it roams freely and widely, even eclectically though not chaotically, to make its case incrementally through the variety and diversity of its topics, many of which are taken from popular American culture. So, this book is not, for example, a monograph on Supreme Court decisions about the separation of church and state. Nor is it primarily a professorial treatment of other scholars' views concerning religion and public discourse. Even less is it a "neutral" analysis of the pros and cons of contemporary religious debate. Such discussions have their place, but this one casts its nets differently by relying heavily on wide-ranging illustrations.

In the 1990s, the attention of American society has been gripped by issues of the kind that are reflected in the newspaper stories, novels, dramas, violence, trials, natural disasters, political debates, and economic dilemmas that appear in the chapters that follow. The book uses varied examples as case studies. Those examples and case studies identify empirically

(1) how public talk about religion can appear and where it can be found, especially unexpectedly (the book's descriptive role); (2) how the presence or absence of such talk affects senses of self, society, and understanding (the book's critical function); and (3) how public talk about religion might be crafted to expand our senses of self and society, including our senses of the whole and the sacred, so that the relationships between our private needs and our public selves are enriched and strengthened (the book's ethical/spiritual task).

The typical academic forms of assertion, argument, and criticism may not be the best tools—clearly they are not the only ones—for getting at these dimensions of experience most effectively. That is why we have stories and narratives and testimonies. I have written about them so that their voices can be heard in new and different contexts. As it emphasizes the diverse and unexpected ways in which religion gets expressed or muted in those voices, the book amplifies how private needs are contextualized by attention to the public dimensions of selfhood, how public selfhood is personalized by private needs, and how talk about religion can help or hinder favorable development of those relationships. Explorations along these lines can contribute, I hope, to a renewed sense of American identity at a time when more forces are dangerously pulling us Americans apart than are constructively bringing us together.

Drawing as it does on simple and not-so-simple feelings and experiences, impressions and stories, and the indirectness of evocations as well as on simple and not-so-simple facts and figures, analyses and theories, and the directness of criticism, this book is partly analysis and argument, partly collage and kaleidoscope. Methodologically, the book's patterns emerge chiefly through the narrative lines that its writing unfolds and the conversational tones its inquiries establish. Because I believe that good conversations depend on good questions, the book's lines and tones will ask many of them. My reason for writing that way is this: What we need to learn by talking about religion in public must be discovered through sharing that involves many voices, not just one. The insights we need will emerge from encounters that depend on your perspective, not my limited one alone. Good questions encourage the needed give-and-take.

Meanwhile here are some of the main points—and there are several—that I hope this book can lead us Americans to consider and discuss. They are at once simple and direct, traditional and ambitious; they are also complicated and ambiguous, controversial and problematic. Only sketched for now, their lines contain nine clusters of thought. Each chapter explores at least one of them in depth, using examples taken from or related to American culture as case studies to do so. The nine themes are as follows:

1. Talk about religion in America involves sharing, evaluating, and searching for loyalties that matter deeply to us. That process includes stocktaking about the direction of American life. Such appraisal requires honesty about our perspectives on American dreams.

2. In the 1990s, many Americans sense that public talk about religion is crucial. To a significant degree, Americans would like more of that talk—not if it produces greater division and contentiousness but if it can be done in ways that foster understanding.

3. In the 1990s, however, most Americans also would largely agree— albeit for very different and often contradictory reasons—that neither the quantity nor the quality of public talk about religion is focused to the nation's best advantage.

4. The inadequacy of our talk about religion reflects the fact that we Americans often fail to see, let alone nurture, some of the most important connections between our private needs and our public selves. Sometimes this is true because our American talk about religion is too private, implicit, or even nonexistent rather than public and explicit. Other times, that talk asserts too much and inquires too little, argues too much and analyzes too little. In still other instances, our talk about religion is not directed toward the common ground that its diversity contains but often masks.

5. Vital connections among our private needs and our public selves can be strengthened and their implications for public talk about religion discerned by sharing the narratives of American lives—sometimes our own, sometimes those that move us as we witness them and find ourselves led to transmit them to others. If we look carefully, we will find that these narratives often contain religious questions and themes.

6. Not only can such sharing reveal that we Americans possess more common ground than we sometimes think, but also it can show what greater religious sensitivity could do to strengthen and expand the bonds that can give us a desirable shared identity.

7. For that strengthening and expansion to happen, we need to explore how the wrong kinds of talk about religion have contributed to an immense wasting of human life at home and abroad and how our talk about religion ought to be affected by those tragedies. Typically the wrong types of talk about religion are ones that dwell too literally on the particularities of one religion's traditions and institutions instead

of taking those particularities, important and valuable though they are, as points of departure that enable us to obtain depths of insight that encompass but also go beyond particularity alone.

8. To be focused in the ways that are needed, our public talk about religion must emphasize qualities that religion itself often leaves in scarce supply: better listening, more give and take, greater openness, increased sensitivity, and a deeper commitment to reflection about the things that matter most to us, the things that deserve to matter most to us, and the possible differences between those two categories.

9. If those characteristics can be found in and encouraged by public talk about religion, Americans will get along better, live and work for the common good more effectively, and benefit from a greater degree of shared memory and hope. Living in the United States would be, in short, more like living in a community in which its members rightly take pride, deepen meaning, and find satisfaction.

Right now, I realize, my sketch raises many more questions than it answers. For example, is talking about religion in public really a good thing, as my outline implies, or would American life be better if people talked about religion less, not more? Why would anyone think that talk about religion, of all things, could bring Americans closer together? Historically, aren't there too many indications to the contrary? Doesn't the sheer variety of American religious expressions, to say nothing of their divisiveness, seem to say so? Isn't religion the great "conversation stopper" of our day, and aren't we better off leaving it that way? Despite our admission that American life needs better listening, more give and take, greater openness, and increased sensitivity, isn't it fantasy to expect such traits to emerge in and through talk about religion, which has typically been rife with contentiousness and dogmatism? In short, is it reasonable to think that talk about religion in public can contribute anything significant to a renewed communal spirit in the United States?

That catalog of questions is already long, but you will probably have no trouble thinking of more that should be added to it. If you do, that is good, because locating the right questions, as well as discussing them each and all, is a key part of the process of talking about religion in public. If Americans—not just "experts," but more and more of us together—can identify and explore the right questions well, that result would go a long way toward showing the validity of the argument I have traced so far. There is a logic in the outlined argument and also in the objections that can rightly be raised against it. What has to be seen is whether that logic, overall, can move beyond paradox, contradiction, and dissonance and into territory that Americans can identify as common ground that they want to share with care.

In the chapters ahead, the claims outlined here and the questions they raise will be revisited in a variety of ways, which, I hope, will add incrementally to the credibility of what I want to say. They will suggest, in particular, that *the primary venue for talking about religion in public can be found whenever and wherever people are willing to share and receive the narratives of their lives.* In this field only the people themselves are experts, and it is precisely the sharing of their expertise that is needed. So, to close this introduction by amplifying that theme, return briefly to the story of Orel Hershiser's baseball comeback.

An American Allegory

When Dr. Jobe diagnosed the condition of the pitcher's shoulder, he told him, "Orel, I'm afraid this is very serious." I found that statement in Bill Plaschke's article from the *Los Angeles Times.* As I studied that narrative, Jobe's comment stood out. It did so because Orel Hershiser's story can be an American allegory.

Like Orel Hershiser's right shoulder, American life has been hurting, showing signs of being worn out. We may have made it through six innings all right, but in the seventh too little may be left. The nation's injuries have accumulated. More than capable of producing a loss in one game, they could be "career-threatening." Health-restoring attention to body and soul is needed, but the diagnosis leaves the future uncertain. Reconstruction and rehabilitation, tenaciously followed, are needed if the country is to keep pitching effectively. "America," the nation's team doctor might say, "I'm afraid this is very serious."

Orel Hershiser came back. Can the United States do so as well? As in the Dodger pitcher's case, the answer involves religion and even talking about religion in public. His religious commitment helped him take the steps that were necessary to correct what was wrong. True, that commitment could guarantee no outcome as specific as pitching success, but there can be little question that religious conviction was important, even indispensable, in his recovery. The fact that Orel Hershiser said so openly, that he talked about religion in public, is significant because his speaking suggests the importance, even the indispensability, of religion in recoveries of other kinds as well.

At least in Bill Plaschke's narrative, Orel Hershiser's talking about religion in public took the form of personal testimony. He spoke movingly about how his own Christian faith had helped him to meet his private needs and encouraged him to recover his public life as a major league pitcher. Hershiser shared his testimony with Plaschke not to convert people to his beliefs, although the testimony's power should not be underestimated and it might have had that effect on some. Rather, he simply told what he had experienced and how he interpreted what had happened to him. His narrative connected the personal and public dimensions of life, illustrated how personal needs and public roles interact, suggested how they can serve each other in beneficial ways. More specifically, his story revealed at least some of the important ways in which religious discourse can be set within a dialectical understanding of the relationship between the public and private self and how such discourse can have helpful unifying roles.

Bearing witness to what one has experienced but not with the presumption that others should necessarily agree—that approach is where public talk about religion might have its most helpful beginning in late twentieth-century American life. From that beginning, other steps can follow. Differences and similarities can be explored. Continuities and discontinuities, including the relations among them, can be studied. Reasons for belief and interpretation can be appraised. New levels of understanding can be reached, or ways for people to deal better with their misunderstanding may be found. Common ground may be discovered, or ways for people to get along better on uncommon ground may be discerned. This work, as Dr. Jobe said of Orel Hershiser's condition, is very serious. Nothing less than the recovery of American life—the reconnecting and reforming of private needs and public selves—is at stake.

NOTES

1. William Dean, *The Religious Critic in American Culture* (Albany: State University of New York Press, 1994), xiv.

2. Ibid., ix. In American philosophy and religious thought, versions of this same concept can be found in an impressive tradition that includes Ralph Waldo Emerson, Henry David Thoreau, Charles Sanders Peirce, William James, Josiah Royce, and Alfred North Whitehead, to name only a few. Dean takes the phrase "sense of the whole" from John Dewey. At the outset, I am leaving aside an important question that will come up later: Is there, can there be, some single set of beliefs and meanings, yearnings and purposes, that defines a distinctively American sense of

the whole? In due course, I will have much to say about the structures of law and government, the ideals of liberty and justice, the ambitions for material success and economic power, and other elements that produce substantive American traditions, which often—but not always wisely or accurately—proclaim the exceptional status of the United States in the world.

Note, too, that my understanding of religion does not entail that anything and everything we care about involves religion. Clearly, each of us has cares and concerns—some of them even expressed through institutions and communities and in narratives and traditions—that have little, if anything, to do with life's profoundest, depths.

3. Orel Hershiser and Bill Plaschke, "Shouldering a Heavy Burden," *Los Angeles Times,* 29 May 1991, sec. C, 1 and 5.

4. Labor-management disputes shortened both the 1994 and 1995 major league baseball seasons when the players went on strike on August 24, 1994. If baseball unites Americans, it can also divide them. The strike pitted two economic elites against each other: the major league franchise owners and the players. As wealth and power clashed, disenchanted fans learned to live, however reluctantly, without the summer games. When play resumed, declining major league attendance figures showed that baseball's reputation as the "national pastime" had suffered.

Ken Burns's PBS television special *Baseball,* which aired in late September 1994, brought historical perspective to the strike. Burns showed how baseball mirrors the state of the country itself and reveals the shared history of all Americans. Like talking about religion in public, baseball's story is too big for any single narrative to tell. Like the story of religion in America, baseball's story is often, but not always, a good one. Its history, again like that of American religion, includes segregation and racism, greed and corruption, their base paths scarring the field of dreams that our American romance with baseball counts on so much. All of baseball, Burns documented, not just the happy parts, tells us Americans where we have been and who we are now. American religion may do the same. Perhaps for that reason John Chancellor, the venerable newsman who narrated Burns's series, concluded that his voice should sound like "God's stenographer," stating a record for the ages, one that might help us to make better sense of who we Americans can be and ought to become. This book argues that the right kinds of talk about religion can play a similar part in the American experience. For further insights about baseball and religion in the United States, see David Chidester, "The Church of Baseball, the Fetish of Coca-Cola, and the Potlatch of Rock 'n' Roll: Theoretical Models for the Study of Religion in American Popular Culture," *Journal of the American Academy of Religion* 64 (Winter 1996): 743–65.

5. Hershiser has also done so in an autobiography. See Orel Hershiser, *Out of the Blue,* rev. ed. (New York: Berkley, 1990). Hershiser is one of a growing number of professional baseball players in the 1990s who are "born-again" Christians. See, for example, "The Gospel vs. the Game," *Baseball Weekly,* 8–14 June 1994, 36–41.

CHAPTER ONE

Mapping America

I promised to show you a map you say but this is a mural
then yes let it be   these are small distinctions
where do we see it from is the question
—ADRIENNE RICH, *"Here Is a Map of Our Country"*

The introduction stated that the quality of American life depends on good talk about religion in public. Such talk involves sharing, criticizing, and searching for loyalties that matter deeply to us Americans as the public and private dimensions of our lives unfold and intersect. To take that conversation another step, the direction of American life needs to be mapped. Where have we been, where are we now, and where are we going? Responses to those issues are rarely impersonal, detached, and "objective." They emerge from the particularities of our lives. Sharing responses to such questions entails understanding how one's background produces the perspectives from which the assessments are made.

This chapter advances that kind of understanding in two ways. First it explains how some of my perspectives have formed. Then, by drawing on those perspectives, I start to specify my interpretation of the directions American life has been taking in the 1990s. Both dimensions of the chapter enable me to suggest further why and how we Americans should weave together our distinctive experiences, places, and stories to inform and produce the good talk about religion that we need.

A Map of Our Country

One of my favorite American writers is the poet Adrienne Rich. Some of her best work appears in *An Atlas of the Difficult World*. In ancient Greek religion, Atlas was a Titan. He challenged Zeus and paid a price. His punishment was to hold up the sky, although he is sometimes pictured as the one who must hold up the earth. Atlas can make us think of strength. Most often, however, the word *atlas* suggests a book of maps. In this sense, an atlas does not hold up the earth, much less the sky, and yet it does suggest strength of another kind. A good atlas helps us to know where in the world we are, where the earth has been, and what has been happening in it. These days, of course, atlases keep going out of date. The map-drawing and map-revising businesses thrive with the many political, economic, geographical, and religious upheavals that the world has witnessed in the last decades of the twentieth century. Good maps, carefully drawn, are needed to help us see where we are going and where we need to be headed.

As the title for a book of poetry, *An Atlas of the Difficult World* suggests a variety of themes: poems as maps, for example, or the poet as Atlas. Rich's poems are about a difficult world, one that she tries to map and perhaps to hold in ways that keep the skies from falling or the earth from going completely out of orbit.

Rich does not view the earth from the sky, however. Whether she writes "From an Old House in America" in Vermont or, in this case, from out west along California's Pacific shore, she stands firmly on American ground. "Here is a map of our country," she begins one entry from her *Atlas*. And then this poetic cartographer lines out words about haunted rivers and seas of indifference, battlefields and shrines, capitals of money and suburbs of acquiescence, blind alleys, crumbling bridges, air inversions, and cemeteries of the poor.[1] Although it expresses concerns that I regard as at least implicitly religious, hers is not a map of America the Beautiful, but of a wasted land, a country that blights nature and corrupts young and old alike, a place that betrays its best ideals and squanders hope. Yet Rich's lamentation is no conventional litany of woe. On the contrary, her yearning for a deeper and higher goodness, her loyalty to truth, justice, and love, makes her map of our country point the way toward the "never-to-be-finished, still unbegun work of repair" (11).

Rich charts poisoned environments. She explores issues of race, class, and gender. Her atlas exposes illusion and disillusionment. But Rich plots all of this decay to protest against the waste that forgets, ignores, or marginalizes "those who could bind, join, reweave, cohere, replenish / . . . those needed to teach, advise, persuade, weigh arguments / those urgently needed for the work of perception" (11).

At first glance, Rich's *Atlas of the Difficult World* is neither religious poetry nor poetry about religion. But depending on where you hear it from, her voice—personal and public at once—speaks about concerns and loyalties that are profoundly important, centers on refocusing and restoring a sense of the whole, and awakens understanding that our private needs cannot be adequately met unless we Americans pay better attention to the public life we share. The themes she elucidates, the dilemmas she probes, the memories and hopes she echoes—all of these elements make contact with deep human yearnings. Especially in the United States, those yearnings and the responses made to them are often rich with religious significance.

I can explain what I mean by focusing on some additional examples from Rich's *Atlas*. One of them is a poem about suicides. Drawing on her Jewish tradition, Rich offers a "Tattered Kaddish," a raveled prayer for the dead. This poem praises life even "though it crumbled in like a tunnel / on ones we knew and loved" (45). Rich's praise is inseparable from grief and even rage. It savors the gift, the goodness of life. "How they loved it, when they could," Rich says in honoring those who lived but could not stand to do so anymore. Yet her "Tattered Kaddish" also questions the gift and, implicitly, the giver of lives that can be so good and yet so broken, so wonderful and yet so full of despair, so filled with love and yet so lonely and bereft.

Rich writes about private needs, but she expresses them publicly. She does so because those needs cannot be understood or addressed without contextualizing them in a world of public selves and also because the issues of public life too often remain abstract and distant until we feel them in our aching hearts. Again, Rich's *Atlas* contains an example of what I mean. In 1942, Rich turned thirteen. Looking back in a 1989–90 series of poems called "Eastern Wartime," she asks,

> . . . what's an American girl
> in wartime   her permed friz of hair
> her glasses for school and movies
> between school and home   ignorantly Jewish
> trying to grasp the world
> through books . . .   (36)

And then this poem jars the reader by quoting a telegram.

Containing information conveyed by German industrialist Eduard Schulte to Dr. Gerhart Riegner, the World Jewish Congress representative in Geneva, the telegram is dated August 11, 1942. Its message, sent through the American legation in Bern, Switzerland, to the U.S. State Department in Washington, D.C., reported the existence of a Nazi plan for the systematic annihilation of Europe's Jews. Those who received the telegram dismissed its message as unbelievable.

I do not know what, if anything, Adrienne Rich knew about the Holocaust while it was actually happening. Clearly, however, that catastrophe decisively marks her identity. For instance, in a 1990 poem called "1948: Jews," she apparently ponders her college experience at Radcliffe when she observes,

> It was a burden for anyone
> to be fascinating, brilliant
> after the six million
> Never mind just coming home
> and trying to get some sleep
> like an ordinary person.   (52)

Rich is intent on remembering, on taking the responsibility to be moved by memory. In profound ways the Holocaust is one of her answers to the question "Where do I see it from?"

Where do we Americans see it from, and what do we see, if our private needs and public selves are voiced in talk about religion? As the case should be in the United States, that question will provoke multiple responses—privately and publicly. Some of those responses will be spoken, others not. Some will be encouraged by religion, others not. Some will be heartened by our country, but others not.

The voice in Adrienne Rich's poetic map of our country responds to puzzlement raised silently: "I promised to show you a map you say but this is a mural" (6). For the poet's purpose, that distinction—map or mural—is small, but not because there are no significant differences between the two. Maps tell where places are, where events happened. Murals show what places look like, what happened there. At least those can be some of their functions, and we need them all. But for the poet's purpose, questions about perspectives and perspectives about questions are more important than distinctions between maps and murals.

Where Do We See It From?

"Where do we see it from?"—that, says Adrienne Rich, "is the question" (6). As I talk about religion in public, I raise and respond to that question in the best ways I know how. I do so hoping to participate in and to learn from the give-and-take that finds good replies to more of Rich's questions: "Where are we moored? / What are the bindings? / What behooves us?" (23). I do so watching for ways to rehabilitate what Rich calls "this segregate republic" (11). Citing her words once more, I do so looking for links that could "join, reweave, cohere, replenish" the soul and spirit of our country. If I say more about what those commitments mean to me, perhaps you will find ways to think and talk about yours as well.

California is home for me. It is one place where I "see it from," and an amazing and complex place it is, too. Consider its population, for example. California is by far the most populous state in the country, its population approaching thirty-three million in the late 1990s. One American in nine now lives in this state, whose population exceeds that of Canada. In the last decade alone, California's population has risen by six million, and only 40 percent of that number is due to a natural increase of births over deaths. The rest comes from immigration, most of which originates outside the United States. For every person who comes to California from another American state, five settle there from abroad. Nearly one Californian in six has been born outside the United States. Much of this immigration, but by no means all, is legal. In the late 1990s, California—especially southern California and the Los Angeles area in particular—has become home for more than two million illegal immigrants, 40 percent of the nation's total.

In a country that is the most multiethnic, multireligious democracy in history, these migrations mean that California is our nation's most ethnically diverse state: more than 25 percent Hispanic, almost 10 percent Asian-American, and 7.5 percent African-American. In Los Angeles alone, more than 150 different ethnic and racial groups can be found. Each year in the 1990s, more than 100,000 children who speak little or no English have entered California's public schools. More than 10 percent of all American children are educated in the California public school system, which in 1996 began to implement plans to reduce class sizes in the lower elementary grades but still has, overall, one of the worst student-teacher ratios as well as one of the highest average class sizes in the nation. Before the twenty-first century arrives, "minorities" will constitute a majority of the state's population. The U.S. census for 1990 separated California's population into fourteen groups and still left 10 percent of the state's population undescribed.

Geographically and economically, California is also huge. If California were transposed to the East Coast, it would stretch from Providence,

Rhode Island, to Charleston, South Carolina. If California were a separate nation, it would have the seventh largest gross domestic product in the world. It would also be the eighth largest importer and eleventh largest exporter of merchandise. Los Angeles has overtaken New York as the nation's busiest gateway for foreign trade. Nearly one-third of California's land is farmland, and eight of the top ten agricultural counties in the nation exist within its borders.

After a deep recession in the first half of the 1990s, its worst in sixty years, California has rebounded smartly. Having created new jobs to replace almost all of the 525,000 that were lost to shrinking construction, aerospace, and military industries, the state's economy accounts for 13 percent of the nation's total. Not without reason, California calls itself the "Golden State." Yet even in its postrecession comeback, this region of our country has plenty of problems. Overcrowded schools and prisons, strained racial relations, congested and crumbling freeways, high costs of living, drug problems, agitation about immigrants legal and illegal, nagging anxieties about job security and welfare policy, as well as a series of devastating earthquakes, fires, and riots in the first half of the decade—all have left the state's physical and social infrastructure in serious disrepair. In Los Angeles alone, four out of ten residents report that they personally know someone who has been shot, stabbed, seriously wounded, or murdered in the city. The California Dream has nightmarish qualities that make it far from purely golden.[2]

Within that state, I live in Claremont, an attractive college town with a population of about 40,000. The town is located on the eastern edge of Los Angeles County, whose more than nine million residents make it by far the most populous county in the United States. Once surrounded by citrus groves, Claremont is now engulfed by the sprawl of Los Angeles. Founded in the late nineteenth century by WASPs who came there from the east, Claremont increasingly reflects the diversity, and to some extent the fraying, of American life. Churches, like the Congregational one that anchored the community early on, are just a few of the community's many centers, which include nearby a mosque and a Jewish temple as well as a wide variety of civic-minded institutions. People of Mexican and African-American heritage have been part of Claremont life from the town's beginning, and long before that, Native American tribes inhabited land that now contains a main street called Indian Hill. Claremont's population has Asian and Middle Eastern members as well. By no means is English the only language spoken in the schools. Many people who settle here tend to stay, or at least they would like to do so if employment permitted, but if the town has more stability than many contemporary American communities, it is still a place of comings and goings. A 1992 report showed that 37 percent of the town's households have been in Claremont less than five years. Very few families have lived there for three generations and not many are likely to do so.[3]

For more than thirty years, my place in this California town has been as a professor of philosophy at Claremont McKenna College, one of the five liberal arts colleges that cluster together to comprise a community known as the Claremont Colleges. During that time, I have also been active in the Claremont Presbyterian Church, which has long enjoyed strong leadership for its well-educated and, on the whole, well-heeled congregation. Officially it numbers 850, but consists, more realistically, of about 650 active members.

On the whole, this church is a strong one, and it wants to be better, a fact that accounts for the no-nonsense self-study that it conducted in the early 1990s. Its findings were less than was hoped for, but they provide a mural about one congregation that may help to map and reorient where at least some American talk about religion needs to be going.

Among the challenges that face this church, whose membership is older, whiter, and more female than its surrounding community, is the increasing diversity of the area and people it strives to serve. This diversity is ethnic, racial, economic, familial, religious—the latter including differing values, beliefs, and expectations among the church's own members. The church's self-study, whose sophistication benefited from the expertise of social scientists who are members of the congregation, showed that although the membership reported very positive feelings about itself, it also had "no unanimity of vision, no consensus of goals or directions, and no readily identifiable sense of who we are and what binds us together."

Rarely did the members of the Claremont Presbyterian Church respond to the open-ended questions of its self-study with answers that were phrased in plural or collective terms, contained discernible theological content, or showed strong feelings or passion. The language its own members used to describe this community of faith was "decidedly secular," suggesting that "we think of our church as more a social community than a religious one."

One upshot of this study has been a renewed emphasis on the congregation's self-definition. The way the Claremont Presbyterian report put the point is worth quoting further, because it maps many—though not all—of the recognitions that need to inform our whole country's spiritual life and its religious discourse in particular:

We need to begin weaving a new story; one that places us in this frightening and challenging time and place in history. Our new story will continue to be informed by Scripture, by our tradition, and hopefully by God's continued work in our midst. This weaving of a new story is, as one might expect, a "bottom-up" undertaking. Our new story cannot be given to us by our General Assembly, our Presbytery, nor even by our pastors. It is something we must concoct ourselves in our daily lives with one another and in prayer and worship and study. We must also find a way, however, to balance this "bottom-up" theology and polity with genuine attempts to create a true *community* of faith with a *unifying* vision and reason for being. In other words, we must take great care to weave a story which is truly communal, rather than individualistic.[4]

"Claremont" is one of my replies when the question is "Where do you see it from?" But my Claremont viewpoint includes horizons far beyond the town's limits. In general, those horizons involve philosophy, which as Plato said, begins in wonder. That word encompasses awe and puzzlement, skepticism and surprise, imagination and yearning, even despair and protest. Provoked by wonder in all of these senses, more specific horizons have come into my view, because life as a teacher and a scholar has led me on a path that forks in two directions. One fork explores American culture and specifically what the concept of "the American Dream" reveals and hides. The other leads into the darkness formed by genocide and, in particular, by the Holocaust, Nazi Germany's planned total destruction of the Jewish people, the actual murder of nearly six million of them, and the annihilation of millions of non-Jewish victims who were also caught in that catastrophe.

When the question is "Where do you see it from?" my answer, still deeply rooted in my hometown, expands beyond Claremont, its Presbyterian Church, and my Claremont McKenna College workplace to dreams and questions. Many of the dreams are visions of American life that continue to be influential in making the United States, and indeed the world, what it is today and will be tomorrow. Many of the questions are posed by Auschwitz and Treblinka—how and why they have scarred the earth. Those senses of where I "see it from" mold my private needs and sculpt my public self. They do so by making me think in a deeply personal way about what is most important about living, how experiences and events hang together, where my loyalties should be placed, and what does—and does not—deserve to be called sacred. But in addition to thinking about these things in deeply personal ways, I have to express socially and live publicly what I feel and believe about them. My religious interests and commitments flow in and out of these personal and public dimensions of my life. Such perspectives and questions about them govern what I can give and, I believe, ought to contribute to talk about religion in the United States.

You also have some place where you "see it from." Like mine, I suspect, your insights depend on your perspective, and your horizons consist, at least in part, of questions. If I say more about mine, yours may become clearer, too.

The Interdependence of All Human Actions

Formerly the commandant of Nazi death camps on Polish soil at Sobibor and Treblinka, a former Austrian policeman named Franz Stangl was sentenced to life imprisonment by a West German court on December 22, 1970. Early in April of the next year, Gitta Sereny, an insightful scholar-journalist, met Stangl for the first time. The result was a memorable series of interviews not only with Stangl himself but also with his family and many of his associates. These ingredients drove home to Sereny what she called "the fatal interdependence of all human actions."[5] That memorable theme would govern her 1974 book, *Into That Darkness: An Examination of Conscience*, which still stands among the most instructive studies of the Holocaust.[6]

Sereny's inquiry emerged from the hope that it might reveal, as she put it, "some new truth which would contribute to the understanding of things that had never yet been understood."[7] Specifically, she wondered, could Franz Stangl have left the path that took him to Treblinka? And if he could have left that path, would it have made any difference?

As Sereny probed her findings, she drew the following conclusions: Individuals remain responsible for their own actions and their consequences, but persons are and must be responsible for each other, too. What we do as individuals, contended Sereny, "is deeply vulnerable and profoundly dependent on a climate of life" that reflects "the fatal interdependence of all human actions."[8]

If Gitta Sereny is correct to speak of "the fatal interdependence of all human actions"—and I think she is—then how might American dreams and Holocaust questions be related? That question keeps moving me. It compels me to wrestle with senses of the whole, with differences between right and wrong, good and evil, with fundamental values that include my identity as an American, a Christian, a son, brother, husband, and father. As these concerns mix and mingle in the private and public aspects of my life, I understand them to have religious aspects. If those features are denied public expression and the benefit that comes from sharing—critical and sympathetic alike—with others, then my personal life shrinks and closes in on itself in ways that deprive me and others of relationships that could build understanding, care, and trust.

Perspectives on the American Dream

Having described how some of my perspectives have formed, I want to begin my use of them in interpreting directions that American life has been taking. So I will start by mentioning that in 1931 the historian James Truslow Adams published a widely read book called *The Epic of America*. One of the first to popularize the concept of "the American Dream," Adams contended that, apart from the Dream, the glory of America's epic would be lost. Indeed he believed this Dream was "the greatest contribution" the United States had "as yet made to the thought and welfare of the world."[9] Adams summed up his vision by referring to "that dream of a land in which life should be better and richer and fuller for every [person], with opportunity for each according to his [or her] ability or achievement. . . . It is not a dream of motor cars and high wages merely, but a dream of a social order in which each man and each woman shall be able to attain to the fullest stature of which they are innately capable, and be recognized by others for what they are, regardless of the fortuitous circumstances of birth or position."[10]

As inviting, elusive, and ambiguous, as tantalizing, optimistic, and yet frustrating as those ideas remain, the Dream appears again and again in American culture. Advertising, books, music, political rhetoric—all of those sources and more reveal that "the American Dream," at least as a concept, still has plenty of life. In the 1996 presidential election, for example, the Republicans titled their party's platform "Restoring the American Dream," and Bill Clinton was only the most recent president to run for reelection by proclaiming that one of his most important goals is "to preserve the American Dream for all of our people."

James Truslow Adams's summation notwithstanding, the contents of the American Dream are not simply identified, let alone easily reconciled or smoothly put into practice. How, for instance, will Americans interpret the words when the Dream is defined to mean a "better and richer and fuller" life for every American? How should we interpret words like those? Are they even credible anymore? When the issue is about having opportunity according to one's ability or achievement, to what extent can people "make it" on their own? How much help do people need to live the American Dream? How much help should Americans expect if the goal is to restore or to preserve the American Dream? What form should help take? Where can help best be found? What roles might religion play in good responses to such questions?

One of the fascinating and potent features of "the American Dream" is that this concept is and always has been composed of many dreams. Many of these dreams are basically economic or materialistic—owning a house, buying a car, finding a well-paid job—the elements promoted most by advertising, in which the concept of the Dream is often used to create visions of success defined in terms of wealth, power, and the creature comforts of an upwardly mobile standard of living. Other versions of the Dream stress moral, political, and religious ideals. They champion human rights, freedom, justice, and honor. Usually these diverse ingredients mix and mingle, but not always clearly, coherently, and harmoniously. The material aspects of the Dream tend to take priority, partly because they are connected to the ideal dimensions. Nevertheless, the ideal dimensions of the Dream cannot be reduced to material considerations. On the contrary, the material aspirations that drive so many of us Americans depend upon ideals that are integral to the Dream but that are too easily and too often taken for granted. Thus, because its meanings are not only shared but also contested, and clashing no less than they are constructed, the American Dream is never far removed from contradiction and conflict.[11]

No single vision has ever totally dominated American imaginations. Abraham Lincoln knew as much during the Civil War when he observed in 1864 that Americans "all declare for liberty, but in using the same *word* we do not all mean the same *thing*."[12] Complementing Lincoln's point as much as it supports Adams's vision of the American Dream, Ralph Ellison's 1952 "epic of America," *Invisible Man,* may well be the best novel ever written by an American. In any case, when Ellison died at the age of eighty on April 16, 1994, the United States lost a national treasure, one of its most profound and gifted writers. A month before Ellison's death, David Remnick hit the mark in the *New Yorker* when he described the appearance of *Invisible Man* as "something entirely new, lasting, and American," and then observed that "in Ellison's view, America is not made up of separate, free-floating cultures but, rather, of a constant interplay and exchange."[13] Written from the perspective of a black American whose individual identity had been denied by his native land, *Invisible Man* protested against the assumption that there should be—or ever was—a one-size-fits-all pattern that answers the question "Who are we Americans?"

"Diversity is the word," Ellison insisted.[14] To him that word—*diversity*—had distinctive meanings for life in the United States. Those meanings comprise the nation's legacy. In an American context, the vast ethnic, cultural, and religious variety of the people would always make us Americans many—pluralistic, different, and to some extent divided. But this same diversity, Ellison affirmed, was also bringing us together. Paradoxically, unexpectedly, ironically, even kicking and screaming and against our will, the diversity of American life would make the American people inexorably and distinctively one. That vision, Ellison also insisted, "is not prophecy, but description" (564).

For Ellison, as Remnick's *New Yorker* article noted, "integration is not merely an aspiration but a given, a fact of cultural and political life."[15] As Ellison knew, however, that fact remains as ambiguous as it is volatile, as much an occasion for frustration and rage as for encouragement and hope. Yes, it is true that American life is one—even integrated—in the sense that we Americans dwell together in a more or less shared geographical, political, economic, and even religious space. We Americans may debate the pros and cons of "multiculturalism" in the nation's schools, colleges, and universities, but the unavoidable fact is that American culture has long been multicultural. As Remnick pointed out, one has only to consider the music we hear, the games we play, the books we read, the clothes we wear, and the food we eat to find evidence of that. The religions we practice should be added as well, but the multicultural aspects of American life mean that the divisions among us are many, too. They run deep and seem to be running deeper. One has only to consider the divisions among the places we live, the schools we attend, the religions we follow, the wealth we distribute, the poverty we permit, the homelessness we ignore, the racism we express, and the violence we unleash to find evidence of that. To the extent that American life is one, the question is how bruised and bloody or how healing and caring it will be. That question is not likely to be answered well unless we deliberate together very carefully. No deliberation will be careful enough to meet the need if it fails to include public discourse that is religious in the broad way that I have defined the concept.

Ellison's invisible man says, "Now I know men are different and that all life is divided and that only in division is there true health" (563). He was right about the first parts, but when he spoke about true health's being found only in division, the words bear watching. As Ellison knew, everything depends on the kinds of division, the styles of diversity, that find expression among us Americans. Ellison was not one who glorified the separatism of an "identity politics" that celebrates some particular "culture" — "white," "black," and so on — to the exclusion of a more inclusive vision of American life. On the other hand, the inclusion he championed had no place for invisibility. As Ellison understood, there can be no meaningful identity without particularity. But when particularity goes unrecognized and unappreciated, invisibility will not be far behind. At some level, we Americans understand such things — or at least we need to do so. Such considerations explain why Ellison could end *Invisible Man* credibly by having his narrator ask, "Who knows but that, on the lower frequencies, I speak for you?" (568).

Ralph Ellison would have agreed with Henry James, the great nineteenth-century American novelist, who stressed that being an American is a complex fate. So many factors make that fate complex. We Americans, for example, trace our roots to many different places. Our history is made up of histories. Those histories involve everything from ethnicity and religion to regional and class differences as well as gender distinctions and sexual preferences. Those particularities from the past give us memories and experiences that do not cohere easily. Thus, there can never be one national narrative that tells every American story adequately. It takes an unfinished, unending multitude of stories to tell our American story. Nevertheless, only by telling, receiving, and sharing them can we establish connections, build human ties, rediscover American ground, and reclaim our common good in ways that give us Americans a better, if forever incomplete, sense of the whole and what is sacred in it.

Testing the Dream

"America," Ellison insisted correctly, "is woven of many strands; I would recognize them and let it so remain. . . . Our fate is to become one, and yet many" (564). Echoing here a basic American ideal — *E Pluribus Unum* (Out of Many, One) — Ellison's invisible man not only expresses both the unity and the diversity of American society; he implicitly acknowledges the complex, sometimes paradoxical texture of the Dream which that society has reflected and perpetuated.

The Dream's diversity is undeniable. Nevertheless that diversity exhibits major strands whose recurrent interweavings have given the Dream a subtle unity. None of those strands is more persistent than a belief in *new beginnings*. This belief exemplifies better than any other the optimism—some would call it the naivete—of Americans and the fundamental reason why rhetoric about the Dream caught on in the United States. From their inception, American self-images reflected the idea that the past did not bind one irrevocably. Fresh starts could be made, tomorrow promised to be better than today, and progress always seemed possible. This strand supports and has been strengthened by others, including affirmation of the unalienable rights enshrined in the Declaration of Independence; trust in the Constitution; conviction that opportunities still remain for individuals to achieve material prosperity and their own versions of happiness; confidence that the United States can successfully meet any challenge; and faith that the nation is sincerely dedicated to human equality, respect for diversity, justice, and freedom of choice.

To what extent can we Americans do what our dreams say? What do we too easily take for granted? How well do we practice what we preach? As a young American dreamer named Stingo experiences a "voyage of discovery" in *Sophie's Choice*, William Styron's controversial novel invites such questions as it explores how the Holocaust tests the American Dream.[16] Initiated by Sophie Zawistowska, a fictional Polish Catholic who, like thousands of her actual Polish sisters and brothers, experienced Auschwitz, Stingo learns in 1947 about a world very different from his own. As Sophie's story unfolds, Stingo undergoes shocks of recognition, including, as he relates the incident, "the absurd fact that on that afternoon, as Sophie first set foot on the railroad platform in Auschwitz, it was a lovely spring morning in Raleigh, North Carolina, where I was gorging myself on bananas" (217). On that day—Styron says it was April Fool's Day, 1943—Stingo was seventeen. He was desperately trying to make the weight requirement for enlistment into the U.S. Marines. He squeaked by. He had not heard of Auschwitz.

American dreams and Holocaust questions—in some ways, these dimensions of life are as different as the experiences of Sophie and Stingo in April 1943. And yet those realities intersect and challenge each other—sometimes producing shocks of recognition—in ways that make one wonder about the interdependence of all human actions, about the sense of the whole, about what is—and is not—sacred and ultimately deserving of loyalty. Exploring those relationships, including the absurdities they sometimes involve, invites and even necessitates religious discourse. Additional lines in Styron's narrative about Stingo and Sophie show how and why.

In Styron's novel, Stingo meets Sophie Zawistowska in "a place as strange as Brooklyn," but their shared experience climaxes in Washington, D.C. "We walked through the evening in total silence," Stingo recalls. "It was plain that Sophie and I could appreciate neither the symmetry of the city nor its air of wholesome and benevolent peace. Washington suddenly appeared paradigmatically American, sterile, geometrical, unreal." The reason, Stingo adds, was that Auschwitz "stalked my soul" (493).

Stingo's experience in Washington, D.C., would have taken place some fifty years ago. Although the city is still paradigmatically American and its symmetry remains, much about our nation's capital has also changed. On the one hand, now there is probably less an "air of wholesome and benevolent peace" than there was then. On the other, perhaps there are today more people walking through the evening in total silence. For now Americans not so different from Stingo are visiting the U.S. Holocaust Memorial Museum in huge numbers—millions since the museum was formally dedicated on April 22, 1993—and thus, like Stingo, they may be finding that Auschwitz stalks their souls, too. If so, what would that presence do to American dreams? Should it make them "paradigmatically American, sterile, geometrical, unreal" or should Holocaust questions make something else of those dreams?

As we Americans consider those questions, it bears remembering that American attention during World War II could not have been completely focused on the European situation because the United States also waged a massive war against Japan in the Pacific. Among the shadows of that campaign, however, something closer to the home of the American Dream also bears remembering. Supported by Executive Order 9066, which President Franklin D. Roosevelt signed on February 19, 1942, just a few weeks after Japan's bombing of Pearl Harbor, Lieutenant General John L. DeWitt, head of the Western Defense Command, took action—supposedly to forestall possible attacks by Japanese agents against strategic installations in the United States—to confine and then "relocate" 120,000 ordinary citizens and immigrants of Japanese descent to ten concentration camps at places such as Tule Lake and Manzanar.

The internment's legality was contested, but only in 1944 did the Supreme Court rule on it. Notwithstanding comments about the melancholy resemblance the evacuation bore to Nazi treatment of the Jews, the Court held that the military, under certain special circumstances, could legally segregate "all citizens of Japanese ancestry."[17] Troubling precedents lurk in that decision, foremost the court's overriding of constitutional guarantees to equal protection under the law for American citizens.

Manzanar, it must be underscored, did not become an Auschwitz, nor was Tule Lake a Treblinka. American policy was far removed from Nazi genocide. In addition, a Civil Liberties Act—passed, however, only in 1988 —led in October 1990 to the first distributions of $1.5 billion in government reparations, which has provided checks of $20,000 and a presidential apology to the more than 60,000 surviving internees or heirs of those who were still living when the law was enacted. Yet, as John R. Dunne, the Justice Department official who supervised the redress effort, has said, "The injustice of the forced evacuation and detainment of citizens without due process of the law was a constitutional travesty."[18] It still stands as one of the nation's worst violations of individual rights.

The United States also retains the dubious distinction of being not only the first but the only power—at least at the time of this writing—to fire nuclear weapons in actual combat. With the atomic bombing of Hiroshima and Nagasaki, however, American military might brought about Japan's surrender. American armed forces also proved essential in bringing the Third Reich to its knees. Yet, even if the history cannot be detailed here, it bears remembering, too, that David S. Wyman, the leading authority on the subject, hits the target when he writes about "the abandonment of the Jews" by the United States during the Hitler era.[19]

In the late 1930s, restrictive immigration policies meant that the American Dream of Emma Lazarus—the Jewish poet whose words "Give me your tired, your poor, / Your huddled masses yearning to breathe free" are inscribed on the Statue of Liberty—would be a dream tragically deferred for many of her own people who might have escaped the Holocaust. "Negative attitudes toward Jews," Wyman shows, "penetrated all sectors of wartime America."[20] Even after public governmental acknowledgment in December 1942 that the Jews were being slaughtered en masse, the American government was not moved to take action specifically directed at alleviating the Jewish plight. Not the least of the reasons for that inaction was American antisemitism, some of it deeply embedded in American Christianity. According to Wyman, polls taken from August 1940 until the war's end showed that 15 to 24 percent of the respondents "looked upon Jews as 'a menace to America.'"[21] Such ingredients conspired to yield a record less noble than the American Dream might like to envision.

Nor does the Holocaust's shadow on American ground stop there. Formerly the director of the Office of Special Investigations, a division of the U.S. Department of Justice established in 1979 to identify and prosecute Nazi criminals in America, Allan S. Ryan Jr. hopes the nation's "record in dealing with Nazi war criminals is not entirely beyond salvage," but he also estimates that hundreds, if not thousands, of German and Eastern European war criminals found a haven here after the Second World War. "The record is clear," asserts Ryan. "Preventing the entry of Nazi criminals to the United States was not a high priority, and was not taken seriously." [22]

Such a report would have saddened but not surprised Ralph Ellison. In 1945 he was working on a different narrative when what he identifies as the "blues-toned laughter" of *Invisible Man* began to dominate his imagination. Eventually the laughter compelled him to give full expression to its voice, which belonged to the invisible man "who had been forged," the author noted, "in the underground of American experience and yet managed to emerge less angry than ironic" (xv).

Ellison's postponed story was to be about an American pilot. Downed by the *Luftwaffe* and interned in a Nazi prisoner of war camp, he was the highest ranking officer there and thus, owing to war's conventions, the spokesman for his fellow prisoners. Like Ellison himself, the American pilot was black. Prisoner of racists and also the "leader" of prisoners who in normal American circumstances would not see him as their equal, let alone as their superior, Ellison's pilot would have to navigate his way between the democratic ideals he affirmed and "the prevailing mystique of race and color." This dilemma, Ellison adds, was to be "given a further twist of the screw by [the black pilot's] awareness that once the peace was signed, the German camp commander could immigrate to the United States and immediately take advantage of freedoms that were denied the most heroic of Negro servicemen" (x).

If Ralph Ellison never finished that story, his pilot's voice, like that of *Invisible Man*, would seem to echo Langston Hughes's 1938 poem, "Let America Be America Again":

> Oh, yes,
> I say it plain,
> America never was America to me,
> And yet I swear this oath —
> America will be!
> An ever-living seed,
> Its dream
> Lies deep in the heart of me. [23]

For *Invisible Man* ends where it begins. Ellison's character is in the underground hideout where American life has driven him. He is awakening from a state of hibernation, as he calls it, and his awakening entails writing.

Thus, in the novel's epilogue—making poetry out of invisibility, it is one of the most insightful writings about the interdependence of private needs and public selfhood ever produced by an American author—Ellison expresses his character's outlook as follows:

So why do I write, torturing myself to put it down? Because in spite of myself I've learned some things. Without the possibility of action, all knowledge comes to one labeled "file and forget," and I can neither file nor forget. Nor will certain ideas forget me; they keep filing away at my lethargy, my complacency. . . . So it is that now I denounce and defend, or feel prepared to defend. I condemn and affirm, say no and say yes, say yes and say no. I denounce because though implicated and partially responsible, I have been hurt to the point of abysmal pain, hurt to the point of invisibility. And I defend because in spite of all I find that I love. In order to get some of it down I *have* to love. I sell you no phony forgiveness, I'm a desperate man—but too much of your life will be lost, its meaning lost, unless you approach it as much through love as through hate. So I approach it through division. So I denounce and I defend and I hate and I love. (566–67)

As Ellison, Hughes, Styron, and others help to show, destructive qualities of mind—certainly not identical but still akin to those that established Auschwitz—also scar American ground.[24] They led Ellison's invisible man to remark—and he speaks for more than himself—that, "I'd like to hear five recordings of Louis Armstrong playing and singing . . . all at the same time":

> Cold empty bed; springs hard as lead; pains in my head;
> Feel like old Ned—What did I do to be so Black and Blue?
> No joys for me; no company; even the mouse ran from my house.
> All my life thru I've been so Black and Blue.
> I'm white inside—it don't help my case.
> Cause I can't hide what is on my face.
> I'm so forlorn;
> Life's just a thorn, my heart is torn.
> Why was I born?
> What did I do to be so Black and Blue?[25]

Auschwitz shadows the American Dream. As it does so, we Americans confront questions about our senses of the whole, about our loyalties, about what deserves to be called sacred and what does not. In William Styron's story about Sophie Zawistowska, an SS doctor gave her a choiceless choice. She could pick which of her two children, Jan or Eva, should go to the gas. "*Ich kann nicht wählen!* [I cannot chose!]," she screamed (483). Sophie could not choose. And yet, so as not to lose them both, she let Eva go.

Limited though it was, Sophie's choice was real. So was her sense of guilt. Set free in 1945, she found her way to the United States. "But," as the lyric from *Les Miserables* so aptly states, "there are dreams that cannot be, / And there are storms we cannot weather." Liberation left Sophie in the shadow of Auschwitz. She found inescapable the conclusion that her own life, even in America where she had hoped to find a new beginning, was not worth living. In 1947 Sophie let it go—also by choice.

Dreams die hard in America. In *Sophie's Choice,* Stingo, the white Presbyterian Southerner, cannot prevent Sophie's suicide. But Stingo endures, having learned much about himself, about American racial guilt, about his own American Dream. Three fragments from a journal he kept in 1947 form the novel's conclusion. *"Someday I will understand Auschwitz"*—like many American dreams, that vow, Stingo reflects years later, is "innocently absurd." *"Let your love flow out on all living things"*—that one is worth saving "as a reminder of some fragile yet perdurable hope." Finally, some poetry: *"Neath cold sand I dreamed of death / but woke at dawn to see / in glory, the bright, the morning star"* (513-15). Facing despair, Stingo finds ways to revive determination to choose life and hope again. If freedom to choose destroyed Sophie, apparently Stingo will try to resist that fate by using choice against itself in a struggle to make life more worth living and not less so.

Words We Need to Hear

Some years after Stingo's fateful encounter with Sophie Zawistowska, Harry Angstrom and his wife, Janice, the principal characters in *Rabbit Run* (1960), *Rabbit Redux* (1971), *Rabbit Is Rich* (1981), and *Rabbit at Rest* (1990)—John Updike's four-volume saga about the ups and downs of American life since World War II—are also struggling to find ways to make life more worth living. In *Rabbit Run,* the earliest of the four novels, Harry suffers from a "closed-in feeling." A former high school basketball star, the Rabbit has since experienced only mediocrity. And Harry cannot abide mediocrity. Consequently, like earlier Americans, he runs. The trouble is, he does not know where to run. Harry has a son, Nelson, and he fathers a daughter, Becky, who drowns while still an infant. Harry also takes up with a prostitute named Ruth and gets her pregnant. Nearly twenty years later—in *Rabbit Is Rich*—Harry thinks he meets his other daughter, but Harry never knows for sure. Meanwhile, the institutions—domestic, social, religious—that the younger Harry has been brought up to believe in fail to satisfy him. Yet he can find no adequate replacements, no new frontiers where he can fan the "little flame" inside him.[26]

The second novel, *Rabbit Redux,* unfolds as America's involvement in Vietnam is being most strenuously criticized. But Harry is not one of the critics. Desperate to believe in something, Harry substitutes America for "a face of God" and stubbornly defends the Vietnam War. "America," he thinks, "is beyond power, it acts as in a dream. . . . Wherever America is, there is freedom. . . . Beneath her patient bombers, paradise is possible."[27] The America Harry truly believes in, however, is an older America, which, as he nostalgically remembers it, was epitomized by family solidarity, Sunday-morning church, and Sunday-afternoon baseball. It is not the nation he inhabits. In the late 1960s, America has penetrated outer space but, to Harry, has failed to fill its spiritual void. In the course of the novel, Harry struggles to come to terms with his feelings not only about Vietnam but also about the sexual revolution, the civil rights movement, the new technology that threatens his employment, the drug culture, and above all the question of how much responsibility he must assume for himself, for others, and for his country as a whole.

At the end of *Rabbit Redux,* Harry and Janice—estranged from time to time—are tenuously reunited. They are not sure this will make things better, not even for themselves, let alone the country: "If it was better," Harry says of the United States, "*I'd* have to be better."[28] But Harry and Janice are trying. They are conducting a vigil; they are waiting to see. "How do you think it's going?" Harry asks Janice. "Fair," she replies.[29]

A decade later, Updike affirms that "Rabbit is rich."[30] Now in his midforties, Harry manages Springer Motors, his wife's family business, and prospers by selling Japanese Toyotas to buyers in his hometown, Brewer, Pennsylvania. Harry has a country-club membership and a new house. His frequently rocky marriage seems to have stabilized. Harry, who thought God "never wanted him to have a daughter," has a new granddaughter, too.[31] But Harry's contentment is not complete. Rabbit cares, and so he still has reasons to wonder whether "the great American ride is ending."[32]

At least for Harry, whose votes went to Ronald Reagan and George Bush, the ride is ending with *Rabbit at Rest.* Although Harry now spends half of the year in Florida retirement, he has found very little domestic tranquility. Springer Motors and his son's family life are both in trouble because Nelson, who ineptly manages both, is hooked on cocaine. Overweight and out of shape himself, Harry seems nearly unable to find the flame any longer, let alone to fan it, for his heart is failing. Not exactly to

Harry's comfort, Janice has found a new lease on life with a career in real estate.

Increasingly, Harry seems preoccupied with the ending of his life. At the fringes of Harry's diminished moods of "stirred-up unsatisfied desire," writes Updike, "licks the depressing idea that nothing matters very much, we'll all soon be dead." [33] And yet, in spite of Harry's flagging energy, in a way even because of it, his dissatisfaction, his yearnings for something better, do reassert themselves. Although Harry wonders "how many fresh starts for him are left," and despite the fact that his life has hardly been a paradigm of order and responsibility, he keeps insisting that "We got to get some order going in this crazy family. . . . There comes a point when you got to take responsibility." [34]

Harry's rest does come. The last words John Updike gives him are a reply to Nelson's cry, "Don't *die,* Dad, *don't!*" "Well, Nelson," he says, "all I can tell you is, it isn't so bad." To which Updike adds, in concluding the novel: "Rabbit thinks he should maybe say more, the kid looks wildly expectant, but enough. Maybe. Enough." [35]

Enough? Until nearly the end, Harry had an ongoing affair with Thelma Harrison, whose husband was one of Harry's high school teammates. "Believe in God," Thelma would urge Harry, "it helps." [36] Harry says, "I don't *not* believe," but clearly sex meant more to him than religion, a woman's embrace more than God's love. And yet that is not the whole story, either. An example of what sociologists call "unchurched Americans," Harry still "sees it from" perspectives informed by private needs and public selves that ask questions and invite spiritual responses that are not fully understandable apart from the expressions of religion.[37]

At Nelson's wedding, for example, Harry feels the public words of the service move him. "*The union of husband and wife,* [the minister] announces in his great considerate organ tones, *is intended by God for their mutual joy.* . . . Laugh at ministers all you want," Updike has Harry think, "they have the words we need to hear, the ones the dead have spoken." Such words, however, are not enough, for Updike notes that Harry hears "the syllables descend, *prosperity, adversity, procreation, nurture* . . . like layers of a wide concealing dust." [38] Nevertheless Harry can also feel that "without God to lift us up and make us into angels we're all trash." He does not want to lose "the rhythm, the dance, the whatever it is, the momentum, the grace" that makes life, at least at times and in places, "a piece of paradise blundered upon, incredible." [39]

"How do you think it's going?" Harry once asked Janice. "Fair," she replied. Janice's appraisal fits the American Dream today, but is fair enough? How does her assessment sound if we wonder about the Dream in relation to talking about religion in public? If the Dream were better, we Americans would have to be better at making talk about religion more prominent in the places where we "see it from."

Brewer, Pennsylvania . . . Raleigh, North Carolina . . . Claremont, California. Washington, D.C., and Auschwitz, Poland. Maps and murals. New beginnings and *Into That Darkness*. Liberty . . . enslavement. Loving . . . hating. Saying yes and saying no. Denouncing . . . defending . . . dividing. Knowing . . . wondering . . . American dreams . . . Holocaust questions . . . the fatal interdependence of all human actions.

One could try to talk about all of those experiences, places, and themes without mentioning religion even once. But such talk would be impoverished. Leaving our private needs and public selves needlessly and senselessly divided, its syllables would descend like Updike's "layers of a wide concealing dust." At least implicitly, all of those words are loaded with religious meaning. Failure to address that fact openly silences too much that we need to share, understand, and evaluate.

Where do we see it from? Talk about religion speaks words we need to hear. Unavoidably, indispensably, persistently, they will either inform the atlas of our difficult world or we shall lack a map of our country to guide us well.

NOTES

1. Adrienne Rich, *An Atlas of the Difficult World: Poems, 1988-1991* (New York: W. W. Norton, 1991), 6. Subsequent page references to this collection are given parenthetically in the text.

2. For my information about California, I am indebted to James Quay, executive director of the California Council for the Humanities, which has its main office in San Francisco. See also "California, Back in the Picture," *The Economist*, 2 Dec. 1995, 55-56, and the *Los Angeles Times*, 8 Feb. 1997, A1, A21, and 10 Feb. 1997, A1, A24.

3. U.S. Census Bureau reports for the mid-1990s indicated that the percentage of Americans who moved from one place to another—16.7 percent in the one-year period that ended in March 1994—was lower than at any time since 1950. Accounting for this change are factors such as the aging of the American population, the increase of two-earner families, and overall economic uncertainty. Those conditions have made American mobility more difficult. However, even if Americans

are less convinced that relocation will improve their lives in the 1990s, the American tendency to find new opportunities and to seek new beginnings still makes us far more likely to move than people in Western Europe or Japan.

4. My information about the Claremont Presbyterian Church comes from the typescript of the final report, dated January 1, 1993, of the church's Strategic Plan Task Force, which was edited by Wendy Menefee-Libey.

5. Gitta Sereny, *Into That Darkness: An Examination of Conscience* (New York: Vintage Books, 1983), 15.

6. Sereny has written a second instructive study based on her encounters with another Nazi war criminal, Albert Speer. See Gitta Sereny, *Albert Speer: His Battle with Truth* (New York: Alfred A. Knopf, 1995).

7. Sereny, *Into That Darkness*, 23.

8. Ibid., 367, 15.

9. James Truslow Adams, *The Epic of America* (Boston: Little, Brown and Company, 1934), viii. Adams wanted to call his book *The American Dream*, but his publisher would not accept that title. For more information about Adams and his view of the American Dream, see Allan Nevins, *James Truslow Adams: Historian of the American Dream* (Urbana: University of Illinois Press, 1968). Additional background on the history of the concept of the American Dream can be found in Anthony Brandt, "The American Dream," *American Heritage*, Apr.–May 1981, 24–25, and Robert H. Fossum and John K. Roth, *The American Dream* (Durham: British Association for American Studies, 1981). See also Robert J. Samuelson, *The Good Life and Its Discontents: The American Dream in the Age of Entitlement, 1945–1995* (New York: Times Books, 1995).

10. Adams, *Epic of America*, 415.

11. For insightful perspectives on these senses of conflict and contradiction, see "Yearning for Balance: Views of Americans on Consumption, Materialism, and the Environment," a report prepared for the Merck Family Fund by the Harwood Group in July 1995. Based on a nationwide poll, plus focus group discussions in Los Angeles, Dallas, Indianapolis, and Frederick, Maryland, this study found that Americans are "paralyzed by the tensions and contradictions embedded in their own beliefs. . . . People seem to be caught in a paradox: they believe in the American Dream, but it keeps expanding—so that even as they gain more possessions and higher levels of wealth, they feel like they are losing ground" (2, 21). Closely related to the perspective of my analysis, the "Yearning for Balance" report states that Americans "share a deep and abiding concern about the core values driving our society; they believe that materialism, greed, and excess characterize the way we live and underlie many of our worst social ills" (23). Americans, the report concludes, crave meaningful talk about these issues.

The "Yearning for Balance" report has led to the establishment of the Center for a New American Dream. With headquarters in Burlington, Vermont, the Center's mission statement speaks about "helping Americans to start a new conversation in the home, at work, in our schools, among our families, friends, and co-workers . . . to reconsider the American Dream . . . [and] to create a better quality of life."

12. This quotation is from an address at Baltimore, Maryland, April 18, 1864. See *The Political Thought of Abraham Lincoln*, ed. Richard N. Current (Indianapolis: Bobbs-Merrill, 1967), 329. The italics are Lincoln's.

13. David Remnick, "Visible Man," *New Yorker*, 14 Mar. 1994, 34, 36.

14. Ralph Ellison, *Invisible Man* (New York: Vintage Books, 1982), 563. Subsequent page references are to this thirtieth anniversary edition of the novel and are given parenthetically in the text.

15. Remnick, "Visible Man," 36.

16. William Styron, *Sophie's Choice* (New York: Random House, 1979), 25. Subsequent page references are to this edition and are given parenthetically in the text.

17. See Justice Hugo Black's 1944 majority opinion in *Korematsu v. United States*. The Court split 6-3 on this case. Writing for the dissenters, Justice Robert H. Jackson said: "A military order, however unconstitutional, is not apt to last longer than the military emergency. Even during that period a succeeding commander may revoke it all. But once a judicial opinion rationalizes such an order to show that it conforms to the Constitution, or rather rationalizes the Constitution to show that the Constitution sanctions such an order, the Court for all time has validated the principle of racial discrimination in a criminal procedure and of transplanting American citizens. The principle then lies about like a loaded weapon ready for the hand of any authority that can bring forward a plausible claim of an urgent need."

18. *Los Angeles Times*, 7 Oct. 1990, A4.

19. For elaboration on these points, see two books by David S. Wyman, *Paper Walls: America and the Refugee Crisis, 1938-1941* (Amherst: University of Massachusetts Press, 1968) and *The Abandonment of the Jews: America and the Holocaust, 1941-1945* (New York: Pantheon Books, 1984). Two other excellent resources are Michael Berenbaum, *The World Must Know: The History of the Holocaust as Told in the United States Holocaust Memorial Museum* (Boston: Little, Brown and Company, 1993), and Deborah E. Lipstadt, *Beyond Belief: The American Press and the Coming of the Holocaust* (New York: Free Press, 1986).

20. Wyman, *Abandonment of the Jews*, 12.

21. Ibid., 15.

22. Allan A. Ryan Jr., *Quiet Neighbors: Prosecuting Nazi War Criminals in America* (San Diego: Harcourt Brace Jovanovich, 1984), 344.

23. Langston Hughes, "Let America Be America Again," in *American Ground: Vistas, Visions, and Revisions*, ed. Robert H. Fossum and John K. Roth (New York: Paragon House Publishers, 1988), 350.

24. Additional significant examples to illustrate this point are identified and discussed by Stefan Kühl in his study of the eugenics movement in the United States,

which helped to encourage and legitimate the Third Reich's racist antisemitism. See Stefan Kühl, *The Nazi Connection* (New York: Oxford University Press, 1995).

25. Although this 1929 song has long been associated with piano man Thomas (Fats) Waller, its words were written by Andy Razaf, a gifted African-American lyricist whose credits also include "Ain't Misbehavin' " and "Honeysuckle Rose." See Barry Singer, *Black and Blue: The Life and Lyrics of Andy Razaf* (New York: Schirmer, 1993).

26. See John Updike, *Rabbit Run* (Greenwich, Conn.: Fawcett Publications, 1965).

27. John Updike, *Rabbit Redux* (Greenwich, Conn.: Fawcett Publications, 1972), 49.

28. Ibid., 153.

29. Ibid., 351.

30. John Updike, *Rabbit Is Rich* (Greenwich, Conn.: Fawcett Publications, 1982), 1.

31. Ibid., 421.

32. Ibid., 1.

33. John Updike, *Rabbit at Rest* (New York: Alfred A. Knopf, 1990), 220.

34. Ibid., 260, 262, 268.

35. Ibid., 512.

36. Ibid., 206.

37. For more on these themes, see Kyle A. Pasewark, "The Troubles with Harry: Freedom, America, and God in John Updike's *Rabbit* Novels," *Religion and American Culture* 6 (Winter 1996): 1–33.

38. Updike, *Rabbit Is Rich*, 226.

39. Updike, *Rabbit at Rest*, 344, 505, 346.

CHAPTER TWO

How Much? What Kind? American Needs for Religious Discourse

> Discussions about personal moral and spiritual beliefs are seldom encouraged. And if you bring them up, you run the risk of offending your hosts.
>
> —PHILLIP BERMAN, *The Search for Meaning: Americans Talk about What They Believe and Why*

An important paradox emerges when one explores American talk about religion. On the one hand, we Americans do talk about religious concerns and about the place of religion in the nation's life. In fact, we do so more often than we may realize at first glance. On the other hand, although Americans do talk about religion in public, we do not do so enough in ways that would best serve our private needs and public selves. In sum, the paradox is that American life is not devoid of talk about religion—to the contrary, much talk about religion can be found—but that talk does not fill the voids in our national life because it does not crack enough of the silences that most need to be broken.

Fortunately, there is evidence not only that we Americans need better talk about religion—talk that would produce deeper understanding instead of greater division and contentiousness—but also that we want it. Examining those possibilities, this chapter addresses two overlapping themes. First, it illustrates further that talk about religion occurs more often than we may think but not always in the conventional places. Second, building on the signs that Americans take talk about religion to be important, this chapter advances the case that we need better religious discourse. That analysis begins with some interesting evidence to support the claim that Americans want better discussion of religion.

Religion News

Stewart M. Hoover and his colleagues Barbara Hanley and Martin Radelfinger have published the results of a significant 1990s study about the coverage of religion in American newspapers.[1] For much of the twentieth century, they found, the coverage of religion in the nation's daily newspapers tended to be marginalized, often restricted to a weekly page or two. If the press is still not quite sure how to cover religion news, partly because when or how a news story involves religion is not always crystal clear, Hoover, Hanley, and Radelfinger also detected a shift toward more diverse and thorough coverage of religion beginning in the mid-1970s. Probably a shift was under way even earlier with the civil rights movement and the Vietnam War debates of the 1960s, but during the period that the Hoover study identified, Jimmy Carter, a born-again Christian, was elected President of the United States. Concurrently the tumultuous stirrings of Islam in Iran and other parts of the Middle East required attention to religion's role in international relations. Conservative religious movements in the United States began to gain ground and assert themselves politically, with the so-called Moral Majority leading a charge that could not be ignored in the daily press. News of this kind defied confinement to a weekly religion page, because these religious expressions were neither neatly institutionalized in traditional religious establishments nor so private and personal as to escape public view.

There will be more to say later about the Hoover study, but first recall just a few major news stories from the 1990s that illustrate how talk about religion is unavoidable because religious issues so deeply penetrate our national life. Ongoing debates about abortion and school prayer come to mind. So does the Million Man March orchestrated by Louis Farrakhan and his Nation of Islam in the autumn of 1995. The same can be said for controversy among Jews—Orthodox, Conservative, and Reform—about who can properly claim Jewish identity. The emergence of the Christian Coalition as a force in American politics has also kept religion center stage. The late March 1997 mass suicide of thirty-nine members of Marshall Applewhite's Heaven's Gate cult in Rancho Santa Fe, California, as well as the fiery conflagration that resulted from the April 1993 confrontation between the U.S. government and David Koresh's Branch Davidians outside Waco, Texas, provide examples that make people wonder whether there will be more events of this kind as a religiously volatile time—the millennium—approaches.

Add to those examples reports about the burning of houses of worship in the United States. In the 1990s, more than 200 cases of arson and desecration in churches, synagogues, and mosques have been under investigation by federal authorities. Only about a third of them have been solved. Half of these cases took place in an eighteen-month period in 1995–96, and about 70 percent of the burnings targeted African-American churches in the southeast. At the time of this writing, no national or regional conspiracy had been detected, but a climate of division and racism has encouraged what *New York Times* religion writer Gustav Niebuhr calls acts of "singular profanity." As Niebuhr correctly explains, the violence of these acts "lies in the attempt to disrupt a community of believers, desecrate their altars and smash the spiritual rhythm of their lives. The arsonist attacks not just the planks and shingles but the space where life's most important transitions are marked, where babies are baptized, marriages celebrated and the dead eulogized."[2]

Responding especially to the 1996 church burnings, President Bill Clinton called for a national month of unity. His proclamation on July 2, 1996, began by noting that "our nation was founded by people who sought the right to worship freely, and religious liberty is enshrined in our Constitution as the 'first freedom' granted by our Bill of Rights."[3] The United States needs much more than a month of unity, but the presidential proclamation is on target nonetheless because religious liberty is indeed the "first freedom." It is first because figuratively as well as literally it involves, as Gustav Niebuhr says, "the space where life's most important transitions are marked." Efforts to rebuild the burned out black churches have been widespread, but the need for those efforts underscores all the more that nothing symbolizes more poignantly and urgently the need for better talk about religion in public than the fact that the American landscape has been lit up by burning houses of worship, not only in the 1990s but for centuries of American experience.[4]

The examples I have cited only start a 1990s list that shows how talk about religion is unavoidable because religious issues so deeply penetrate our national life. Going on and on as it could do, that list might also include stories that are not overtly about religion at all. Consider, for instance, all-too-frequent episodes of disaster and catastrophe—the explosion of TWA Flight 800 off Long Island and the bombing during the XXVI Olympiad in Atlanta in July 1996, or the demolition of the federal building in Oklahoma City in April 1995, to cite only three from recent memory. The randomness of that destruction and the grief caused by the devastation question meaning and shake our sense of the whole as we ask "Why?" in ways that are not far removed from religious impulses or protests.[5] One never knows when apparently nonreligious news can or will lead us unexpectedly to talk about religion.

We may also be led to wonder and to talk about religion when we receive news about scientific discoveries and breakthroughs. In the summer of 1996, for example, reports from NASA indicated that there may once have been life on the planet Mars. Less than a year later, another important scientific story reported that Scottish scientists had successfully cloned an adult mammal, a sheep named Dolly who is the exact genetic duplicate of the animal whose DNA was used in the cloning process. Such news raises profound questions about the nature of the universe and our human place and responsibility in it. When those topics come up, talk about religion is not likely to be absent for long. Returning to more overt examples, talk about religion is also contained in and provoked by accounts that deal with the efforts of a Southern California school board to mandate the teaching of biblical creationism in its public schools' science courses; the emergence of "Promise Keepers" as a significant religious movement among American men; the scandal and disillusionment caused by allegations that a Roman Catholic priest molested children; the impact of Islam in the United States; the ways in which religious teaching about sin may be affected by genetic theory; and the question "Do children need religion?"[6]

In addition, there have been important stories in the 1990s about feminist issues and religion, the role of religion in the "ethnic cleansing" and genocide in the former Yugoslavia, the ways in which religious institutions, leaders, and debates figure in our country's struggle with issues concerning gay men and women, and religion's part in deliberations about abortion, health care delivery, and of course the AIDS epidemic. In every case, the personal feelings of individuals as well as concerns about the public good are at stake. How these issues are covered and discussed—or not—affects the quality of American life at every turn.

Relatively few of these stories are found only in the conventional weekly religion sections of American newspapers. Even the sermon excerpts published in the *Los Angeles Times* often turn up in the Monday morning opinion pages. The special religion sections that usually appear in the nation's Saturday newspapers also have significant news, but news about religion unavoidably spills well beyond the columns that earlier were expected to hold it.

More significantly, Hoover and his associates discovered that the reading public would welcome much more coverage of religion. Utilizing a method they call "elaboration," the researchers employed a variety of polling techniques that could "amplify and cross-reference one another"—in-depth interviews, for example, as well as quantitative measures.

Their study unfolded step by step. First, by means of personal interviews, Hoover, Hanley, and Radelfinger conducted a national random-sample survey of 1,100 adults. It sought to measure religious interest and commitment among the nations's newspaper readership. Next, they used in-depth interviews with members and leaders of four local congregations: two urban parishes, one Methodist and the other African-American Baptist; and two suburban parishes, one Roman Catholic and the other an Assemblies of God church. These congregations were of similar size but had different theological perspectives and socioeconomic profiles. Third, with qualitative questions refined by the in-depth congregational studies, the Hoover project surveyed a second national probability sample of 1,100 adults. This survey measured opinion about the quality of religion coverage, definitions of what constitutes religion news, and preferences about various kinds of news coverage. Still more information came from interviews with religion writers and their editorial supervisors from eight daily newspapers, four larger and four smaller ones. Hoover and his colleagues also got input from consultations with twenty prominent religious journalists and observers of American religious life.

The first national survey indicated that more than 70 percent of Americans read a newspaper every day.[7] The vast majority of that group, the Hoover survey found, regard religion as "very important" or "fairly important" in their lives. Following up on the finding that most daily readers of newspapers are religious people, the researchers determined that few daily readers go to overtly religious publications for their news about religion. On the contrary, they look primarily to their daily newspapers, and thus 66 percent of those who read a paper every day believed it "very important" for newspapers to cover religion.

When their respondents emphasized that it was "very important" for newspapers to cover religion, Hoover, Hanley, and Radelfinger wanted to find out more about the meaning of that claim. Having determined that readers discriminate among the different kinds of news a paper contains—front-page, "hard news," for example, in comparison to back-page sections that typically contain features and "softer" news—they asked their second national survey's respondents to rank in importance nine "special interest" topics.

Religion came out in the middle. Interest in stories about education, health, business, and food led religion, but entertainment and, especially surprising, sports as well as the arts and personal advice features trailed behind. When asked to pick which of the nine topics they were actually most likely to read on a given day, the respondents ranked the topics nearly the same. A significant shift occurred, however, when people were asked about the quality of the coverage of the nine "special interest" topics in the papers they read. Sports, which religion surpassed in the previous two inquiries, went to the top. Lack of satisfaction with religion's coverage pushed it to the very bottom of the list.

Apparently American newspaper readers want more and better coverage of religion, but the inquiry about "special interest" topics did not do full justice to the question about what more and better coverage of religion means. Hoover and his colleagues explored that definitional issue by using a list of sixteen "types" of religion coverage. Their working hypothesis was that people would favor local and parochial news. So their "types" presented those options first and gradually moved toward national and international concerns.

In what they call "the most surprising result of the entire survey," Hoover and his associates observed that reader interest was less local and parochial than the survey's working hypothesis assumed. Respondents tended to define religion coverage broadly. They wanted national and international as well as local perspectives. Especially interesting for the outlook of this book, they recognized that religion affects and is affected by news—political and economic, for example—that cannot be confined to the religion page. To use the Hoover study's word, "mainstreaming" of religion news was what many American readers wanted in their papers.

In multiple ways, such mainstreaming would require improved quality as well as greater quantity and variety of talk about religion in public. The mainstreaming would do so by changing press coverage, and that change, in turn, would affect public discourse because people tend to talk in public about what newspapers deem worthy of attention.

Newspapers, of course, are only one medium, and their readers' response to the coverage of religion news is only a single source of evidence that talk about religion in public is widespread, important, interesting, and also in need of improvement. But there are many other sources to consider as well. Take television: in January 1994, for example, the ABC network hired Peggy Wehmeyer to work with anchor Peter Jennings, who wanted to add a new dimension to *World News Tonight*.[8] At the time, that appointment made Wehmeyer the only regular religion correspondent in network television. A devout Christian, she is theologically trained, and her ABC reports have included stories on prayer in the schools and antisemitism. Her position does not signify a sea change—one 1993 study showed that only 211 of 18,000 network news stories focused specifically on religion—but Wehmeyer's presence on ABC news does make that network's coverage more comprehensively American.

More than major network newscasts, publications such as *Newsweek, Time,* and *U.S. News and World Report* often focus on religion.[9] Occasionally their cover stories even feature it. Books do their share, too, among them, for example, the *Catechism of the Catholic Church.* The first new Catholic catechism since the Council of Trent in 1566, this 750-page compendium of Roman Catholic doctrine reached bookstores in the summer of 1994 and enjoyed best-selling status. By the end of 1994, Pope John Paul II's *Crossing the Threshold of Hope* topped the nonfiction bestseller list, and *The Celestine Prophecy,* James Redfield's spiritual novel, held the same spot for fiction, signaling bestseller status that would last for months.

Reading, Writing, and Religion

Substantial shelf space in major bookstores is devoted to books that talk about religion in one way or another. Many specialty stores prosper by concentrating on that trade. A few comments about seven books can sharpen the focus on the range and variety of discussion about religion and spirituality that have been found in the United States during the mid-1990s. Start with one by Phillip Berman. During a three-year period, he traveled 35,000 miles and interviewed some 500 Americans about their beliefs. The result was *The Search for Meaning: Americans Talk about What They Believe and Why.* Appearing initially in 1990, the book was issued in a popular paperback edition three years later.

Berman was impressed by "the diversity of the American moral imagination," which he found to include everything from hedonism and nihilism to strict practice of biblical injunctions.[10] Nevertheless, much of the time he saw a striking similarity in basic outlooks. Americans repeatedly affirmed a more or less religiously inspired version of the Golden Rule: Treat other people as you would like to be treated. He discovered something else, too, and it is a key factor in the argument I am making in favor of talking about religion in public.

While working on his book, Berman reports, he became aware that it focused on "what may be the last taboo of American life" (5). What Berman meant is that the perspectives displayed and the questions raised by *The Search for Meaning* are, as he put it, "seldom a topic of conversation at the typical American dinner party, or even in intimate talks among friends, where people focus more often upon work, family problems, and the political and economic issues of the day. Discussions about personal moral and spiritual beliefs are seldom encouraged. And if you bring them up, you run the risk of offending your hosts" (5).

Here it is crucial to underscore an important nuance in the perspective that I share with Berman. When he spoke—correctly, I believe—about "the last taboo of American life," his point was *not* that Americans fail completely to talk about religion. Nor was he ignoring the fact that religion is a topic covered by pollsters, journalists, scholars, clergy, and other "experts" of one kind or another. What Berman and I sense instead is that we Americans are too often reluctant to share and evaluate our deepest feelings and experiences, thoughts and hopes, commitments and loyalties about what deserves to matter most, about what, if anything, ought to be held sacred, and about our sense of the whole. As Berman's book suggests, Americans of all kinds—not just specialists and "experts" in the study of American religion—have important things to say about these matters. As people who experience joy and pain, happiness and grief, and who strive to cope with the ups and downs and even the tedium of everyday life, how could we not, for we all have the stories of our own lives to tell and share. When the right opportunities present themselves, Americans can and will express themselves along these lines—often with amazing eloquence and power. Yet too often for our own good these lines of communication remain constricted, inhibited, and jammed. Fear of embarrassment, a sense that such matters are too "private" to be shared, worry that values might be "imposed," or that attempts at conversion might be involved—those reasons are only a few of the blocks that impede the kinds of talk about religion in public that Phillip Berman and I have in mind. Those reasons can be valid, too, and so the point is to keep looking for good ways to talk about religion, ones that can overcome fear, reveal that all of our lives are impoverished if we hold back too much, and encourage ways of speaking that replace imposition with searching for common ground and conversion with seeking for a common good.

Appropriately, Berman's study convinced him that Americans are never going to reach a neat, national consensus about what they believe religiously or otherwise. But he also stated correctly that our souls, individual and collective, are likely to wither unless we allow each other the opportunity to peer into ourselves and thereby to peer into the spirit of America as well.

Care of the Soul: A Guide for Cultivating Depth and Sacredness in Everyday Life achieved bestseller status in the 1990s for Thomas Moore, a psychotherapist writer who lives in New England.[11] Drawing on insights from Jungian psychology and the world's religions, including practical self-help approaches that he finds in spiritual traditions from the Middle Ages and the Renaissance, Moore identifies and works to treat what he calls "loss of soul," which he regards as "the great malady of the twentieth century, implicated in all of our troubles and affecting us individually and socially." Moore believes that "when soul is neglected, it doesn't just go away; it appears symptomatically in obsessions, addictions, violence, and loss of meaning."[12] To that list of troubles he adds others that he often hears in his therapeutic practice: emptiness, vague depression, disillusionment about marriage, family, and relationship, a loss of values, yearning for personal fulfillment, a hunger for spirituality.[13]

Soul, admits Moore, is difficult to define, but he thinks that we know intuitively that it has to do with genuineness and depth, attachment, love, and community. He wants his book to help people bring "soul back into life," and he is convinced that doing so "means we have to make spirituality a more serious part of everyday life." That work, in turn, requires development of "a religious sensibility."[14] Proper care of the soul, he warns, "is not a project of self-improvement nor a way of being released from the troubles and pains of human existence."[15] Such care does not aim to solve, once and for all, life's puzzles; "quite the opposite," he says, "it is an appreciation of the paradoxical mysteries that blend light and darkness into the grandeur of what human life and culture can be."[16]

By calling attention to soul, we make a first step in caring for it. Talking about religion in public may work that way as well. By calling attention to talk about religion in public, we make a first step in caring about it. And if Moore is right about the importance of soul, then talking about religion in public is important, too, because religious sensibilities and the spirituality they encourage are not merely private affairs. A soul is not a private possession but a center of relationships. Hence, we are not likely to have souls that are well cared for unless we have communities and institutions—religious ones among them—that express and nurture such caring. At least in part, moreover, those communities and institutions cannot exist, let alone thrive, unless people discuss honestly and openly their most fundamental concerns, recognizing that these views will involve differences but also common ground that can help to keep us Americans together.

In the 1990s some of the most potent and provocative talk about religion in public is being done by women. Rebecca Chopp, Mary Daly, Elisabeth Schüssler Fiorenza, Susannah Heschel, bell hooks, Audre Lorde, Sallie McFague, Elaine Pagels, Rosemary Radford Ruether, Letty Russell—those names are just a few of the most prominent women's voices in American religion during this decade.[17] Another belongs to Elizabeth Johnson, an award-winning Roman Catholic scholar who teaches at Fordham University in New York.

"What is the right way to speak about God?" Johnson asks in her book *She Who Is*.[18] Her answer expresses the widespread and growing view that "it is indeed right to speak about the mystery of God in female metaphor" (xii). Among the reasons that such speech is crucial, she goes on to explain, is that "while officially it is rightly and consistently said that God is spirit and so beyond identification with either male or female sex, yet the daily language of preaching, worship, catechesis, and instruction conveys a different message: God is male, or at least more like a man than a woman, or at least more fittingly addressed as male than as female. The symbol of God functions. Upon examination it becomes clear that this exclusive speech about God serves in manifold ways to support an imaginative and structural world that excludes or subordinates women. Wittingly or not, it undermines women's human dignity as equally created in the image of God" (4–5).

Johnson rightly stresses that no talking about religion in public can ever be fully adequate to the burning mystery that our language signifies when it tries to grasp what is sacred. But she is also correct to suggest that Americans can and should find more inclusive ways of speaking that bear "ancient wisdom with a new justice" (273).

If American religious discourse needs to reflect a more inclusive sense of care for our souls, individual and collective, then care for children must be a high priority, too. That concern was on the mind of Martha Fay, who published a 1993 inquiry entitled *Do Children Need Religion? How Parents Today Are Thinking about the Big Questions*. Raised Catholic, Fay gradu-

ated from college in 1968. Religious identities were shattering around her—
"most of the people I knew," she says, "having jettisoned the religious identity they had grown up with, were emphatically *not* something." [19] As she
and her friends moved into their mid-thirties and children came along, Fay
found that the young parents she knew seemed to talk about almost everything but "their spiritual plans for their children" (xi). When Fay began
to raise that question with her friends and thereby for herself as well, she
found "the issue of religion—of belief, of observance, of tradition, and the
desire or reluctance to pass it on—had not disappeared but simply gone
underground, to become, it seemed, the last unshared secret of our extraor-
dinarily confessional generation" (xi).

Fay wrote her book to explore "the muddle in which a large number
of people unexpectedly find themselves by virtue of becoming parents: the
obligation to think about what they believe and how they wish to transmit
those beliefs to their children in a time when such an obligation is easily
sidestepped" (xiv). She could not write her book alone, however. She had
to talk to people and listen to them, children included, to find out what
they felt. She had to get them to talk about religion before she could answer
the questions that were on her mind and—silently at times but really nonetheless—on theirs. Fay's book clarifies why she advocates raising children
without the "certainties" that she equates with most conventional religion,
but she emphasizes that the best part of writing the book—and perhaps of
the finished volume itself—was "the rich and still unfinished conversation
it opened with friends and family" (233).

What Fay's conclusions suggest is that by sharing our uncertainties and
living our questions together, including those that make us ask whether
we and our children need religion, we Americans might find that our unfinished conversation can make us more like friends and family than we
might have imagined.

According to Wade Clark Roof, a sociologist of religion at the University of California, Santa Barbara, Martha Fay would be a baby boomer,
a member of that American generation—seventy-six million strong and
about a third of the nation's population—born between 1946 and 1964.
Coming of age not only in the turbulent 1960s but also in the 1970s, with
that decade's evangelical and charismatic revivals, and in the 1980s, with
its New Age spiritualities, this huge, diverse, and much-analyzed cohort
has been dubbed everything from "Hippie" to "Yuppie," "Grumpy," or
"Dink," but Roof finds that they defy those caricaturing generalizations
because "this is a generation of seekers." [20]

Roof's extensive study of the boomers locates "widespread ferment today that reaches deep within their lives" (4). That appraisal may sound strange when one considers that this generation, which started to turn fifty in 1996 at the rate of one every seven and a half seconds, tended to reject in record numbers the religious upbringing it had received. But "now in the 1990s," says Roof, "when many in this generation are rearing children and facing midlife, we observe yet another phase of their religious and spiritual saga. . . . The generation may well be remembered, in fact, as one that grappled hard in search of a holistic, all-encompassing vision of life and as a spiritually creative generation" (243). If the reemergence of spirituality among the boomers is real, their spiritual creativity, Roof believes, will have much to do with a burgeoning pluralism that makes one's religion— or lack of it—very much a matter of choice. That creativity is likely to surface, too, in what Roof calls "multilayered belief and practice," an innovative borrowing and blending of elements from diverse traditions. Although he thinks that only segments of this spiritually divided generation will "return to religion" in the most traditional and conventional senses of that phrase, Roof does expect that as the boomers move into midlife and then toward old age and death, there will be an increasing emphasis on "sharing, caring, accepting, belonging" that will reflect spiritual sensitivity and affect the nation's continual restructuring of its religious life (252). By inviting discussion of religion and its place in American life, especially where the boomers are concerned, Roof encourages not only a generation but an entire nation to become the spiritual seekers that Americans need to be.

In the 1990s the boomers have had to compete for attention with the generation of Americans that follows them. Called twentysomethings, Generation X, the Thirteenth Generation, or "whatever" (one of their favorite words), this cohort spans the birth years of 1965 to 1980. There are some forty million of them. Unfairly, they have been called slackers and whiners. More likely they will be pragmatic, no-nonsense Americans, perhaps, as a *Newsweek* essay put it, making their own innovations through "a mix of '50s values and a '90s knowledge of the world."[21] One of their number, a Dallas attorney named Michael Lee Cohen, found that this generation also has hopes and fears about the American Dream.

Like Phillip Berman, Cohen took to the road, got twentysomethings talking, and tried to learn what his generation thinks about the American Dream. Among the reasons he picked that topic, Cohen explains, was the fact that "no matter what people think about the concept of the American Dream, it is such a potent and longstanding part of our national mythology that virtually everyone has something to say about it. The American Dream is a Rorschach test for our individual and national psyches, a blank screen onto which we project our personal and collective hopes and aspirations." [22] Cohen found the concept "a good conversation starter," one that could open up the private needs and public selves of a generation that has so often seemed enigmatic to itself as well as to its elders.

What did Cohen discover about the twentysomething American Dream? First, his generation joins every other in American history in placing a high premium on material prosperity and comfort. Cohen also found that his assessment of twentysomethings as the "dis-" generation rang true: "We *are* disenchanted, dissatisfied, disenfranchised, disgruntled, disillusioned, disconnected, disgustful—and frighteningly distrustful," he concluded (296). Those attitudes apply to religion as well as to government and business. "Although virtually everyone I met expressed a belief in God or some higher spirit or force," says Cohen, "almost none of them attend religious services regularly. More than a few think formal religion is as corrupt as formal politics. . . . Most people believe that as long as they know right from wrong and have some sort of personal relationship with God, that is enough" (301–2).[23]

Cohen found the public selves of the twentysomethings—his "dis-" generation—ill defined. "We must find something to inspire us to enlarge our circles of concern to include people beyond ourselves, our families, and our close friends," he insists, adding as his last words that "the people I met seem to be waiting—not only for a hero, but also for a mission. . . . The people in this twentysomething generation see the challenges, but they do not have a clear vision of how to overcome them" (302–3, 307).

Echoing some of Cohen's perspectives on the American Dream, sociologists Barry Kosmin and Seymour Lachman reported that "Americans in general believe that there is a moral crisis in society." [24] That sentence begins their account of what they call "the largest and most comprehensive poll ever on religious loyalties" in the United States (2). The National Survey of Religious Identification (NSRI), conducted by the Graduate School of the City University of New York, used computer-generated telephone calls to reach a representative sample of 113,000 people during a thirteen-month period early in the 1990s.

Their profile of the U.S. adult population, which numbered about 250 million at the beginning of this decade, showed that 86.2 percent of Americans identify themselves as Christians, and another 3.3 percent identify themselves as either Jewish (1.8), Muslim (0.5), Buddhist (0.4), Unitarian

(0.3), Hindu (0.2), or "miscellaneous" (0.1). According to NSRI, 8.2 percent of Americans claimed no religious identity, and another 2.3 declined to participate in the poll. NSRI also found that 80 million Americans attend worship services on any given weekend. Yet the 1990s have also been a time in which our country's rates of violence, drug addiction, and crime are notably higher than other Western industrialized nations.[25] Millions of Americans have been incarcerated in jails and prisons during this decade.

What do these data mean, Kosmin and Lachman ask, in a nation that claims religion—as the United States seems to do—to be "important for the maintenance of the social order" (12)? Is American behavior affected by religion and worship? Interestingly, instead of answering that question with a simple yes or no, Kosmin and Lachman pose another: "Is it possible that the situation would be worse if religion were not there?" (1). That question is not one that any poll can really answer, but, as Kosmin and Lachman say, it is definitely one worth talking about "as we approach a new millennium with all its hopes and fears for the future" (283).

Religion in the Air

Discussion and debate about religion, of course, are not confined to print. They permeate American culture.[26] Although evangelical Christian programs proliferate on certain channels, television is usually regarded as indifferent, if not antithetical, to religion. Yet, contrary to that impression, talk shows, newscasts, documentaries such as Randall Balmer's study of evangelical religion, *Mine Eyes Have Seen the Glory*, and explorations such as Bill Moyers's "World of Ideas" and "Genesis: A Living Conversation" series and Hugh Hewitt's 1996 series, "Searching for God in America," are only a few examples of television's testimony that religious trends, themes, and traditions are vital parts of the life Americans share. To mention but five examples from the 1990s, movies such as *Breaking the Waves, Pulp Fiction, Dead Man Walking, Unforgiven*, and *Schindler's List*, the latter two Academy Award winners for best picture in 1993 and 1994, respectively, show that religious motifs are more common in the film world than we might at first think.[27]

Nor does the spectrum stop there. If we Americans sometimes sing what we hesitate to say, then American music talks, or at least can be heard as talking, about religion, too. Listen to "America, the Beautiful," for example, or "God Bless America." Consider the lyrics of country-western songs—one of my favorites says that "some of God's greatest gifts are unanswered prayers," and another warns us not to be "parched, standing knee-deep in a river, dying of thirst." "Christian rock" and "Gospel rap," to say nothing of all the hymns that are sung in religious observances every week, also talk about religion in public. Although its origins were far from American, it is also fascinating to note what happened when a two-disc CD called "Chant" was released in the United States in March 1994. Hot-selling (by the end of 1994 sales approached three million copies), this collection of Gregorian chants, recorded in the 1970s and 1980s by monks in a Benedictine monastery in northern Spain, reached number one on the American classical charts and then shocked the pop charts by breaking into the top ten.

If much American music cannot be appreciated without encountering the memories, tragedies, and hopes that religion involves, consider also the symbolism and rhetoric that surround national holidays such as Memorial Day, the Fourth of July, and Thanksgiving. Or revisit the aura of places — I think of commemorative battlefields such as the one at Gettysburg or the U.S. Holocaust Memorial Museum that opened in Washington, D.C., in April 1993. The impact of those public times and places is linked to history that is infused with religious feeling, commitment, and conflict.[28]

When immigrants become naturalized citizens, they swear to "support and defend the Constitution and laws of the United States against all enemies, foreign and domestic." This oath of allegiance ends with the words, "so help me God."[29] Apparently no American president can conclude a speech without the obligatory, "God bless you" or "God bless America." Although such rhetoric often seems perfunctory, that appearance may reveal only part of the truth. It is neither accidental nor arbitrary that such oaths are required from new citizens and such benedictions are expected even from supposedly secular leaders.

These illustrations suggest only a few of the ways in which talk about religion in public happens frequently in less than obvious ways and places all over the country. As one notes these happenings, something else also bears watching. Even where its presence is less obvious than in the examples already cited, religious discourse may be implicit if not explicit, waiting to happen if it is not occurring already.

In concluding this chapter, what I have in mind is this: Certainly not everything we Americans say or do is directly religious — far from it. Nevertheless, it is also true that very little happens that does not involve and influence religion. Politics or philosophy, economics or entertainment, family life or friendship, science or sex—take almost any event or topic you want. Somehow or other, it will either react to or reflect religion, and religion, in turn, will be affected by it.

Religion is like the air we breathe. It is all around and within us, because our deepest loyalties and concerns are intertwined unavoidably with the inquiries that religion invites and the responses it makes to the yearnings we possess as individuals and as a people. That perspective does not mean that everything and everybody is somehow "religious" in any conventional or institutional sense of that word. But it does suggest that no one's life is completely untouched or unaffected by religion, even when that fact, like the air we breathe, goes unnoticed.

Religion's importance, again like the air we breathe, gets taken too much for granted. True, people may be able to live without religion, whereas they cannot live without air. Yet if religion were removed from our environment, it is not clear that human life would be recognizable, because our actual, historical identities have depended so heavily on religion's reality— and they still do. Critics of religion might welcome the opportunity to have life made strange in that way, but it is not certain that such a new beginning would be desirable even if it were possible.

It is true that the worst that people do is often intensified by religion's ingredients. But, likewise, it is not easy to account for what is good and right about human life without taking religion's positive contributions into account. The difficulty is that, again like the air so many of us actually breathe today, religion is hard to keep unpolluted, fresh, and clean. Religion's strengths and weaknesses, its good and bad features, are not easily separable. Link that reality to the fact that religion is a potent, even explosive, part of life and you have one of the reasons why religion is such a fascinating subject to study and such a significant topic to discuss.

Everywhere Americans turn, the topic of religion can come up. It often does, and in many cases where it does not, it should. One basic reason for saying so is because people constantly face situations—personal and social—that require them to decide what they ought to do. Some of those decisions are much more momentous than others, but whenever forms of the questions "Should I do this?" or "Should we do that?" confront people, moral considerations or the lack of them come into play.

Implicitly if not explicitly, those considerations involve differences between what is right, just, and good and what is wrong, unjust, and evil. That point holds even if a person simply decides "I am going to do this because I feel like it" or a group determines merely "We are going to do this because we want to." Practically every decision we make has moral implications.

American moral sensibilities, or the lack of them, are profoundly connected to religion. That fact holds because moral sensibilities are always informed to a significant degree by social influences, and, at least historically, one cannot separate American society from religion. Consequently, talk about religion in public is possible whenever Americans have to judge what they ought to do. Such talk may be especially appropriate, even essential, in circumstances where the nation's basic well-being is on the line. Thus, as this chapter has argued, the need for more and better talk about the place and significance of religion in American life looms especially large as the twenty-first century approaches.

NOTES

1. Stewart M. Hoover with Barbara Hanley and Martin Radelfinger, "Who Reads Religion News?" *Nieman Reports* 47 (Summer 1993): 42–47. This issue of *Nieman Reports* features a variety of articles on the topic "God in the Newsroom." Focusing on the points that are particularly relevant for the issues at hand, the discussion that follows summarizes overall results from the surveys described in "Who Reads Religion News?" and does not attempt to recapitulate the carefully nuanced detail of the surveys that Hoover, Hanley, and Radelfinger conducted. Their findings, of course, revealed some significant differences with respect to the respondents' gender, region, particular religious persuasion, and other factors.

2. See Gustav Niebuhr, "Church Fires: Real Target Is Souls, Not Just Shingles," *International Herald Tribune*, 25 June 1996, 7.

3. The quotation is taken from the July 2, 1996, text of the presidential proclamation as provided by the U.S. Information Service.

4. Noting that independent black congregations have existed in the United States since the late eighteenth century, Jim Campbell, a Northwestern University historian, observes that "for as long as there have been separate black churches, there have been whites determined to destroy them." For more detail, see Jim Campbell, "Burning Black Churches: A Dismal Historical Cycle," *International Herald Tribune*, 21 June 1996, 9.

5. See Martin Marty, "When Meaning Eludes Us," *Los Angeles Times*, 28 July 1996, M1, M3.

6. *Newsweek* focused cover stories on some of these topics. See, for example, the magazine's features on "Death Wish" and "Sex and the Church," which appeared in the issues of May 3, 1993, and August 16, 1993, respectively.

7. More recent reports emphasize that in the mid-1990s many American newspapers have been downsizing, cost cutting, merging, and closing. Newspaper circulation dropped about 3 percent nationally from 1992 to 1995. The percentage of adults reading daily newspapers declined from 78 percent in 1970 to 64 percent in 1995, figures that put the Hoover study's statistics right in between. For young Americans aged sixteen to twenty-four, slightly more than 50 percent read a newspaper daily. Between 1992 and 1995, the number of daily newspapers in the United States dropped from 1,570 to 1,532. More and more newspapers are adapting to new technologies, including the Internet. Meanwhile, more than 50 percent of American households still receive a daily newspaper. Newspapers continue to be an important and influential presence on the American scene. See "Read All about It," *Time*, 21 Oct. 1996, 66–69.

8. Peter Jennings's views about television news coverage of religion can be found in "The Media's Challenge in Covering Religion," *Religious Studies News,* Nov. 1996, 15.

9. To illustrate this claim, 1994 can serve as a typical year. *Newsweek*'s cover story for November 28, 1994, focused on "The Search for the Sacred: America's Quest for Spiritual Meaning" (see 52–62). This *Newsweek* analysis indicated that although "the seekers fit no particular profile, . . . millions of Americans are embarking on a search for the sacred in their lives." Religious retreats, courses on spirituality, and lectures on religious themes—all are receiving burgeoning responses. According to *Newsweek,* increasing numbers of people are trying "to find answers to profound questions, to understand their place in the cosmos."

In conjunction with its report, *Newsweek* conducted a national poll on November 3–4, 1994. Basing its conclusions on the 756 randomly selected adult respondents, *Newsweek* found that 60 percent of Americans believed that experience of the sacred depends on belief in God, 58 percent reported a need for spiritual growth, 33 percent have had a religious or mystical experience, 20 percent claimed a revelation from God in the past year, and 13 percent have felt the presence of an angel. Fifty percent of those polled indicated that they encountered the sacred "all or most of the time in church or at religious services." Outside of those environments, 68 percent experienced the sacred at the birth of a child, 45 percent during meditation, and 26 percent during sex.

U.S. News and World Report's cover story for April 4, 1994, focused on "Spiritual America: In God We Trust—Testing Personal Faith in a Cynical Age" (see 48–59). The magazine's story noted that the United States has more churches per capita—one for about every 900 Americans—than any other country. Voluntary giving to American religious communities has been about $38 billion annually, a figure that exceeds the gross national product of many countries. Those figures are explained, at least in part, by polls that show that 93 percent of Americans believe in God or a universal spirit, and 68 percent of Americans belong to a church or synagogue. The religious institutions that Americans belong to, however, change considerably from generation to generation. Less than half of the American public remain in the religious group they were born into. Nor is church membership alone an especially reliable measure of the religious depth that may or may not exist in the lives of individuals, communities, or institutions. That observation fits with an additional *U.S. News and World Report* finding, namely, that 80 percent of Americans think that attending a church or synagogue is not necessary for being a good Christian or Jew.

As sociologist Robert Wuthnow pointed out in this *U.S. News and World Report* account, we Americans seem increasingly inclined to set aside institutional religion and its theological grounding in lieu of making up our own faiths as we go along. In addition, the magazine's findings showed that although 62 percent felt that religion's influence in their personal lives had been increasing, 65 percent believed that religion is losing influence on American life, and almost 90 percent (among them 85 percent of those who describe themselves as not very religious) believe that the nation is declining morally.

What do such numbers mean? That question is important, but it cannot be answered, at least not well, unless we Americans do a better job of talking about religion in public.

Highlighting "The Death of Jesus," *Newsweek*'s cover story from April 4, 1994, discussed the light and shadow that contemporary biblical scholarship casts on the New Testament accounts of the death and resurrection of Jesus (48–54). Observing that the passion and death of Jesus "may well be the world's best known story," Kenneth L. Woodward's article also indicates how current scholarship makes the Gospel narratives increasingly problematic—at least if they are interpreted as direct, historically accurate, eyewitness accounts. The best scholarly evidence, Woodward explained, continues to support the view that the Gospels, written thirty-five to seventy years after Jesus' crucifixion, "are proclamations generated by the early church. They were based on memories and traditions kept alive through the oral traditions of preaching and teaching. Even now, scholars are unable to identify the actual authors or pinpoint where the men called Matthew, Mark, Luke and John wrote their stories." Such findings raise a host of questions, among them, Woodward points out, "Who really was responsible for the death of Jesus? Exactly what crime did he commit? Why do the four Gospels differ in the stories they tell? Can they really be trusted?" Americans, in particular, have a long heritage that takes the Bible seriously. But how to take it seriously and how seriously to take it—those are issues that *Newsweek*'s story invites us to take seriously by talking about them in public.

The March 1994 issue of *Life* featured a cover story on "The Power of Prayer: How Americans Talk to God" (54–63). Utilizing the results of a poll conducted by the Gallup organization on December 17–19, 1993, *Life* concluded that Americans pray in astonishing numbers—as many as nine out of ten. Of that number, 75 percent pray at least daily. American prayers tend to be brief—most take five minutes or less. Although their contents range widely, asking for help and giving thanks are prominent, and there is steady focus on family, forgiveness, and healing. When asked if their prayers have ever been answered, 95 percent of Americans, *Life* found, would answer yes. (In *Time*'s June 24, 1996, cover story on "Faith and Healing," polling results showed that more than 80 percent of Americans express confidence in the healing power of personal prayer; more than 70 percent affirm that praying for someone else can help to cure that person's illness; and more than 60 percent think that doctors should join their patients in prayer when patients ask them to do so.)

Some of these percentages were not so high in the data *Newsweek* reported in its January 6, 1992, cover story on "Talking to God: An Intimate Look at the Way We Pray" (38–44). Its findings showed that 15 percent regularly receive a definite answer to a specific prayer, 27 percent never have, and 25 percent have once or twice. Still, citing studies done by sociologist of religion Andrew M. Greeley, *Newsweek* reported that 78 percent of all Americans pray once a week, 57 percent pray once a day, and among those who identify themselves as agnostics or atheists, one in five still prays daily. *Newsweek* noted, too, that "many Americans are embarrassed to speak about their personal prayer life," but reading about prayer may be another matter: "Astonishingly," said *Newsweek* in 1992, "the current edition of *Books in Print* lists nearly 2,000 titles on prayer, meditation and techniques for spiritual growth—more than three times the number devoted to sexual intimacy and how to achieve it."

Five years later, *Newsweek*'s March 31, 1997, issue featured another cover story on prayer whose polling results basically agreed with similar studies from earlier in the decade: 25 percent of adult Americans reported that they pray once a day, and another 29 percent indicated that they pray more than once a day. According to this poll, Americans typically pray for health or success for a child or family member (82 percent) or for strength to overcome personal weakness (75 percent). The *Newsweek* poll found that 87 percent of adult Americans believe that God answers prayer, at least some of the time. See Kenneth L. Woodward, "Is God Listening?" and Jerry Adler, "Unbeliever's Quest," *Newsweek*, 31 Mar. 1997, 56–65.

There is a widespread conviction in the United States that prayer is important, perhaps even one of the most important things that people do. Probably that conviction helps to explain why school prayer remains such a hot issue in American politics. Gallup polls taken in May and June 1995 indicated that 71 percent of Americans would favor a constitutional amendment to permit spoken prayers in the nation's public schools, whereas 25 percent would oppose such a measure, a difference of opinion that has remained quite consistent for a decade. More controversial is the kind of prayer that might be preferred. Disagreement rises in direct proportion to the sectarian nature of prayer; the compromise position becomes "a moment of silence," but enthusiasm for that option is much less intense. See Michael Golay and Carl Rollyson, *Where America Stands 1996* (New York: John Wiley, 1996), 191–92. If so many Americans pray so much and so seriously—in private and in public alike—and if so many Americans believe that prayers are answered, then it is intriguing to ask: Why do Americans not talk about prayer even more than they do? That question could be a good invitation to talk about religion in public.

Many of the 1994 cover stories about religion appeared during the seasons of Passover and Easter. With its religious holidays of Hanukkah and Christmas, December is another time of year when such features can be expected. In 1991 and 1992, for example, *Time*'s cover stories talked about religion in public by raising questions: "One Nation, Under God: Has the Separation of Church and State Gone Too Far?" (9 Dec. 1991, 60–68) and "What Does Science Tell Us about God?" (28 Dec. 1992, 38–44). Maintaining the holiday tradition, *Time*'s cover story for December 18, 1995, asked "Is the Bible Fact or Fiction?" and explored what archaeology can show about biblical history. Four months later, during the seasons of Easter and Passover, *Time*'s cover story (Apr. 8, 1996) dealt with "The Search for Jesus," coverage that featured news about the latest scholarly research concerning the "historical Jesus." By October, *Time*'s cover spotlight (Oct. 28, 1996) was on the biblical book of Genesis, a story prompted by the PBS launch of what *Time* called "the most ambitious Bible-study class ever to air on nationally broadcast television: a two-month series called *Genesis: A Living Conversation*, with Bill Moyers as host" (68). For Christmas in 1996, *Time* (Dec. 16) followed up with a cover story about "Jesus Online," which explored how the Internet influences faith and religion.

For its pre-Easter 1997 issue, *Time*'s cover story asked "Does Heaven Exist?" (24 Mar. 1997). Considering heaven to be "where people live forever with God after they die," most adult Americans polled in March 1997 said yes (81 percent). Of those who said yes, 61 percent believe they will "go directly to heaven" immediately after death, 85 percent think that life in heaven will be "totally different" from life on earth, but 88 percent believe they will meet friends and family members there. All of these questions and concerns are as interesting as they are significant. They deserve the best dialogue and debate that we Americans can muster.

10. Phillip L. Berman, *The Search for Meaning: Americans Talk about What They Believe and Why* (New York: Ballantine Books, 1993), 4. Subsequent page references are given parenthetically in the text.

11. This book has been followed by two others that elaborate and extend themes in *Care of the Soul*. See Thomas Moore, *Soul Mates: Honoring the Mysteries of Love and Relationship* (New York: HarperCollins, 1994) and *The Re-enchantment of Everyday Life* (New York: HarperCollins, 1996).

12. Thomas Moore, *Care of the Soul: A Guide for Cultivating Depth and Sacredness in Everyday Life* (New York: HarperCollins, 1992), xi.

13. If bestseller book lists make a good indicator, American hunger for spirituality reached ravenous proportions in the summer of 1994. For example, writing for the *New York Times* News Service, Veronique de Turenne spoke of "the summer of the soul," as she noted that "two of the top five hardcover novels on the *New York Times* bestseller list deal with the spiritual world. Six spiritual books grace

the nonfiction hardcover list, while the top-selling paperback is *Care of the Soul* by Thomas Moore." According to Turenne, booksellers report that such books—they may deal with everything from near-death experiences to angels and magic as well as more traditional topics—are becoming more mainstream than trendy. What do such findings reveal about us Americans? That question, too, is worth talking about in public. See Veronique de Turenne, "Soul Searching Appears to Be Latest Theme for Summer Books," *Inland Valley Daily Bulletin,* 3 July 1994, A24.

14. Moore, *Care of the Soul,* xiv–xv.

15. Ibid., 304.

16. Ibid., xix.

17. Here it is worth noting that an important conference, "Re-imagining . . . God, the Community, the Church," was held in Minneapolis, Minnesota, on November 4–7, 1993. Planned in conjunction with the World Council of Churches' "Ecumenical Decade: Churches in Solidarity with Women," it attracted 2,000 people from thirty-two Christian denominations, forty-nine states, and twenty-seven countries. Among them were women theologians from ten denominations, twelve countries, and diverse racial and ethnic backgrounds who addressed a variety of religious topics from feminist perspectives. The talk at this conference, which included urging the use of *Sophia* (meaning Wisdom) as a name for God—something that Elizabeth Johnson and many other feminist theologians have proposed for some time, has produced responses in American churches that range from strong approval to vociferous dissent, with nearly all the shades of difference in between. The Re-imagining Conference intended to provoke dialogue and discussion. It has surely done so. The quality of that dialogue and discussion will have much to say about how talking about religion in public is nuanced and engendered in the future.

My information about the Re-imagining Conference comes from the Office of the General Assembly of the Presbyterian Church (USA). It is contained in a document entitled "Resolution of the Assembly Committee on General Assembly Council Review in Regards to the Re-imagining Conference."

18. Elizabeth A. Johnson, *She Who Is: The Mystery of God in Feminist Theological Discourse* (New York: Crossroad, 1992), 3. Subsequent page references are given parenthetically in the text.

19. Martha Fay, *Do Children Need Religion? How Parents Today Are Thinking about the Big Questions* (New York: Pantheon, 1993), xi. Subsequent page references are given parenthetically in the text.

20. Wade Clark Roof, with the assistance of Bruce Greer, Mary Johnson, Andrea Leibson, Karen Loeb, and Elizabeth Souza, *A Generation of Seekers: The Spiritual Journeys of the Baby Boom Generation* (New York: HarperCollins, 1993), 8. Subsequent page references are given parenthetically in the text.

21. Jane Bryant Quinn, "The Luck of the Xers," *Newsweek,* 6 June 1994, 67. Quinn's essay is part of a larger cover story analysis of "The Myth of Generation X: Seven Great Lies about 20somethings"; see 62–72.

22. Michael Lee Cohen, *The Twentysomething American Dream: A Cross-country Quest for a Generation* (New York: Dutton, 1993), 6. Subsequent page references are given parenthetically in the text. Cohen makes no claim that his book is a thorough sociological study. He interviewed 161 people in fifty-one cities and towns across the country between October 1991 and June 1992. His discussions with forty-three of them appear in the book. About half of these men and women have college degrees, which is twice the national average. A random sampling Cohen's book is not, but the issues raised by the people with whom he spoke remain significant nonetheless.

23. David W. Machacek's sociological studies of Generation X complicate and dispute Cohen's views at this point. Machacek finds that Americans born between 1963 and 1976 are more favorably disposed to and active in religious life than Cohen's comments suggest. Machacek found them about as religious as the baby boomers, and in some respects more so. See David Briggs, "Studies Show Generation X Keeping Faith," *Inland Valley Daily Bulletin,* 18 Jan. 1997, B4. Briggs is an Associated Press religion writer.

24. Barry A. Kosmin and Seymour P. Lachman, *One Nation Under God: Religion in Contemporary American Society* (New York: Harmony Books, 1993), 1. Subsequent page references are given parenthetically in the text.

25. Contributing to these conditions, American civilians tote a staggering amount of guns. According to estimates by the federal Bureau of Alcohol, Tobacco, and Firearms, there were some 220 million of those weapons on our streets in 1996.

26. Although it is beyond my expertise to do more than mention the topic, the Internet and the World Wide Web are additional places where talk about religion in public may increasingly be found. The possibilities that this medium holds are vast, and they are worthy of a much more thorough analysis that I am capable of giving. For further information about this subject, see Mark A. Kellner, *God on the Internet* (Foster City, Calif.: IDG Books Worldwide, 1996). This book is billed as "a complete guide to enhancing your spiritual life via the Internet and online services." Kellner estimates that 250 million people will be accessing the Internet by the year 2000, a considerable potential for public discourse about religion. See also Quentin D. Schultze, *Internet for Christians* (Muskegon, Mich.: Gospel Films, 1997), and Stephen D. O'Leary, "Cyberspace as Sacred Space: Communicating Religion on Computer Networks," *Journal of the American Academy of Religion* 64 (Winter 1996): 781–808. More information can be found in *Time*'s religion coverage (Dec. 16, 1996), which included articles entitled "Finding God on the Web" and "Can Thor Make a Comeback" (60–69). In the aftermath of the mass suicide of the Heaven's Gate cult in late March 1997, it became apparent that the diversity of religious groups making use of the Internet is vast. Religious cults in the United States are estimated to number between 2,000 and 3,000 in the late 1990s. Many of them have Web sites and Internet "chat rooms."

27. For an insightful study of moral and religious themes in films, see Mar-

garet R. Miles, *Seeing and Believing: Religion and Values in the Movies* (Boston: Beacon Press, 1996). Miles thinks that Americans are more likely to gather around movie and television screens than in conventional religious institutions to reflect on basic moral problems.

28. Some of the best work on the sacredness of special American places has been done by Edward Tabor Linenthal. See, for example, his *Sacred Ground: Americans and Their Battlefields,* 2d ed. (Urbana: University of Illinois Press, 1993). Also helpful in this regard is William Zinsser, *American Places* (New York: Harper-Collins, 1992). For an insightful interpretation of the U.S. Holocaust Memorial Museum, see Linenthal's *Preserving Memory: The Struggle to Create America's Holocaust Museum* (New York: Viking Penguin Books, 1995). Another significant study of Holocaust memorialization is James E. Young, *The Texture of Memory: Holocaust Memorials and Meaning* (New Haven: Yale University Press, 1993).

29. The U.S. Immigration and Naturalization Service reported that more than one million new citizens—75 percent of them living in the regions of Los Angeles, New York, Miami, Chicago, and San Francisco—took this oath in fiscal year 1996, making it the biggest year in American history for naturalizations. These people have become American citizens at a time when political controversy about immigration policy in the United States has been running high. Some critics contend that the criteria to become a naturalized citizen are too lax. Presently those criteria are: five years of residence in the United States; no convictions for a serious crime; the ability to read, write, and speak basic English; and a passing mark on an American history and civics test. Most Americans, of course, receive citizenship as a birthright. See Maria Puente, "Naturalizations at All-Time High," *USA Today* (International Edition), 8 July 1996, 3A.

CHAPTER THREE

Virtue and Religion

People should be able to speak [of] their religious conviction in a forthright way, explaining it, talking about it.
But there's not much public discourse about it.

—GEORGE H. GALLUP JR.

Thus far, we have been primarily exploring two major themes. First, as it
involves fundamental concerns about our senses of the whole, about what
deserves to be called sacred, and about our most basic loyalties, religion
pervades American life and by no means always in expected ways. Second, we Americans express our views about religious issues. We do so frequently and pluralistically. Evidence shows that Americans would like to
know even more about religion's roles in our lives.

In addition, we have been alluding to a third theme: Neither the quantity nor the quality of public discourse about religion in America meets
our needs in the best ways possible. We ought to have more and better discourse about our personal religious concerns and the place of religion in
our public lives.

More needs to be said about what these propositions mean and how they
fit together. If religion is so widespread in American life, and if we Americans—including scholars, critics, clergy, pollsters, and other "experts"—
express our views about religion as much as we do, then what, in particular, could be lacking? Concentrating on that question, this chapter suggests

that the lacking element is a combination of ingredients. The point is not simply that we need more talk about religion in public, but that we need more of certain kinds of discourse about religion. The "more" and "better" are perhaps aptly written "more-and-better," for in the case at hand these dimensions are inseparable. Not only are the quantitative and qualitative aspects connected, but they need to be interrelated even more thoroughly. They intersect most importantly at the places where Americans of all kinds find ways to share, understand, and criticize constructively their feelings and thoughts about what matters most.

Specifically, this chapter advances reflection in those directions by considering important connections between virtue and religion. Drawing on some definitive traditions of American government, the chapter illustrates and examines connections between virtue and religion by interpreting words that most Americans know, the Pledge of Allegiance to the flag, and by evaluating something that most Americans want to experience, the American Dream. This inquiry elaborates how the fact and fiction, the remembering and forgetting of basic American promises and dreams require us Americans to make talk about religion more deeply and widely shared if we are to move beyond fantasy, deception, and nightmare to enhance the vision, insight, and hope that life in the United States offers.

The American Dream and the Common Good

As a point of departure, come along with the countercultural writer Hunter S. Thompson. Although his angles of vision differ from Adrienne Rich's, Thompson looked for, and in a way created, a map of our country when he published his 1971 novel *Fear and Loathing in Las Vegas*. Detailing what Thompson's subtitle called "a savage journey to the heart of the American Dream," the story follows Dr. Duke and his attorney as they blast eastward from Los Angeles through the desert in a "huge red Chevy convertible . . . rented off a lot on the Sunset Strip."[1]

Eventually the two explorers find themselves "somewhere on the Northeast outskirts of Las Vegas—zooming along Paradise Road" (161). Headed toward Boulder City, they stop at Terry's Taco Stand, USA, to find their way. "Let me explain it to you," Dr. Duke's attorney tells the waitress, "let me run it down just briefly if I can. We're looking for the American Dream, and we were told it was somewhere in this area. . . . We were sent out here from San Francisco to look for the American Dream, by a magazine, to cover it" (164–65).

The directions given by the Taco Stand's waitress and its cook, whose name is Lou, are not too clear. In one of its manifestations, however, the American Dream may once have been a discotheque previously known as the Old Psychiatrist's Club. Following those leads, Dr. Duke and his attorney finally locate what's left of the place: "A huge slab of cracked, scorched concrete in a vacant lot full of tall weeds," writes Thompson. "The owner of a gas station across the road said the place had 'burned down about three years ago' " (168).

If we Americans consult our private needs and public selves for directions about the Dream, where will we end up? What will we find? Is the Dream somewhere in our area, in yours or mine? Can anybody "cover it"? Is it cracked, scorched, full of tall weeds, "burned down about three years ago"? And what might questions such as those have to do with talking about religion in public?

In the spirit of Hunter Thompson's journey to locate the American Dream in Las Vegas, a circuitous route can provide a good case study to focus those issues. So note that American calendars designate June 14 as Flag Day. Unlike Thanksgiving, Memorial Day, or the Fourth of July, Flag Day means business as usual for banks, post offices, taco stands, and other establishments. Still, even if "a flag is only a bit of cloth," sociologist Émile Durkheim was certainly correct when he added, "a soldier will die to save it."[2] The American flag is one of the nation's most potent symbols. Quite literally, people will kill and die for it. Thus, even if June 14 is not an official national holiday, Flag Day has significance nonetheless.

The exact origins of the Stars and Stripes are obscured by legend and tradition. Historians, for example, have never documented that Betsy Ross first made "the American flag" at the request of George Washington. Yet the story persists. Every year thousands of Philadelphia visitors track down the Ross house to pay respects. Better proved than the Betsy Ross legend, a resolution was adopted by the Continental Congress on June 14, 1777. It specified that the flag of the United States should be "thirteen stripes, alternate red and white; that the union be thirteen stars, white in a blue field, representing a new constellation." A century later, Congress called for public displays on June 14, 1877, to commemorate the flag's one-hundredth anniversary. World War I was under way on May 30, 1916—Decoration Day (later Memorial Day)—when President Woodrow Wilson proclaimed Flag Day an annual national observance.

The flag is designed to be a symbol of national unity, although its power in that regard is often questioned.[3] One of the ways (again, often questioned) in which the flag unites involves the Pledge of Allegiance: "I pledge allegiance to the flag of the United States of America and to the Republic for which it stands, one nation under God, indivisible, with liberty and justice for all." Probably like you, I cannot remember when I committed those words to memory, but I expect that one of my early Midwestern school teachers taught them to me. We were expected to know the Pledge of Allegiance by heart. Daily repetitions made that certain. For a long time, nearly every American child has had that experience.

Even if the pledge is taught and learned with care, most recitations of it are thoughtless. Like the language of much religious ritual that many Americans have memorized at some time in their lives, the words are uttered without thinking. Nonetheless, the pledge's simple statement has much to say, and it highlights much of what we Americans should talk about. The pledge can provide a compass that helps us to read a map of our country. Before those words can do so, however, attention to their meanings must be paid.

Consider, first, that the Pledge of Allegiance begins differently than other texts—the Declaration of Independence, for example, or the Constitution, or even the National Anthem—that are supposed to have a uniting function in American life. "We hold these truths to be self-evident," says the Declaration as it identifies individual rights that people are to share equally. "We the people," affirms the Preamble that ordains and establishes a Constitution for the United States of America. As for the National Anthem, it begins by asking whether *you* can see the star-spangled banner. In contrast, the pledge's first word is "I."

The current form of the pledge developed from a version that appeared originally on September 8, 1892, in a Boston weekly called the *Youth's Companion*.[4] Published initially as part of a national commemoration of the four hundredth anniversary of Christopher Columbus's "discovery" of the "New World," Francis Bellamy's text was soon used widely in patriotic school exercises. Directed toward young Americans, its language was intended to be personal. Indeed, the original version simply spoke of "my flag," not "the flag of the United States of America," a substitution made in 1924.

A pledge is a promise. In the case of the Pledge of Allegiance, the promise is an oath of loyalty. Thus, it is no accident that it was war time—1942—when the federal government officially recognized the pledge. Nor can it have been accidental that, for all its first-person significance, the pledge is rarely said silently or in private. The pledge is recited publicly. Others, but also oneself, are supposed to hear and be informed by the I who speaks. The speaking I confers responsibility on the I who hears. As the listening I accepts what is heard, a private need to be true to oneself is underwritten. Thus, the personal nature of the pledge, the private need it is designed to intensify, deepens because the pledge's purpose is public. It is something to be said, heard, shared, and reinforced in ways that make us public selves, people who profess loyalty—each and all—to a country we inhabit together.

According to the pledge, the country we inhabit together has a flag that stands for a *republic*. Most Americans know something about the Republican party, but it would be difficult even for most Republicans to specify what the word *republic* means. In fact, if the Pledge of Allegiance disappeared, most of us Americans would not have *republic* in our vocabularies. Even when the word is pronounced in that context, *republic* remains one of those words that gets recited thoughtlessly. It just does not mean much to us anymore.

In his saga about Harry Angstrom, John Updike says that there are certain words we need to hear. In spite of, indeed because of, our deafness to it, *republic* belongs among them. Here is why.

In American political history, the term refers primarily to a form of government. Such usage is embedded in the Constitution itself, whose Fourth Article guarantees "to every State in this Union a Republican Form of Government." That form places a premium on ingredients such as (1) a government of laws, not rulers, to secure liberty and justice; (2) the sovereignty of a people who are free; (3) representative democracy; and (4) a mixed political structure that checks and balances legislative, executive, and judicial authority.

Those elements stress process. They map *how* a republic should work. Granted, such forms are more than the means to an end, for these elements are to some extent ends in themselves. But only to some extent if they are taken by themselves, for American history also draws deeply on traditions that add other key elements to the formal republican vision. Two of those elements are especially important.

To discern them, recall that the word "republic" derives from the Latin *res publica,* meaning "the public thing." By themselves neither the Latin phrase nor its English translation clarifies much, but both do point to the elements I have in mind: first, "the public" and, second, "the thing" that is public.

In Latin, *public* meant "of the people." It did not refer to generic, unidentified people but to *the* people. Particularity, identity, unity—terms such as those help to specify the meaning. One belongs to "the people." In the republican tradition, moreover, the people *inhabit* a place. Inhabitation means that they do more than live there. The people establish a way of life in the territory of their dwelling. Their practices invest it with history and tradition. But the relationship goes the other way as well. The place inhabits the people. Its horizons define what is possible and what is not, what is permitted and what is not. Membership in "the people," participation in its traditions, and recognition of its shared memories, values, and hopes entail responsibilities as well as privileges.

At least on American ground, a republican people is one whose inhabitation commits them to the practices and values of government by law, popular sovereignty, representative democracy, and the separation of powers, to name a few of its main traditions. But political philosophers, including the founders of the United States, have always added a fundamental warning: A republican way of life depends mightily on the *virtue* of the people.

Here it is worth noting that *The Book of Virtues* spent months on the nation's bestseller list when it appeared in 1994. Edited, with commentary, by William J. Bennett, former secretary of education, chairman of the National Endowment for the Humanities, and director of the Office of National Drug Control Policy, this 800-page anthology, Bennett explains, is "a compendium of great stories, poems, and essays from the stock of human history and literature."[5] Some of that history and literature, though by no means all, comes from biblical sources and explicitly religious writers. Whatever their sources, Bennett rightly observes that "this book reminds us of what is important. And it should help us to lift our eyes."[6] As he explains what he means, it is more than coincidental that he turns to biblical language, specifically to words from Paul's New Testament letter to the Philippians (4:8): "Whatever is true, whatever is honorable, whatever is right, whatever is pure, whatever is lovely, whatever is of good repute, if there is any excellence and anything worthy of praise, let your mind dwell on these things."

Self-discipline, compassion, responsibility, friendship, work, courage, perseverance, honesty, loyalty, and faith—those virtues are the ones that *The Book of Virtues* singles out for our American minds to dwell on. What these virtues can and should mean in contemporary American life is a key issue for us to think and talk about. Not only that, as he introduces his book's selections on faith, Bennett makes a succinct and persuasive case to suggest that the identification of those meanings is strongly connected to the importance of talking about religion in public: "Faith is a source of discipline and power and meaning in the lives of the faithful of any major religious creed," he writes. "It is a potent force in human experience. A shared faith binds people together in ways that cannot be duplicated by other means. . . . A secular world stripped of all vestige of religion," he says, "would assuredly have no 'religious wars,' but it by no means follows that it would be a world at peace. We do faith a disservice in laying at its doorstep the fundamental causes of faction. . . . A human being without faith, without *reverence* for anything, is a human being morally adrift. The world's major religions provide time-tested anchors for drifters; they furnish ties to a larger reality for people on the loose. Faith can contribute important elements to the social stability and moral development of individuals and groups."[7]

The contents of Bennett's book have been around for a long time. Most are very old; hardly any are very new. So why did *The Book of Virtues* and its sequels achieve such widespread attention in the mid-1990s? Bennett begins his book by saying that he developed it "to aid in the time-honored task of the moral education of the young."[8] That is a gently understated way of saying what the cover story of *Newsweek* highlighted on June 13, 1994, when 76 percent of the American people described the United States as being in a moral and spiritual decline.[9] Such news, of course, was scarcely surprising to Bennett, who documented that decline in his 1994 book, *The Index of Leading Cultural Indicators: Facts and Figures on the State of American Society.* "Over the past three decades," claims Bennett, "we have experienced substantial social regression. Today the forces of social decomposition are challenging—and in some instances, overtaking—the forces of social composition. And when decomposition takes hold, it exacts an enormous human cost. *Unless these exploding social pathologies are reversed, they will lead to the decline and perhaps even to the fall of the American republic.*"[10] Although not everyone will share the conservative, Heritage Foundation perspective from which Bennett sees the nation, his warnings are ignored at our peril.

Bennett's *Index* notes that in 1992 nearly 900 million "music units"—CDs, for example, cassettes, and music videos—were sold, an increase of more than 50 percent since 1982. Country music grew fastest, but rock led the market, and "between the seventh and twelfth grades, the average teenager listens to 10,500 hours of rock music, just slightly less than the entire number of hours spent in the classroom from kindergarten through high school."[11] Whether *The Book of Virtues* can do very much about that remains to be seen, but the songs we know and sing—or that we have ignored or forgotten—do tell much about who we are. So it is significant that Bennett's book contains words that make important music. They are not by 2-Live Crew but John Newton ("Amazing Grace"), not by Pearl Jam but Julia Ward Howe ("The Battle Hymn of the Republic"), not by Bad Religion but Samuel Smith ("America"), not by Madonna but Katherine Lee Bates ("America the Beautiful").[12]

Construed politically, virtue means what Katharine Lee Bates had in mind when one of her stanzas in "America the Beautiful" speaks of those "who more than self their country loved."[13] That understanding of virtue, however, is incomplete, for the idea runs deeper by pointing to the moral characteristics that individuals must develop in mutually supportive ways to make one's country *worthy* of such love. Bates's text sums up those traits when it sings about "brotherhood from sea to shining sea."

Attention to "the public"—the people—leads to reflection on "the thing" that is public. Earlier in American history, the word *commonwealth* was often used to designate it. As that old term suggested, a people have shared interests and concerns, hopes and aspirations, or they are not "the people" at all. Some of those public interests involve respect for the fulfillment of private needs, but many of those interests show that our selves are public. They are constituted by communal ties.

There is no society without individual men and women, but as people live together, a social reality that is more than them, individually or collectively, manifests itself and exerts its influence. Individualistic Americans tend to lose sight of the fact that living together in the United States binds people together by social ties that elude reduction to individual choices and decisions, likes and dislikes. Nevertheless, even individualistic Americans can recognize the importance of traditions that emphasize the crucial importance of the good of the whole. That emphasis contends that there is a public interest or, better still, a *common good*.

Such a good is social. More than the sum of individual efforts and parts, this good involves a sense of the whole and of what is sacred in it. The health of the public interest or the common good cannot be entrusted conveniently to "invisible hands" that will secure it—somehow or in the long run, the optimistic assurance always says—as individuals pursue self-interest. The tuning of human loyalties toward what deserves fundamental respect is essential for that outcome. Such loyalties emphasize realities that all Americans need—individually and collectively. Among them are justice, truth, and compassion. Such qualities are not abstractions. We feel their presence or absence in the particularities of our lives, even as those qualities transcend such particularities by giving us the perspectives we need to understand, judge, and improve the specific times and places in which we live. More persistently than any other aspect of human experience, religion identifies such qualities as essential to the sense of the whole, as key elements in our understanding of what deserves to be called sacred. More insistently and publicly than any other aspect of human experience, religion urges loyalty to those values as well. To advance the influence of those values in our lives, religious discourse and talk about the place of religion in the nation's life are crucial, and the quality of that deliberation makes a huge difference in the health of the common good.

Here it is important to underscore that the common good is not separated from self-interest, especially when self-interest is "rightly understood," an important qualification that properly makes a distinction between self-interest and selfishness. To be "rightly understood," self-interest must reveal that we are public selves. We have our private needs, but our selves are public nonetheless, because our private needs always have public dimensions. Unless our self-interest is so rightly understood that the common good is cared for in its own right and attended to for its own sake, the significance of life, for each and all, will be less than it can and ought to be.

Thus, for Americans to pledge allegiance to a flag that stands for a republic is no trifling matter. In the words with which the Declaration of Independence concludes, doing so implies that "we mutually pledge to each other our Lives, our Fortunes, and our sacred Honor." Doing so signifies a promise to look after the common good. This means, in turn, that we have a responsibility to look after the health of American religious discourse because its quality and the nation's are so closely dependent on each other.

Our American tradition might have developed very differently, but its republican roots run deep. The nation's difficulties in the late twentieth century may exist in large measure because we Americans have lost sight of them. So it is worth figuring out next what the Native American novelist, N. Scott Momaday, has in mind when he observes, "Where words touch the land, there is place."[14] The country we Americans inhabit together unavoidably involves the land, but much more than geography is involved, because words have touched the land. Some of those words have broadened the land's horizons, adding prospects and possibilities to a country that creates hope. Others have narrowed the land's horizons, diminishing prospects and possibilities in a country that breeds despair. Together those words have transformed land into many places. The many places have become a country that is itself a place—a place of many places. Such multiple senses of place bring people together and pull them apart, because those senses of place are infused with yearnings, aspirations, and histories that we return to in our minds.

"No real culture," Daniel Kemmis adds to Momaday's insight, "can exist in abstraction from place." [15] In turn, Kemmis explains what he means by drawing on Wendell Berry's *The Unsettling of America*. There Berry remarks that "we and our country create one another, depend on one another, are literally part of one another; . . . our land passes in and out of our bodies just as our bodies pass in and out of our land; . . . therefore, our culture must be our response to our place, our culture and our place are images of each other and inseparable from each other, and so neither can be better than the other." [16]

The Pledge of Allegiance interacts with the land in that way. Touching the land, the pledge's words seek a political culture, a common good on common ground, that involves much more than land. The pledge contains words that have helped to make the land a place of American dreams.

One Nation under God?

Originally, the pledge envisioned allegiance to a flag that stood for a republic that would be "one nation indivisible, with liberty and justice for all." Touching the land, those few words express a dream of immense proportions and implications, especially when history and ideals collide, revealing contradictions between what is preached and what is practiced. The part about "liberty and justice for all" is the pledge's best remembered, most often quoted, and most problematic and unsettling phrase. As expansive and open as the land touched by those words, the pledge's dream was supposed to hold Americans together, not only because we pledged allegiance to it but also because American life would grow in those directions.

Individual liberty has long been the nation's watchword. But if liberty came ahead of justice in the pledge's ordering of values, that point only intensifies the tension within the pledge. Its emphasis is no less on what is "for all," on what will make the land into "one nation indivisible." Therefore no "pledge word" that touches the land is more important than *justice*. Justice is so crucial because, without it, the Declaration's sense that people are created equal becomes a mocking abstraction. Only as Americans treat each other with respect and fairness does equality have practical significance. Only as equality has practical significance can the United States make good its dream of providing "for all" its citizens a sense of belonging to and of being at home in a country that can rightly be called "one nation indivisible."

Could putting the nation "under God" help to make it one and indivisible, with liberty and justice for all? Many Americans apparently thought so in 1954, the year that President Dwight D. Eisenhower convinced Congress to add those words to the pledge, requiring schoolboys like me to undo memory and to learn a different rhythm in the words, one that at times still seems strange to me because it was not the way the words came to my memory first. For good measure, Congress also specified a code of conduct to govern the pledge's recitation: Allegiance to the flag was to be pledged standing tall, hats off, right hand over the heart.

The year 1954: Cold War time. More or less united in its deadlock with the USSR's atheistic Communism, the nation was also more or less divided by suspicions about Communist conspiracies within. Nearly fifty years later, the world looks different. The USSR is gone; the Cold War is over. But a congeries of ethnic conflicts abroad have replaced the divisions based on those old realities. There is even some nostalgia for the Cold War's "good old days." Their uncertainties could be mapped and perhaps even managed more easily than the dilemmas of a world that is globalized, tribalized, and often terrorized all at once. At home it would be simpler to cast about for supposed Communist conspirators than to cope with the divisions of race, party, class, and gender that have moved from smoldering latency to open eruption since the time that we revised the Pledge of Allegiance and learned to say, with right hands over our hearts, that the nation was "under God."

The idea that the nation is "under God" is, of course, nothing new, although the conditions that prompted the pledge's 1954 revision may have been so at the time. Belief that the United States is "under God" has been a part of our nation's life from the beginning. The Declaration's signers, for example, put their names on a document that professed "a firm reliance on the Protection of Divine Providence." The meaning of that idea for those late eighteenth-century sons of the Enlightenment, the fervor and sincerity with which they endorsed it, no doubt varied considerably. But the fact that the Declaration enshrines such language illustrates how religion has permeated the American Dream—sometimes by legitimating, other times by subverting, and still other times by correcting, what Americans wanted the Dream to be. Thus, how much that idea has unified or divided American life is hard to say. With poet Carl Sandburg as a guide, a visit to Chicago—perhaps the most American of all the nation's cities—can help to show why.

"Bareheaded, shoveling, wrecking, planning, building, breaking, re-building"—that is how Sandburg saw Chicago in 1916. Under the city's wrist, he wrote, "is the pulse, and under his ribs the heart of the people." "Coarse and strong and cunning," Chicago is still proud to be alive in its "stormy, husky, brawling" way.[17]

As cable television has proliferated channels for the viewing public, the CNBC network came to American life. On Flag Day, 1993, some of its pro-gramming was "live" from Chicago, the place that Sandburg called "Hog Butcher, Tool Maker, Stacker of Wheat, Player with Railroads and Freight Handler to the Nation."

At the time, CNBC's motto, "Information That Hits Home," meant "Money All Day. Talk All Night." Later that motto became "First in Busi-ness. First in Talk." Either way, from June 14 to 18, 1993, all of those net-work themes found expression in what was widely hyped—popular maga-zines such as *Newsweek* and *Time* carried full-page announcements about it—as "an unprecedented cable TV event." Hosted by Tom Snyder and Jane Wallace, the kickoff happened at Chicago's Park West Theater.

The week's topic on CNBC was "Achieving the American Dream." More precisely, the opener posed a question: "Is the Dream still possible?" Promotion for the show offered mixed perspectives. One example pictured a multiethnic group trying to climb a craggy peak. There was not much room at the top, definitely not enough for everybody. Tenuous footholds, strained faces, one person grabbing another to get ahead or to pull the other down, exhaustion, fear—the climbers' trek looked rough.

Prose bordered this publicity picture. It suggested that the climb was about a home, a college degree, equal rights, a safer world for your chil-dren, diversity in the workplace, equal opportunities—any or all of the above. CNBC's week-long series, the promotion went on to say, would address "what it takes to make it in America today." The Snyder-Wallace opener, billed as a dynamic town meeting, promised to explore "the chal-lenges and choices facing the ethnic and cultural groups of our day as they strive to make their dreams come true."

Joining the hosts on that Flag Day evening were some noted pundits, among them Patricia Ireland, the president of NOW (the National Orga-nization for Women); the ex-NFL star and African-American activist Jim Brown; Luis Gutierrez, then a freshman congressman from Chicago; and the syndicated columnists Bob Greene and Cal Thomas. Henry Cisneros, secretary of housing and urban development in the first Clinton adminis-tration, and Ben Chavis, then head of the NAACP (National Association for the Advancement of Colored People), the nation's oldest and largest civil rights organization, were also on hand via satellite from Washington, D.C.[18]

The show began with Tom Snyder's comment that dreams were simpler in the 1950s than they are nearly fifty years later. Earlier, he suggested, the American Dream meant having a job, a house, and a family. Nostalgic film clips backed up that impression. In the 1990s, he continued, although the Dream still contained those elements, its meaning was much less clear.

What followed proved Snyder to be a master of understatement. CNBC's "town meeting" parodied itself. For the most part, "audience participation" was eclipsed by the "experts" or cut off by the hosts. Special interest point-scoring, much of it driven by racial differences, muted probing discussion and put the staking out of positions at center stage. Unrelenting commercial "time-outs"—there were about forty of them—ensured that no trains of thought, such as they were, lasted for more than ten minutes. Even when Jane Wallace announced that the sponsors—which included American Dream interests such as Paine Webber and Charles Schwab, Embassy Suites and Anheuser-Busch, Mercedes Benz and BMW—had generously decided to let the program run for two hours instead of the originally scheduled ninety minutes, one got the impression that the airing of more commercials was at least as important as giving the frustrated audience a few more minutes to ask a question or to make a comment.

Well-intentioned though CNBC may have been, its "unprecedented cable TV event" on the American Dream was a classic example of what public discourse ought not to be. Claiming rather than clarifying, interrupting instead of inquiring, lecturing not learning, posturing in place of pondering, quarreling instead of questioning, scoring rather than sharing, undermining instead of understanding, winning in place of wondering, deferring to "experts" and advertisers rather than to a broader and less commercial set of voices—those are only some of the contrasts that come to mind. The point is not that differences and disagreements have no place. Nor is it that every voice deserves identical prominence. Nor is it that standing one's ground, speaking out, or even "acting up" are out of place. On the contrary, there are times for all of those moves and more. But where the questions include "Is the American Dream still possible?" and "How might religion affect that subject?" a style of discussion more thoughtful, more sustained, more open and democratic was needed than CNBC's Flag Day format in Chicago afforded. The lesson in that judgment was made clear by the frustration level that mounted as the Snyder-Wallace show unfolded.

As entertainment, which it was surely designed to be, the show may have been a minor success, but the main impression it left was that the important questions it raised had received attention that was as unsatisfying as it was undistinguished. In fact, the program seemed to frustrate all of its participants, not least the guest pundits and their hosts. All of them, however—experts and hosts alike—ended up hopeful about the Dream. Well they might, too, for in large measure their individual lives had achieved it. Not to endorse the achievability of the Dream would have been blatant hypocrisy, betraying themselves and the Dream alike.

For many Americans in the Chicago audience and elsewhere, the reactions would not—could not—have been so full of gratification and hope. CNBC helped to document that fact. In preparation for its American Dream programs, the network teamed up with the Gallup polling group to sample public opinion. The questions asked were less than crisply precise. Nor did CNBC explain the nature of the polling sample very well. Yet the questions and findings of the CNBC-Gallup poll about the American Dream are instructive nonetheless.

When asked, for instance, whether it will be easier for the next generation—including the children of the 1990s—to achieve the Dream, 80 percent answered "harder," whereas only 15 percent and 5 percent, respectively, answered "the same" or "easier." The results were more optimistic when the question was "Compared with your parents, what are your chances of achieving the Dream?" Forty-three percent answered "better," and another 28 percent could say "the same." But 27 percent saw their odds as "worse." (By 1995 those figures would deteriorate as Gallup poll results showed that 35 percent regarded themselves as better off than their parents and 52 percent regarded themselves as worse off.)[19] Meanwhile, the CNBC poll revealed the widespread assumption that a yearly income of $50,000, a figure about $12,000 higher than the median income for American families at mid-decade, is needed to achieve the Dream.

Further complications intruded when questions about race came up. When asked how race affected a person's chances of experiencing the Dream, 22 percent of whites acknowledged that their race helped, 66 percent reported no effect, and only 11 percent indicated that their race hurt them. By contrast, 49 percent of nonwhites said that their race was a hindrance, whereas 33 percent reported no effect, and only 15 percent indicated that their race helped them to achieve the American Dream.

Gender-related questions produced related outcomes. When asked how gender affected achievement of the American Dream, only 6 percent of the male respondents thought that their gender hurt them, whereas 64 percent reported no effect, and the remaining 30 percent judged that being male helped them. Women told a different story. Although 56 percent of the female respondents testified that their gender had no effect on achieving the American Dream, only 6 percent thought that being a woman helped them, and 36 percent contended that their gender hurt them.

Beyond these poll results, beyond the opinions expressed and the contentious confusion that reigned during CNBC's Chicago explorations of the American Dream, the entire enterprise had another facet that was as significant as it was intriguing. Explicit references to religion were not conspicuous by their absence, they were just absent—period. Race, gender, sexual preference, AIDS, political policies, economic realities, high ideals, material standards of living—the talk that night covered a vast array of topics, however inadequately. At least by implication, all of those topics were related to the American sense of the whole, perspectives about what deserves to be called sacred, and loyalties to those convictions, but with precious few exceptions, religion was not even explicitly alluded to, let alone discussed in depth. Conservative opinion editorialist Cal Thomas made some tentative efforts to bring religion directly into the discussion, but they were essentially lost in the shuffle as more liberal speakers took him to task for his politically incorrect positions on the condition of American family life and the nature of racial tensions in the United States.

Why was direct talk about religion absent when the American Dream, a topic that has so many implications for and about religion, was under discussion? Did the participants care so little about religion that the topic was deemed irrelevant? Or were they embarrassed, ill equipped, or afraid to talk about religion in public? Or is religion just too private and personal to be discussed very well in an open and public forum?

All of those factors may have played a part in the scant attention that religion received directly on this occasion, but as justifications or arguments for that silence, they do not work very well. One way or another, most of us Americans have strong feelings about religion. At least in part we have such feelings because we know that what people believe affects how they live, and how they live is a public as well as a private matter. If we Americans are too embarrassed, ill equipped, or fearful to talk in public concerning what we feel and know about religion, then that is not a justification for silence but an argument in favor of learning how to engage in discourse about religion more frequently and more effectively.

Talk All Night

Perhaps CNBC thought the issues raised by its American Dream program were thorny enough without introducing directly the added controversy that religion might spark. Maybe the sponsors did not want religion on their hands. Maybe Tom Snyder and Jane Wallace thought it more prudent to sail the relatively calmer waters of secular politics than to navigate debate through the stormy surf of religious pluralism. Responses to those possibilities were not forthcoming from CNBC, its promises about "Information That Hits Home" notwithstanding. But what would happen if there were "Talk All Night" about religion and the American Dream?

For one thing, we Americans would probably rediscover how individuals and groups have disagreed markedly because of the contents and priorities emphasized in our particular versions of the Dream and the place of religion in them. The resulting controversies would show that the American Dream is not only an ideal to rally around but also a convenient target for criticism. Differences about the Dream, many of them charged with diversity about religion, affect American identity so much that they are unlikely to cease. For although Americans—famous or obscure, extraordinary or ordinary—may cherish and want to believe in their dreams, they are also frequently skeptical, even cynical, about realizing them. Whether American attitudes about religion are pro, con, indifferent, or mixtures in between, they complicate the patterns of that kaleidoscope. This complication has been present all along, because no actuality could ever exactly correspond to the lofty ideals, religiously informed or not, that the United States has set for itself.

If talk all night about religion and the Dream would remind us Americans how much faith and skepticism, conviction and uncertainty, dissent and disagreement wax and wane throughout the nation's history, the recollection could provide good reasons not to back away from such debate but to pursue it further. For in doing so we might discover something more. We might locate what we care about together, what we share in spite of and even because of our differences. We might find out, too, how religion could support that common good and even how religion would be most loyal to its best impulses and teachings when it does so.

Pollster George H. Gallup Jr. and Timothy Jones broke the silence by speaking openly about such matters in *The Saints among Us,* a study of American attitudes about religion.[20] Later it will be important to revisit their work in more detail, but some of Gallup's comments about the book's findings provide a good way to conclude this chapter.

On the negative side of the ledger, Gallup found that Americans apparently feel besieged by a "bewildering array of problems."[21] These problems include "not only discouragement at the failure of the material world but disenchantment with lifestyles that we fall into. Loneliness is a factor," Gallup claimed. "We're acutely lonely. We're searching for meaningful relationships." These findings, he contended, involve in at least some dimensions "the failure of the American dream." Those findings persist, moreover, even though tens of millions of Americans are in churches, synagogues, or other places of worship each week. For the most part, in fact, Gallup detected little difference between the typical "churched" person and the "unchurched"—except that the former seem to possess a "brighter outlook and be more active in civic affairs."

Gallup's picture differed dramatically, however, when it focused on those Americans who scored highest on what he calls the "depth dimension" of religious commitment. That 13 percent, claimed Gallup, is "a breed apart." Those people, he affirmed, are "more involved in charity, more tolerant, more ethical, and much happier"—indeed more likely to be concerned for a better society—than the rest of the population.

Strangely, Gallup went on to suggest, these results are a bit like lights hidden under the proverbial biblical bushel. His analysis of that phenomenon was striking because of an ironic outcome of religious pluralism. Gallup put it this way:

[Those who score highest on the "depth dimension" of religious life seem] unable to defend their faith. A climate of pluralism has stifled them, stifled their religious convictions. People are afraid to talk about it. There's a feeling they have to go underground. That's sad. On college campuses, students should be discussing and debating from their own religious traditions. But you don't find it. So nobody learns, nobody is served. People should be able to speak [of] their religious conviction in a forthright way, explaining it, talking about it. But there's not much public discourse about it. Part of the problem is that many people are so ill-informed about their faith and tradition. They're ill equipped to engage in discussion.

If not anticipating the pollster, Robert N. Sollod, a psychologist from Cleveland State University, certainly echoed Gallup when he wrote about "The Hollow Curriculum" in the March 18, 1992, issue of the *Chronicle of Higher Education*.[22] Although he directed his points specifically to universities and colleges, Sollod's comments can be broadened to highlight one key point that I am making as far as talking about religion is concerned.

Sollod stressed that it is not the proper function of universities and colleges to "indoctrinate students with specific viewpoints or approaches to life." I would add that what I mean by talking about religion in public does not have that purpose, either. But Sollod was profoundly and rightly concerned that "the curricula that most undergraduates study do little to rectify the fact that many Americans are ignorant of religious and spiritual teachings, of their significance in the history of this and other civilizations, and of their significance in contemporary society." In the humanities, he argued, religion tends to be downplayed by multiculturalists and traditionalists alike. In the social sciences, Sollod lamented, the situation may be even worse—those disciplines still tend to treat religious commitments as pathologies of one kind or another.

Sollod's claim is bold and therefore debatable, but surely if we Americans were to share talk all night about religion in public, the following words of his would deserve to be on the agenda, both in their specific applications and in their wider implications about what is needed for Americans to do a better job of achieving a dream that offers liberty and justice for all:

Much has been written about the loss of ethics, a sense of decency, moderation, and fair play in American society. I would submit that much of this loss is a result of increasing ignorance, in circles of presumably educated people, of religious and spiritual world views. It is difficult to imagine, for example, how ethical issues can be intelligently approached and discussed or how wise ethical decisions can be reached without either knowledge [of] or reference to those religious and spiritual principles that underlie our legal system and moral codes. . . . National debate and discussion about the best way to educate students concerning religion and spirituality are long overdue.

There will be more to say on these matters, but let this part of the conversation end by winding its path back to Chicago once more. When Carl Sandburg surveyed that place, his language mapped hearty action: brawling and breaking, for example, or building and rebuilding. Most of all, though, Sandburg described Chicago *laughing*.

According to Sandburg, Chicago's laughter sings. Showing "white teeth," maybe going on all night, its laughter is public, out in the open. Its laughter is young, too: the kind, Sandburg says, one might hear from "an ignorant fighter . . . who has never lost a battle." Nevertheless, Chicago's laughter, bragging though it may be, senses what the poet calls "the terrible burden of destiny." [23]

For all its boisterousness, then, Chicago's laughter sounds serious. It does so because meaning, commitment, and a nation's future are at stake.

Involved are deliberations about the sense of the whole, about what deserves to be regarded as sacred, and about loyalties that ought to be most fundamental. Without saying it in so many words, the laughter Sandburg rolls from Chicago's mouth suggests that the health of American dreams and places depends on finding good ways to "talk all night" about religion and virtue.

NOTES

1. Hunter S. Thompson, *Fear and Loathing in Las Vegas: A Savage Journey to the Heart of the America Dream* (New York: Warner Books, 1982), 3–4. Subsequent page references are to this edition and are given parenthetically in the text.

2. Émile Durkheim, *Sociology and Philosophy,* trans. D. F. Pocock (New York: Free Press, 1974), 87. The statement is from "Value Judgments and Judgments of Reality," Durkheim's 1911 article in the *Revue de Métaphysique et de Morale.*

3. Public desecration—especially burning—of the flag has a history sufficiently long and widespread that during the Vietnam War protests of the late 1960s, Congress passed legislation to provide penalties of up to a year's imprisonment or a $1,000 fine or both for publicly burning or otherwise desecrating the flag. Supreme Court decisions in 1989 and 1990 struck down flag desecration laws on the grounds that such laws violated the First Amendment's guarantee of free speech. In the aftermath of the Court's 1990 decision, which involved a 5-4 split, there have been renewed, but thus far unsuccessful, calls in Congress for a constitutional amendment that would make prosecution of flag burning possible.

4. For the following historical information about the Pledge of Allegiance, I am indebted to Diane Ravitch, ed., *The American Reader: Words That Moved a Nation* (New York: HarperCollins, 1991), 182.

5. William J. Bennett, ed., *The Book of Virtues: A Treasury of Great Moral Stories* (New York: Simon & Schuster, 1993), 13. Capitalizing on the considerable popularity of this book, Bennett also edited and published a sequel called *The Moral Compass: Stories for Life's Journey* (New York: Simon & Schuster, 1995). In addition, he produced *The Children's Book of Virtues* (New York: Simon & Schuster, 1995). The latter books enjoyed brisk sales in 1995 and 1996. Although Bennett has long been a critic of PBS, he was pleased nonetheless to have that network air a television series of children's stories from *The Book of Virtues.*

6. Bennett, *Book of Virtues,* 15.

7. Ibid., 741–42. Among Bennett's many provocative entries in *The Book of Virtues'* section on faith is one called "Going to Church," which Theodore Roosevelt wrote for the *Ladies Home Journal* in 1917 (see 798–99). All ten of Roosevelt's reasons for affiliation with religious institutions are still worth talking about in public. Although it would need to be interpreted in a less exclusively Christian manner

to fit the nation's increasing religious pluralism, Roosevelt's first reason especially invites talk about religion in public as we Americans think about the relationships between our private needs and public selves. "In this actual world," wrote Roosevelt, "a churchless community, a community where men have abandoned and scoffed at or ignored their religious needs, is a community on the rapid downgrade. It is perfectly true that occasional individuals or families may have nothing to do with church or with religious practices and observances and yet maintain the highest standard of spirituality and of ethical obligation. But this does not affect the case in the world as it now is, any more than that exceptional men and women under exceptional conditions have disregarded the marriage tie without moral harm to themselves interferes with the larger fact that such disregard if at all common means the complete moral disintegration of the body politic."

8. Ibid., 11.

9. See Howard Fineman, "The Virtuecrats," and Kenneth L. Woodward, "What Is Virtue?" *Newsweek*, 13 June 1994, 31–39.

10. William J. Bennett, *The Index of Leading Cultural Indicators: Facts and Figures on the State of American Society* (New York: Simon & Schuster, 1994), 8. Bennett's selections on responsibility in *The Book of Virtues* create sharp contrasts with and antidotes to many of the declining conditions he describes in his *Index*. One example that comes to mind is by a man from Maryland named William Tyler Page. In 1917, he won a national contest for his version of "the best summary of American political faith." On April 3, 1918, the U.S. House of Representatives adopted it as the American's Creed, but, Bennett goes on to say, "today very few people have even heard of it" (*Book of Virtues*, 219). Here is how it goes:

> I believe in the United States of America as a Government of the people, by the people, for the people; whose just powers are derived from the consent of the governed; a democracy in a republic; a sovereign Nation of many sovereign States; a perfect union, one and inseparable; established upon those principles of freedom, equality, justice, and humanity for which American patriots sacrificed their lives and fortunes.
>
> I therefore believe it is my duty to my country to love it; to support its Constitution; to obey its laws; to respect its flag, and to defend it against all enemies.

11. Bennett, *Index of Leading Cultural Indicators*, 111–12.

12. See Bennett, *Book of Virtues*, 772, 797–98, 718–19, and 722–23. John Newton, eighteenth-century slave trader–turned–abolitionist minister, wrote about "Amazing grace, how sweet the sound, / That saved a wretch like me! / I once was lost, but now am found, / Was blind, but now I see." Julia Ward Howe's "Hymn," written in November 1861, first became popular with Union troops during the Civil War. As it sings about "the glory of the coming of the Lord," it also warns that God is "sifting out" our hearts "before His judgment seat." In a bit of American-style subversion, Samuel Smith turned the tune to "God Save the King" into "America."

Smith's words let us Americans sing of our country—"sweet land of liberty"—and also to God, who is hymned as the "author of liberty." The words of such hymns are not only worth singing—public expression of religion occurs whenever we do sing them. They are also worth talking about in public because they involve affirmations and questions about matters as important as any concerns can be.

13. See ibid., 722–23, and Ravitch, *American Reader*, 185. A professor of English at Wellesley College, Bates wrote "America the Beautiful" in 1893, revising the lyrics in 1904 and again in 1911. Her words were set to music by Samuel A. Ward. The song is really a hymn. Each of its stanzas invokes God. They ask God to shed grace on America, to mend the nation's flaws, and, metaphorically speaking, to refine its gold. Its religious tones help to explain why "America the Beautiful" has often been proposed as a substitute national anthem. Those same tones may help to explain why "America the Beautiful" has not—and probably will never—replace "The Star-Spangled Banner." But here is another topic that could invite instructive talk about religion in public in the United States.

14. Momaday made this remark in the 1993 Public Humanities Lecture that was sponsored by the California Council for the Humanities in San Diego on June 4, 1993.

15. Daniel Kemmis, *Community and the Politics of Place* (Norman: University of Oklahoma Press, 1990), 7.

16. Wendell Berry, *The Unsettling of America* (New York: Avon Books, 1977), 22. Cited in Kemmis, *Community*, 7. Restless Americans have long had a literary tradition that emphasizes travel and the making of fresh beginnings by leaving old terrain behind and setting out for new territory. As the reflections of Momaday, Kemmis, and Berry suggest, however, many Americans also yearn to find themselves in places where roots can grow deeply and where meaning is closely tied to specific locations. This literature of place often expresses profoundly spiritual insights. Three poignant examples of such writing from the 1990s include: David Mas Masumoto, *Epitaph for a Peach: Four Seasons on My Family Farm* (San Francisco: HarperSanFrancisco, 1995), Kathleen Norris, *Dakota: A Spiritual Geography* (Boston: Houghton Mifflin, 1993), and Scott Russell Sanders, *Staying Put: Making a Home in a Restless World* (Boston: Beacon Press, 1993).

17. The quotations are from Sandburg's "Chicago," which is reprinted in Ravitch, *American Reader*, 232.

18. On August 20, 1994, the NAACP, the nation's oldest black civil rights organization, removed Chavis as its executive director. The dismissal occurred because of his management of the organization's finances and his handling of a former aide's sexual discrimination complaint. In late 1995, Kweisi Mfume, a member of the House of Representatives from Baltimore who had led the Congressional Black Caucus, was named president and chief executive officer of the NAACP.

19. See Michael Golay and Carl Rollyson, *Where America Stands, 1996* (New York: John Wiley, 1996), 167.

20. George H. Gallup Jr. and Timothy Jones, *The Saints among Us* (Harrisburg, Pa.: Morehouse Publishing, 1992).

21. Gallup's prepublication commentary about *The Saints among Us* comes from "Gallup Says Media Should Focus on Religion — The 'New Frontier,' " an article in the *Los Angeles Times,* 14 Mar. 1992, F18-19.

22. The quotations that follow are from Robert N. Sollod, "The Hollow Curriculum," *Chronicle of Higher Education,* 18 Mar. 1992, A60.

23. Ravitch, *American Reader,* 232.

CHAPTER FOUR

American Beliefs: Popular Opinions and Religious Inclinations

We are looking for total honesty. There are no right or wrong answers. We are concerned only with what you believe.

—JAMES PATTERSON AND PETER KIM,
The Day America Told the Truth

If Americans are to have better public discussion about religion, we need to identify what matters most to us and why. We need to share, understand, and evaluate our deepest yearnings. This chapter takes steps in that direction by exploring important beliefs that Americans have expressed, directly or indirectly, in the 1990s. It uses the mapping provided by census data and public opinion polls as case studies. Although those elements do not produce a flawless picture of American beliefs and religious inclinations, the facts and figures do indicate trends that are important for helping us to understand who we are and where we need to go. Specifically, they reveal a nation in need of and to a considerable degree searching for a sense of the whole and for understandings of what is sacred within it. They reinforce the need for public discussion about religion and amplify some of the major themes that discourse needs to dwell on. Those themes emphasize trust, commitment, service—key values for holding Americans together.

Who We Are

As we head for the polls, recall that George Washington served the first two terms as president of the United States after leading his troops to victory in the American Revolution. When he left office in 1796, he gave a now famous "Farewell Address." It was a plea for unity. Washington urged his contemporaries to understand "the immense value of your national union to your collective and individual happiness." He also emphasized how the name "American" referred to a single people who had worked and fought together. With only "slight shades of difference," he added, "you have the same religion, manners, habits and political principles."[1]

Not only did Washington underestimate the nation's shades of difference, including the fact that the land contained countless people—slaves among them—who could not think of themselves as American at all, he could scarcely have imagined the variety those shades of difference would come to contain. Homogeneity has never been a dominant American characteristic. Nor will it be. Unity will always be a rhetorical theme for American presidents—arriving, departing, or in between—because its depth and quality cannot be easily presumed.

Mandated by Article 1, Section 2, of the Constitution of the United States, the first American census occurred in 1790, shortly after Washington became president, and it has continued at ten-year intervals ever since. That initial counting was comparatively simple. Its mapping included only free white males aged sixteen or older, free white males under age sixteen (to calculate how many men would be available for military duty), free white females, all other free persons (including Native Americans who paid taxes), and slaves. The census of 1790 registered the American population at about 3.9 million, including about 750,000 slaves (nearly 20 percent of the total).

Two centuries later, the figures for the 1990 census have been contested, particularly by municipal and state officials who argued that its count skipped people in urban areas, the poor, and minorities. Although the tally may be off by a figure larger than the total for the 1790 census, Americans in 1990 numbered about 250 million, an increase of 10 percent from 1980. Nearly a million more Americans citizens could be found living abroad.

Updates by the U.S. Census Bureau show that the population of the United States in 1996 was about 265 million, which included an increase of 2.5 million persons in 1995 alone. Of that number, 720,000 were legal immigrants. The population of the state of Texas in 1996 was 18.7 million, which put it ahead of New York but still second to California. The American people are the most diverse of any nation on earth. The next census, in 2000, will reveal increasing variety as the nation grows more complex and crowded. Looking ahead still further, demographers anticipate even more diversity in an American population that is expected to reach more than 320 million by 2020 and more than 390 million by 2050. Meanwhile, Sam Roberts, urban affairs columnist for the *New York Times,* offered the following picture in his 1993 book, *Who We Are: A Portrait of America Based on the Latest U.S. Census:* "Today, the average American is a 32.7-year-old white woman who lives in a mortgaged suburban home that has three bedrooms and is heated by natural gas. She is a married mother, with some German ancestry, on the cusp of the MTV generation—roughly the thirteenth to come of age since Benjamin Franklin's. She graduated from high school and holds a clerical job. She moves to a new home more frequently than residents of any other developed nation." [2] Echoing the Chinese American author, Gish Jen, who commented on *Typical American,* her 1991 novel, by noting that "there is no longer any one typical American, if there ever was," Roberts hastened to add that his picture was one of a mythical and, strictly speaking, nonexistent American. As Roberts argued, the United States is too much a country of contrasts, it consists of too many parts, to let us speak meaningfully of *the* typical American. What Roberts could say with accuracy, however, was that "the nation's complexion changed more starkly in the 1980s than in any previous decade, and twice as fast as in the 1970s" (7).

According to the government's midcensus estimates, by 1995 whites were estimated to make up about 74 percent of the American population, but that shrinking majority is far from homogeneous, and it has declined from 83 percent in 1980 and 80 percent in 1990. By 2050, that majority will be little more than half of the American population. In the mid-1990s, African-Americans numbered some 33 million, about 13 percent of the population, an increase of almost 14 percent from 1980. In 1995, there were nearly 27 million Americans of Hispanic origin, an increase of 83 percent since 1980 and about 10 percent of the nation's total population. Another 4 percent of the American population is Asian, a number that more than doubled between 1980 and 1995.

Significantly, the country's population is also aging. In 1990, one in five Americans was at least 55 and one in eight was at least 65. The number of people over age 60 nearly equals the number under the age of 14. Moreover, "between 2010 and 2030," Roberts found demographers predicting, "the number of Americans 65 and older will mushroom by 30 million as Baby Boomers turn the age pyramid upside down" (233).

Language and religion tell similar stories of change and diversity. The number of people in the United States whose usual language or mother tongue is other than English rose from 28 million in 1976 to 34.7 million in 1990 and will likely reach 39.5 million by 2000. Spanish will be increasingly important in the United States. Asian languages are becoming more prominent, too. Such diversity has prompted debate about legislation, or perhaps even a constitutional amendment, to make English the explicit official language of the United States.

As for religion, although the Southern Baptist Convention has 15.6 million members, making it the largest Protestant denomination, the days of the old white Anglo-Saxon Protestant (WASP) hegemony in the United States are declining. Roman Catholics—more than 60 million of them—are the largest Christian denomination. In addition, there are about 6 million Jews in the United States, a number now rivaled by Muslims. In fact, there are more Muslims in the country than Mormons or Episcopalians. Often bolstering the political clout of the conservative Christian Coalition, the popularity of evangelical, Pentecostal, and fundamentalist Christian movements—enhanced by extensive television coverage and more than four hundred "megachurches" that each pack in more than two thousand worshipers weekly for everything from sermons to seminars and aerobics classes—continues to make religious news. Meanwhile there is a resurgence of interest in Native American religious traditions, and the appearance of "New Age" spirituality combines with other so-called new religions and the increased influence of Asian religious practices—especially those of Buddhism—to expand the varieties of American religious experience even further.

In a chapter called "Why We Count," Sam Roberts's *Who We Are* observes that *census* is a word "derived from the French verb for 'to assess'" (18). Perhaps the most important reason for an American census/assessment each decade, he reminds us, is "to make democracy more representative and responsive" (17). For that outcome to occur, we Americans also have to reckon with pollster George Gallup's findings about American life in the 1990s, some of which were noted in the previous chapter. Bewildering problems, disappointment with materialism as a measure of success, acute loneliness, the search for meaningful relationships—Gallup reported frequent encounters with all of those factors and more as he explored our private needs and public selves.

Truth Telling

Unfortunately, if we Americans are telling and listening to the truth about ourselves, Gallup's list only begins to detail what has been going on. At least that was my reaction when I followed a lead from *The Saints among Us*, the book that Gallup and Timothy Jones coauthored after extensive field studies about the varieties of American religious experience in the 1990s.

Immediately in their book's introduction, Gallup and Jones mention three items from surveys conducted by two other map makers, James Patterson and Peter Kim, the authors of a provocative book called *The Day Americans Told the Truth*.[3] Tracking American opinion as the 1990s began, Patterson and Kim found that 70 percent of the American people believed that the nation has no living heroes. A similar number thought that American children have no meaningful role models. More than 90 percent reported that they—and they alone—determine by themselves what is morally right or wrong. Such data intrigued me. Deciding to find out more, I supplemented my study of *The Saints among Us* by discovering further what Patterson and Kim had uncovered. The three items mentioned by Gallup and Jones proved to be closely linked.

In an age of heroes, ordinary folks look up to people who act as guides. That guidance may provide images of success or fame to emulate, but usually heroic status includes moral authority, too—qualities such as good character, traits of mind and spirit that tell the difference between right and wrong, the courage to defend what is just and to resist what is not. *The Day America Told the Truth* suggested ours to be a post-heroic age. In the mid-1990s, for example, probably no Americans have been better known than the irrepressible Madonna or NBA basketball star Michael Jordan. As countless fans, young and old, keep testifying, their success is alluring, their celebrity tempting. But such success does not translate easily into ethical leadership. As far as providing moral examples is concerned, their celebrity is wanting, too. Americans may be dazzled, teased, and aroused to emulate the likes of them, but Patterson and Kim found that most of us know better than to confuse the Madonnas or Michael Jordans of the world with moral authorities. In *The Day America Told the Truth*, famous athletes and entertainment personalities ranked near the bottom of the list of people Americans regard as having some right to tell them what is right or wrong.[4]

Where moral authority is concerned, however, that news was about as good as it got in *The Day America Told the Truth*. If only one in five Americans thought a Madonna or a Michael Jordan has authority to tell them what is right or wrong—and less than half that number would accept moral advice from such sources without question—the percentages for college professors and Supreme Court justices, churches, synagogues, the Bible, and your local police force did not fare much better. Only three to five out of ten Americans ranked any of them as genuine moral authorities, and by no means was their word to go unquestioned by those who were inclined to hear what they had to say. Best friends, grandparents, and parents ranked somewhat higher. Spouses and lovers topped the list: 77 percent agreed that they had some right to tell us what is right or wrong, although only 55 percent concurred that the moral counsel of a spouse or lover should be received without questioning.

Could this rejection of moral authority be virtuous, at least in part? Perhaps, for such a mood might show that American life evades a choking conformity, maintains a healthy skepticism about anyone or anything that tries to "tell me what to do," and revitalizes independent thought, self-reliance, and individual conscience. But this coin has another side, and its message is less optimistic. We make a sad comment when our self-evaluation indicates that most Americans, for one reason or another, just do not see many morally admirable people out there where heroes were supposed to be.

Left to our own devices, and there are quite a few vices among them, we Americans have immense freedom. That point can be a cause for celebration, but this coin also has another side. It shows that Americans are prone to immense confusion and considerable loneliness, and that moral consensus has been lacking in the 1990s. *The Day America Told the Truth* gives us Americans reason to pause before concluding that having "me, myself, and I" as our three most important moral authorities bodes well for our individual lives, let alone for the common good.

The full picture provided by Patterson and Kim supports such judgments. Meanwhile the three items mentioned by Gallup and Jones only scratch the surface and, compared to the additional data that awaited me in *The Day America Told the Truth*, are not necessarily the most jarring, either. The mural of our country that Patterson and Kim map is not a pretty picture. One reason is that they did not detect overwhelming evidence that the view from the far end of the nineties would be better. On the other hand, *The Day America Told the Truth* is not completely overcast with threatening clouds of gloom and doom. Periodically Patterson and Kim locate rays of hopeful light. In their 1994 sequel, *The Second American Revolution*, they highlight those rays. Still finding that American opinion voiced a great deal of anger, frustration, bitterness, disillusionment, and fear, the mid-1990s listening done by Patterson and Kim made them think that American public opinion had galvanized around six main issues. Americans were eager for (1) new leadership that could (2) rejuvenate the economy, (3) improve American schools, (4) provide better health care access, (5) make our cities safer, and (6) curb drug abuse. Gallup polls taken at mid-decade revealed a similar profile. Americans were most anxious about violent crime, drug abuse, declining moral values, the federal budget deficit, the nation's welfare and health care systems, public education, and the economy.[5]

Although *The Second American Revolution* is more hopeful than *The Day America Told the Truth,* it unfortunately fails to follow up on the parts that religion might play in the new American revolution. In their earlier book, Patterson and Kim explicitly asked Americans about their religious views. In the sequel, they simply let people express their concerns. The result is that the second book has less to report about religion than the first.

That outcome, however, does not mean that religion is irrelevant. On the contrary, if Americans consider *why* improving schools, making cities safer, and curbing drug abuse are critical items on an American agenda, and if they ask *how* people are to be motivated to make the personal sacrifices that may be essential for achieving those public goods, then religion is back on the table, too.

First, religion is on the table by implication. We may not say so explicitly as much as we should, but things like better education, safer cities, and the curbing of illicit drug use are important because they fit with our sense of what is good, honorable, true, and sacred about American life. Those qualities fit with a sense of the whole that is deserving of loyalty. Second, that same American agenda puts religion on the table explicitly, too. It does so because without religious commitments to help us pursue such goals, it is unrealistic to think that Americans will achieve as much as they could. That fact stands because religious commitments often moderate the selfishness that impedes the common good, and they can increase the understanding that personal fulfillment and public service go together.

In *The Day America Told the Truth,* Patterson and Kim openly shared Gallup and Jones's conviction in *The Saints among Us,* namely, that public discourse about religion is important because it could lead in those directions. Getting to that part of the story, however, requires navigation through stormy weather, because every public opinion poll should be taken with several grains of salt. Snapshots that they are, all polls have margins of error. Nor do their findings agree precisely, even when the polls use comparable questions and are taken at the same times. The population samples they use, however random, are still so small as to make one wonder about the validity of the inferences drawn from them. Furthermore, poll results can be affected by the wording of questions and the order in which they are asked. There is also the issue of a poll's "shelf life." Public opinion changes. So how soon does the data from any single poll become stale? When should it be tossed out completely? Nor should another question be begged: Can you trust what people say, especially when the poll is asking Americans to evaluate themselves?

In the late twentieth century, it must also be acknowledged, public opinion polling, statistical analysis, and cross-checking and updating of empirical data have become quite advanced. Imperfect though they are, polls measure perspectives and perceptions. Those views may not be those of "experts," but they do belong to ordinary Americans who are located all over the country. The feelings and thoughts of such people are important, for their outlooks are not merely perceptions but facts that affect the nation's social, political, and religious "humanscape" as well as its landscape.

In the polling process, steps can be taken to encourage honest self-evaluation. Even after taking a discount for change and fallibility, public opinion polls can help us Americans to see who we recently have been and also who we are, for at least implicitly their results invite us to consider whether we presently agree with the findings or not. So, taking some grains of salt along, let's keep going to the polls, not to find some absolute truth about ourselves, but to discover and discuss what Americans have felt and thought and to find out how all of those views might affect and be influenced by the importance—and the difficulty—of talking about religion in public.

What Do We Think of Ourselves?

Most opinion polls, Patterson and Kim suspected, are too public to permit the privacy required for people to talk with impunity about their most private needs, feelings, and convictions. Thus, for *The Day America Told the Truth*, the two researchers devised their "cathartic method" of inquiry. Although it could not guarantee complete candor, this method minimized the obstacles against truth-telling by ensuring complete anonymity and privacy for the participants.[6] Conducted in fifty geographically diverse places during one week's time as the nation entered the 1990s, the Patterson-Kim survey polled a randomly selected sample of 2,000 adult Americans. Each participant answered more than 1,800 questions out of some 200,000 that Patterson and Kim had sifted for use in the survey. Many other people responded to shorter versions of the questionnaire. Thousands more were interviewed by phone. Patterson and Kim may not be exaggerating when they claimed at the time that theirs was "the most massive in-depth survey of what Americans really believe that has ever been conducted."[7] The results revealed area differences, which Patterson and Kim clustered in nine "moral regions." Most of that detail is beyond the scope of this discussion, but an incidental link to what has gone before is the note that the laughter of poet Carl Sandburg's Chicago may not be so youthful anymore. Patterson and Kim found Chicago in the "Rust Belt." With its capital in Detroit, this region—which includes western New York and Pennsylvania, along with Ohio, Indiana, Michigan, and most of Illinois—is one that has been frequently associated with the nation's economic uncertainties. People who live there, observed Patterson and Kim, ranked last among all Americans in believing that the nation still has heroes. They ranked first, however, when it came to affirming "my country, right or wrong." Their rate of belief in God was above the national average, too.[8]

Be that as it may, when the participants received their surveys, they found a "warning label." It advised that they would be asked "highly sensitive and very personal" questions, ones that would probe "your innermost feelings about some of the most important moral issues of our time." No "surface answers," no "white lies," please—the warning label implored—"we are looking for total honesty. There are no right or wrong answers. We are concerned only with what you believe."[9]

Patterson and Kim's warning did not add that taking the survey might endanger the participants' health. Nevertheless the authors' "concern" about the participants' beliefs ended up well beyond the neutrality of social scientific disclaimers about "no right or wrong answers." Patterson and Kim saw that their survey's findings were decidedly dangerous to the nation's health and therefore to every individual American's well-being, too. Some examples show how and why.

First, when Americans were asked what they would most like to change about themselves, neither increased intelligence nor improved employment topped the list. The idea of becoming a "better person" did not make the rankings at all. Instead, a substantial majority thought outward appearance more important than the inner self. They wanted most to be rich and thin—the American Dream of the nineties, Patterson and Kim suggest.[10]

Many Americans, moreover, quite literally could be bought if the price were right. About 25 percent of those polled by Patterson and Kim, for example, indicated they would abandon their entire family for $10 million. Seven percent (representing about 36 million Americans) would consider committing murder for even less.[11]

Money does not have many serious competitors for Americans' attention, but one definite contender is sex. As the authors put it, "If sex were an expensive restaurant, contemporary Americans would give it a rating of two and a half stars out of four: good eats, but skimpy portions . . . we want more." [12] Fifteen percent of adult Americans may prefer watching television to having sex, but they are the exceptions who prove Marlene Dietrich's rule: "In America, sex is an obsession. In other parts of the world, it is fact." [13] Patterson and Kim found that 92 percent of sexually active people have had ten or more lovers; the lifetime average is seventeen. The age for beginning sexual activity was declining, too, with a majority of American young people losing their virginity by the age of sixteen, and probably 20 percent having done so before the age of thirteen.[14] In response to the question "Whatever happened to childhood?" Patterson and Kim suggested that a Los Angeles elementary school teacher got it right when she remarked, "Children are skipping it."

If children are skipping childhood, Patterson and Kim found large numbers of married adults skipping fidelity. *The Day America Told the Truth* testified that "almost one-third of all married Americans (31 percent or about 77.5 million people) have had or are now having an affair." Less than 30 percent of that number intended to end their marital cheating any time soon. Meanwhile, the 44 percent of Americans who expected that most marriages will end in divorce were on target, because in the mid-1990s the divorce rate topped 50 percent.[15]

This picture is at least somewhat balanced by a landmark study—perhaps the most comprehensive analysis of the subject ever—conducted by a team of researchers led by Edward O. Laumann. Its findings present a much more conservative profile.[16] This 1994 report indicates that Americans have sex once a week on average, and more than 80 percent had only one sex partner or no partner at all during the past year. According to this study, the median number of sexual partners for American men over a lifetime is six. The median for women is two. Almost all Americans marry, and 75 percent of married men and 85 percent of married women say they have remained faithful to their spouses.

If the sexual practices in American bedrooms are more modest than reported in *The Day America Told the Truth,* such restraint seemed not to extend to the country's mean streets. Violence, psychic and physical, runs far and wide in American society. According to Patterson and Kim, one out of seven Americans testified that they were sexually abused as children. Of that number, 75 percent were women.[17] Twenty times more rapes are reported in the United States than in Japan, England, or Spain.[18] Patterson and Kim also discovered that one-third of the people they surveyed owned handguns, and almost as many have rifles or shotguns. They judge that one-seventh of all Americans carry weapons on their persons or in their cars.[19] Among the world's industrialized nations, the United States is by far the most violent. The homicide rate in our country is twenty times higher than in Western Europe, forty times higher than in Japan. Guns were used in 75 percent of those killings as compared to 25 percent of those in other industrialized nations.[20] As for violence in American entertainment, *The Day America Told the Truth* reported that children's television programming averages twenty-five violent acts every hour, a rate up 50 percent from the early 1980s.[21] It also debunks the comforting conventional wisdom that most Americans think there is too much violence and sex in the movies: "Not true," wrote Patterson and Kim, "in our interviews, people admitted that they like plenty of both in their escapist fare."[22]

The data on job satisfaction and work performance were just as dreary. Only 10 percent of Americans were satisfied with their jobs; only three in ten affirmed loyalty to their companies.[23] Testifying that "the so-called Protestant ethic is long gone from today's American workplace," Patterson and Kim found that only one in four Americans gave work their best effort, a disturbing discovery made more so by the revelation that less than 20 percent of Americans believed that our nation will be the world's economic leader by the year 2000. In response to questions about reasons for that decline, there was widespread agreement among bosses and workers alike that "the perceived low ethics of management is a major cause of our problems in the business world."[24]

There is more, far too much to sum up here: One out of three respondents to the Patterson-Kim survey, for example, have seriously contemplated suicide, most of them more than once. Extrapolating from the survey's numbers, apparently some 2.2 million Americans are quite certain they have AIDS; an additional seven million consider themselves at high risk. Most of the people in both of those categories are heterosexual.

Several other points are crucial, too. For instance, one series of questions posed by Patterson and Kim—it is one of several questionnaires included in their book—asks "Are you true to yourself?" The last question in this series of twenty wonders, "Did you lie a little on the test? If so, don't you think that you'd better take it again?"[25] That question does not get scored in the results, but the series of questions is designed to determine how much, about what, and to whom Americans lie. Such a test might belie the validity of the Patterson-Kim survey, but combined with the safeguards built in for anonymity and privacy, the results suggest that the "cathartic method" produced accurate disclosures in this case as well as in the others. If so, the truth is that Americans lie a lot, and when we refrain from lying, less than half of us do so simply because we know it is wrong to lie. "We're talking about conscious, premeditated lies," the authors emphasized, and not just lies about small, inconsequential matters.[26] In fact, the better we know someone, the more likely we are to have told them "serious" lies— self-serving ones that deeply betray trust, hurt others, or have legal consequences. Afterward Americans often regret such lies, and yet "the majority of Americans today (two in every three) believe that there is nothing wrong with telling a lie. Only 31 percent of us believe that honesty is the best policy."[27]

According to Patterson and Kim, institutional confidence and community involvement fared little better than personal honesty. Trust in the nation's institutions and leaders—political and spiritual, educational and economic—may recently have been at an all-time low. Certainly the two researchers found it in decline between 1973 and 1989. Whether one considered the executive and legislative branches of the federal government, organized religion, the nation's educational system, the military, the media, or business, banking, and organized labor, the percentage of Americans who expressed a great deal of confidence in our major institutions declined substantially during that period.[28] That decline was especially sad because, far from being a time of American optimism, 1973 was discouraging in its own right: the humiliation of the Vietnam War was being driven home, oil prices and inflation were soaring, and the scandals of Watergate were starting to unfold.

When Patterson and Kim asked their survey participants to evaluate some seventy American occupations, the results echoed the decline of confidence in American institutions. Congressmen, Wall Street executives, labor union leaders, lawyers, and TV evangelists join organized crime bosses and drug dealers in the twenty occupations that Americans rated lowest for honesty and integrity. Of the twenty occupations that ranked highest in that regard, many were neither prestigious nor high-paying.

The U.S. presidency, for example, did not make that cut, tying for only twenty-eighth in the Patterson-Kim reckoning and just slightly ahead of the nation's often-maligned press. Roles such as fireman or paramedic topped the list instead, with educators, physicians, scientists, airline pilots, and flight attendants joining Catholic priests, Jewish rabbis, and Protestant ministers to round out most of the list. Even in the top twenty list, however, the highest grade point average was no better than a B (3.07 out of 4.0).

Turning to community involvement, *The Day America Told the Truth* showed that two-thirds of Americans never gave time to community activities or to solving community problems. One-third of Americans had never given money to a charitable cause, and among those who did give, the average American donated less than 1 percent of his or her annual income.[29] Just a little over half of the American population felt a moral responsibility to help the poor, with some 42 percent convinced that people are poor because they are lazy or due to other faults of their own.[30]

As for racism, Patterson and Kim detected "fewer hardcore racists than ever before," but they did find a "new racism" directed toward African-Americans in particular. It holds that blacks now have the same chances for success as anybody else in America, and if blacks cannot make it here, then they have not taken advantage of the opportunities that the nation offers.[31]

By their own admission, of course, most of the Americans who spoke in *The Day America Told the Truth* have a diminished sense of the opportunities that the nation offers. Their map of our country reveals a place "colder, greedier, meaner, more selfish, and less caring" than it used to be. Such judgments were reflected again at mid-decade. Gallup polls takes in July 1995 showed that 65 percent of the American people were dissatisfied with "the way things are going in the United States." Not long after, in January 1996, Gallup found that only 31 percent believed that the nation "would be in better shape in the year 2000."[32] Nevertheless, Patterson and Kim would hasten to add, we Americans remain deeply in love with our country. More than 90 percent of us think of ourselves as patriotic; more than four out of five (81 percent) affirm that the United States plays a special part in the world; and 75 percent think more patriotism is needed. Although most Americans doubt that the country will be better off in the near future, 95 percent have what Patterson and Kim call "a deep-down favorable opinion" of the place. That opinion may have much to do with a paradox no less perplexing than it is peculiar: Most Americans believe their personal lives will improve even though the nation's life as a whole does not, an opinion echoed by Gallup poll findings in 1995, which reported that 62 percent of the American people described themselves as "very happy."[33]

Are we Americans deceived, unable to detect self-contradiction, or just dim-witted in supposing that our personal lives can get better even if the nation's life as a whole does not? The answer could be "yes, any or all of the above." It could also be "no, my American Dream can come true in spite of —even because of—the fact that other people's dreams do not or cannot." But something else might be going on, something instead of, or at least in addition to (1) foolish ignorance about the fatal interdependence of all human actions or (2) crafty disillusionment, if not cynicism, which simply accepts the realism that bad times for some mean good times for others.

No Regrets?

The logic that links individual confidence and national uncertainty might go beyond naivete or cunning to a significant sense of *regret*. Perhaps that wistful, even melancholy mood is not what appears on the surface, but *The Day America Told the Truth* suggested its presence repeatedly, at least between the lines. What I mean by regret in this context is simply stated: Regret means that Americans—certainly not all, but a very substantial majority—feel distressed, dismayed, and disappointed. What produces this regret is the feeling that our hopes for personal advancement do not support the well-being of our country well enough. Very few Americans completely overlook the ways in which their successes and hopes depend on opportunities that our national life provides. To the extent that personal advancement and national decline are linked together, even the greediest among us would probably admit that the times are out of joint.

Traditionally, our American ideal has been that individual success and national accomplishment belong together. We Americans are unlikely to give up that dream without regret. Listening to Americans—carefully— suggests that we do not and even that we will not. If that hearing is accurate, the regret of which I speak is important. Regret implies that events did not have to turn out as they have, or it makes little sense at all. If the past is not determined, then the present and the future are not foreclosed, either. Americans do not have to settle for deals that make individual success and national degeneration the best package we can get. Regret could motivate resistance against that disaster.

Significantly, *The Day America Told the Truth* contained little satisfaction or joy about the nation's perceived state of decline. We Americans rationalize our often shoddy ways by thinking "everyone else is doing it," but that justification sparks no celebration. As a people, we have lost a great deal of trust in our leaders and institutions. A sense of significance in work eludes us. We cheat, lie, and steal a lot, too. Few Americans deny that multiple forms of violence wreak havoc in the United States. Surely none of those realizations makes us glad and proud. Granted, *The Day America Told the Truth* revealed that many Americans feel little guilt or shame these days, but even those reports neither exclude regret nor show that guilt and shame are entirely lacking among us. Profoundly private though American morality may be, Patterson and Kim discovered that "Americans still have a lively sense of what sin means. And if there is one ideal that underlies our definition of sin, it is the oldest, most universal principle of them all—the Golden Rule. Sin, as most of us see it today, is doing unto others what we don't want done unto ourselves."[34]

There may be some rare exceptions, but they would only prove the rule that Americans do not want to be cheated, lied to, beaten up, ripped off, raped, mugged, or murdered. Very few Americans, moreover, would put such acts at the top of their list of things that, ideally, they would most desire to do to others. Nor, in general, do we Americans like having untrustworthy leaders, dysfunctional institutions, and jobs in which, as the old rock anthem puts it, we can't get—or give—"no satisfaction." Whatever individual advancements may accompany it, national decline, in short, is not our hope. Instead, we tend to regret that our lives have come to such a pass.

That regret may not be enough to make us Americans change our ways so that the fit is better between individual well-being and national health. Yet Americans also still tend to recognize that there is truth in the old saying, "What goes around comes around." The equilibrium is far from perfect, but conduct that does unto others what we do *not* want done to ourselves has a way of boomeranging back on us. Instead of building self-esteem and making us "feel good about ourselves," such conduct produces pain and sorrow, calls for help, desires for something better. The difficulty is that ways to effect change for the better are neither easily discerned nor neatly implemented. So despair and indifference often leave their marks. But even when they do, Americans as a whole do not cheer that fact. They incline to show concern instead.

The Day America Told the Truth bears witness to such claims. Nearly six in ten Americans indicated that they would gladly give three weeks annually to do volunteer work that would help to solve the nation's basic problems. A similar percentage would accept—even if not so gladly—a heavier tax burden to improve American education and to safeguard our environment, two aims that Patterson and Kim identify as "unifying causes through the 1990s and on into the next millennium."[35] Probably their optimism on those points was excessive, for Americans are deeply divided about how to improve education as well as about what it means to safeguard the environment in circumstances where economic interests conflict with that ideal. Nevertheless, the areas of education and the environment are two examples in our national life where Americans are united substantially in the belief that special attention must be paid.

If the Patterson-Kim poll is to be believed—and on this point how could we Americans afford not to believe it?—there are literally millions of us who would respond to the right kind of call for help. Waiting for wise leadership, efficient organization, and moral vision to tap them, there are tremendous reservoirs of American energy that can serve the common good. That recognition may help to explain why Patterson and Kim found that "the overwhelming majority of Americans (81 percent) want schools to teach morals to our children."[36] Whose "morals" and what content those values should contain are, of course, questions far more easily asked than answered. Yet the strong consensus reported about the importance of such teaching in *The Day America Told the Truth* shows key ways in which private needs and public selves are linked. That same consensus suggests other key ways in which private needs and public selves can and ought to be linked to involve religious discourse.

Turning to Religion

Turning explicitly now to that phase of their study, Patterson and Kim found a mixture of news when they asked their survey participants about religion. Perhaps because Americans think of God in so many different ways, and perhaps because most of those ways connect God with the idea of a creating goodness ("a kind word, a helping hand, forgiveness" is the way one woman described God), the researchers found that "ninety percent of the people we questioned said that they truly believe in God."[37] A Gallup poll taken in February 1995 found American belief in God to be an even-higher 96 percent.[38] Life after death was also affirmed by 82 percent. The latter affirmation entertained the reality of hell as well as heaven, but only a few (4 percent) seriously thought they might be destined to spend eternity with Satan.[39] That belief, however, did not mean that Americans take Satan lightly. On the contrary, Patterson and Kim found that 55 percent of us testified not that Satan is merely a figurative or symbolic power but instead that Satan is particular, even personal, and all too real. In fact, the number of Americans who hold this belief may be growing. A 1995 *Newsweek* poll indicated that 66 percent of adult Americans and 85 percent of evangelical Protestants affirm the Devil's existence.[40]

Despite those high percentages, probes into them reveal neither a very definite consensus about religious meanings nor a clear indication that such beliefs make much difference in people's attitudes and actions about a variety of important public issues. Six out of seven Americans, for instance, think it is all right not to believe in God. Interest in God's will is lukewarm at best, at least if allegiance to the Ten Commandments or the teachings of organized religion are any measure of such concern. Most Americans do not know, to say nothing of consciously obeying, the public policy positions held by the country's major religious institutions.[41] Americans even pick and choose among the Ten Commandments and apparently expect to do so with impunity as far as divine judgment is concerned. Although we Americans still tend to have a sense of sin, we also tend to define sin for ourselves, an outcome that fits the fact that half of the American population has not attended a religious service in the last three months and one in three has not done so in the past year.[42] In fact, if being "religious" is defined to mean that people not only consider religion important but also attend weekly services, then the number of "religious" Americans is about 35 percent.[43]

What Patterson and Kim discovered about American religious experience did not end there, however. They also found a marked difference between those who are superficially religious and those who are really serious about religious commitment. Most Americans belong in the former category, but Patterson and Kim noted that 14 percent of the American people described themselves as "very religious." It was this group that Gallup and Jones explored and to which they devoted their entire book, *The Saints among Us.* By contrast, *The Day America Told the Truth* devoted only a few pages of their study to this group. Yet what Patterson and Kim had to say about those people revealed an importance far exceeding the attention it received.

The Patterson-Kim profile of "very religious" Americans looked like this: The vast majority of them (99 percent) were under age 65. Their educational level was quite high—one in four had graduated from college, two out of three had done some college work. Women outnumbered men. Patterson and Kim found the latter point perfectly consistent with other important results of their survey, which repeatedly revealed the fact that "women are more moral than men, and religious people are more moral than the national average."

Compared to those who defined themselves as "not religious at all," continued Patterson and Kim, "the very religious scored much higher than did other people on moral questions that most of us would accept as defining citizenship in a civilized society."[44] The "very religious" were not perfect, but *The Day America Told the Truth* showed them to be significantly more truthful and committed to their families than were the nonreligious. Less prone to drug use or criminal activity, they were also less likely to carry weapons, to rationalize behavior because "everybody's doing it," or to "have a price." The poll also showed that deeply religious Americans are significantly more dedicated workers, confident of their moral worth, satisfied with their lives, and prepared to die for their beliefs than their nonreligious counterparts.

Given the map of our country that Patterson and Kim provided, given the regret about American life that can be found in and around its lines, even given that the testimonies of deeply religious Americans may be less than 100 percent true, these findings cry out for more discussion in public. So Gallup and Jones and their *Saints among Us* picked up where Patterson and Kim left off.

American Saints?

The Gallup-Jones project had neither the scope nor the detail of Patterson and Kim's work. Its goal was to identify "Americans for whom God is a vibrant reality." The researchers went looking specifically for "people who demonstrate that Christian commitment makes a difference in how they actually live," an aim, they acknowledge, that oriented their book toward "the framework of Christian faith and practice" and "made it difficult to draw conclusions about Jewish and Muslim believers."[45] Using polling techniques developed by the Gallup organization over the course of six decades, their survey relied, first, on a set of twelve questions that were asked of a nationally representative sample of 1,052 adult Americans. Responding by means of a "strongly agree"/"strongly disagree" spectrum that ranged from 1 to 5 with a "don't know" option as a sixth possibility, the participants replied to questions about specifically religious beliefs and practices. ("My religious faith is the most important influence in my life," for example, or "I seek God's will through prayer.")[46]

Gallup and Jones found that 13 percent of their sample answered "strongly agree" or "agree" to that first set of questions. Within that group, more than half (7 percent of the U.S. adult population) answered "strongly agree" to all twelve questions. Those figures are much smaller than the 94 percent of Americans who Gallup and Jones report believe in "God or some kind of unseen spirit," or the 88 percent who sometimes pray to God, or the 76 percent who state that prayer is "an important part" of daily life, or the 70 percent who believe in life after death, or the 43 percent who "claimed they attended church in a typical week," or the 33 percent who stated that they have had a powerful religious experience, or even the 22 percent who indicated that religion is the "most important" influence in their lives.[47]

Clearly, however, there is a great deal of religious interest and personal piety in the United States, much more than the conventional wisdom about the secularization of American society may want to admit. True, fewer Americans say that religion is "very important" in their lives (56 percent in May 1995, for example, compared to 75 percent in 1952), and between March 1957 and May 1995 the percentage of Americans who believed that "the influence of religion on American life is rising" dropped from 69 percent to 36 percent. Nevertheless, Gallup poll results still show that more than 80 percent of Americans regard religion as a significant factor in their lives, and 64 percent affirm that religion could remedy most, if not all, of the nation's problems.[48] That sign could be a very hopeful one for American life, although the depth of religious commitment and the difference it makes in the United States remain fundamental questions. Thus, Gallup and Jones decided to baptize only the 13 percent as "saints among us," according "supersaint" status to the 7 percent who answered "strongly agree" to all of the survey questions. Yet, projecting from their poll results, they estimated that in an adult U.S. population of 182 million, there are some 24 million of those folks, a considerable number whose significance grows when one considers Gallup and Jones's remark that "they can be found in virtually every neighborhood, public school, office building, and congregation."[49]

Although Gallup and Jones do not explain when they decided to call these people "saints," it seems unlikely that they did so simply because of particular scores on a single set of twelve questions. Being a saint depends on *doing* at least as much as on believing. So the researchers used a second questionnaire to gain insight about the comparative behavior of the 13 percent and the rest of us. Utilizing the traditional "strongly agree"/"strongly disagree" spectrum, these six questions probed whether "I would not object to a person of a different race moving next door," for example, or if "I spend a good deal of time helping people in physical, emotional, or other kinds of needs." [50]

The results confirmed that there was a distinctly positive correlation between what deeply religious Americans believe and how they act: the deeply religious are less likely to be racially prejudiced and more likely to be kinder and more optimistic, giving, and forgiving than the rest of us, especially when compared to those who answered "disagree" or "strongly disagree" to the first twelve questions. For instance, among the latter—a group that, interestingly enough, comprised just 3 percent of the American population—only 42 percent indicated that they regularly help those in need, whereas 73 percent of the saints and a striking 85 percent of the "supersaints" did so. Far from being Karl Marx's often-quoted "opium of the people," the religion of the saints does not hinder compassion and caring but instead can be a vital catalyst for social change. [51]

Even with all of that data, Gallup and Jones might not have decided to confer "sainthood" until they took the next step, which moved beyond anonymity and privacy to conversation—by mail, by phone, and face-to-face—on a personal basis with representatives from the many walks of life and regions of the country who comprise that special 13 percent. What Gallup and Jones found out in these meetings probably clinched the case. These people are indeed saints among us—not because they are naive do-gooders or pie-in-the-sky escapists whose stereotypical sanctimoniousness has given sainthood an undeserved "bad name," but on the contrary because, as Gallup and Jones put it, "they are the salt and light of our world." [52]

What do the saints among us look like? Don't expect to find them all in one place or group, Gallup and Jones cautioned, but their research indicated that the saints are more likely to be women than men, more likely black than white. They are found more commonly in the South than elsewhere. They are more likely to earn $25,000 or less per year than to be rich. They are also more likely to have a modest amount of formal education than to be holders of advanced degrees, and they are found more commonly among people who are over fifty years old. If they are not typically among the most powerful and prestigious, well heeled and well educated, their lives are more full of loyalty, more focused on what deserves to be called sacred, more dedicated to respect and compassion for others, and more blessed by feelings of satisfaction than most of the rest of us Americans can honestly claim.

The saints among us differ, too, in testifying that their lives embody those gifts because of the centrality of religion in their daily experiences. More specifically, they report God's presence in their lives. That experience, however, is not a cause for absolute certainty. The saints may have their doubts. They do not claim to understand things perfectly. The evil in the world sometimes makes them want to scream at God. Nor is their religious experience a cause for smugness. Rather it promotes a spirit of humility born from awareness of failures, shortcomings, and inadequacies—some of the saints would speak quite simply about sin—that intensify a hunger for God's love and a thirst for God's grace. The saints bear witness not only to receiving that love and grace but also to experiencing the joy that comes with them.

Gallup and Jones found that the saints staunchly affirm the worth of life. Specifically, they sustain hope in the midst of adversity because, in spite of the apparent odds, their sense of the whole involves trust that God's goodness will ultimately prevail against evil. They also communicate to God their thanks as well as their needs—frequently through words of prayer uttered on the run—and they feel God's plan is guiding them, too. In addition, they underscore that spiritual sensitivity has to be nurtured and encouraged. It does not come automatically, all at once, or on the spur of the moment. Rarely does it come to one all alone, either. The saints know that one has to decide to seek God, intend to persist in that direction, and keep trying to do one's best in that regard. But they are not "rugged individualists" who believe that spiritual growth is a do-it-yourself project, the result of personal willpower or mastery of some technique. They depend on nurture from other people, including religious congregations, and on help from God. They know especially the importance of sharing, interdependence, service, community, and mutual support—the human ties through which God's presence moves, can be understood, and made visible to others.

Above all, their religious life leads them to act. It can do so in various ways, but sense of duty, gratitude to God, and feelings of being God's partner in mending the world are among the "spiritual reasons" that the saints often cite as motivations for helping others. Those reasons do not exhaust the list of motivations. The saints also act because of their feelings of civic responsibility, the personal satisfaction that helping gives them, or simply because they see human needs that ought to be met. But there is no mistaking the fact that religion is a major source of their energy, one that intensifies all the other motivations at work within them.

Put in the Christian terms that characterize Gallup and Jones's book, the saints tend to agree that Jesus' most important teaching is the parable of the Good Samaritan, which emphasizes the importance of helping those in need, loving one's neighbor as oneself, even—indeed especially—when the needy person or the neighbor is outside one's customary circle of obligation to family and friends.

Such points make a good segue to others accented at the beginning of the twentieth century by the American philosopher William James, who affirmed that public discourse about religion was of vital importance. He devoted extensive portions of his 1903 classic, *The Varieties of Religious Experience,* to a study of the nature and value of saintliness. On the whole, he concluded, saintliness belongs among "the best fruits of religious experience," and those, he emphasized, "are the best things that history has to show." [53]

As true now as it was when James stated it, another of his major themes was that saintly persons can be found in many different religious traditions. Those women and men, he contended, can be identified in a "composite photograph of universal saintliness." As James developed that photograph, he saw that saintliness involved (1) a feeling, not merely intellectual, that a wider life and an Ideal Power—Christians, but not everyone, would call it God—exist beyond "this world's selfish little interests"; (2) a sense of our "friendly continuity" with the Ideal Power, which combines with self-surrender to its guiding influence; (3) an awareness of freedom from the limits imposed by narrow self-interest; and (4) a turning outward of the self in the direction of serving needs other than one's own. [54]

The completeness of James's outline may be debatable, but it contextualizes *The Saints among Us* and complements the work of Gallup and Jones in three ways. First, James supports their belief that not all saints are Christians any more than all Christians are saints. Next, James reminds us that the language Gallup and Jones used to describe the saints reflects the particularity of Christian perspectives. Third, James suggests that although an essentially Christian vocabulary would be inappropriate for describing the religious experience of people from other faiths, the world's religious traditions have much in common where saintliness is concerned.

The saintliness that religious traditions share, James thought, is "indispensable to the world's welfare." [55] Apparently Gallup and Jones, Patterson and Kim, could not agree more, especially if we focus James's claim closer to home so that it also reads "indispensable to America's welfare." But what about the rest of us? Do we agree?

We Americans should talk about these matters, and we should do so in public.[56] By example, the saints among us press these issues, for their lives give voice to religious expression that integrates their private needs and their public selves so that the common good is served. The challenge that the saints among us pose is clear, direct, and full of immense implications. If the United States still needs what Abraham Lincoln called "a new birth of freedom," especially when "freedom" is understood to entail higher ethical standards, more compassion, better racial relations, and less violence, then the more Americans imitate the saints among us the better, and the less we do so the worse off we are likely to be. Americans need to talk seriously about that proposition. If we fail to do so because the idea seems "too religious" and therefore is regarded as unsophisticated, foolish, unfashionable, or politically incorrect, then we will miss an essential opportunity to sort out our American priorities in ways that make private needs and public selves mutually supportive.

Going to the polls in the 1990s raises questions that are as troubling as they are timely. Have we Americans changed substantially—for better or worse?—since *The Day America Told the Truth*? At the very least it is hard to argue convincingly that there have been substantial changes for the better. Is *The Saints among Us* more or less true of us than when it was published? If the answer is "less true," then the need for saints among us is greater than ever. Are Gallup and Jones's saints the heroes we Americans need in our post-heroic age? Should we be adding to their number? Could I be one of them? Should you? The answer to those last four questions ought to be an emphatic yes.

We Americans need to be educating ourselves for sainthood, or for something akin to it if full sainthood seems improbable for most of us. The nurturing of saints, or something like them if we cannot all achieve that standard, ought to be a national priority. But we will not make much headway on such goals if we fail to talk about them. Carrying on that conversation will require debate about the forms that such education might take. It will require discussion about what religion means, about what religion should and should not emphasize, and about the traditions that would serve us best. This sort of religious discourse would help us Americans to understand with greater sensitivity the old habits and new paths that need to be broken. It would clarify the kinds of leaders and institutions that ought—and ought not—to take the lead.

One song that most Americans know how to sing in public is "When the Saints Go Marching In." We usually sing only the chorus, but the song has several verses, too. One of them says, "I'm just a weary pilgrim, plodding through this world of sin." On days when Americans tell the truth, a lot of us can identify with that theme. But the saints do not plod—they march. They may get weary but nevertheless they keep mending the world. "I want to be in that number," the chorus says, "when the saints go marching in." By better imitating the saints, we Americans could go a long way toward building a sense of the whole that could rightly increase our pride and joy about who we are.

Gallup and Jones affirmed that their book contains good news. "Sainthood is alive and well," they said. "What we can learn holds great promise for us and for those we live and work with and serve."[57] The saints among us seem to show that when sainthood gets expressed and connected with public life, it directly addresses—and for some Americans even solves— the dilemmas at the heart of American culture. We must talk about these prospects in public. Better still, we need to act on them. We cannot just go to the polls for the responses we need. We don't have the time.

NOTES

1. George Washington's "Farewell Address" can be found in *American Ground: Vistas, Visions and Revisions,* ed. Robert H. Fossum and John K. Roth (New York: Paragon House, 1988), 86–98. See especially 88.

2. Sam Roberts, *Who We Are: A Portrait of America Based on the Latest U.S. Census* (New York: Times Books, 1993), 3–4. Subsequent page references are given parenthetically in the text.

3. Since the appearance of *The Saints among Us* and *The Day America Told the Truth,* Patterson and Kim have coauthored a sequel called *The Second American Revolution* (New York: William Morrow, 1994).

4. See James Patterson and Peter Kim, *The Day America Told the Truth: What People Really Believe about Everything That Matters* (New York: Prentice Hall Press, 1991), 209.

5. See Michael Golay and Carl Rollyson, *Where America Stands, 1996* (New York: John Wiley, 1996), 1–12.

6. The authors explain their methodology in detail at the end of their book. See Patterson and Kim, *Day America Told the Truth,* 243–53. Essentially the method involved carefully developed, self-administered questionnaires, which included both closed-ended, multiple-choice questions as well as many open-ended inquiries that follow-up questions probed more deeply. Demographic data on the participants

were carefully gathered, but a premium was placed on each individual's anonymity and the participants' awareness that their privacy would be scrupulously respected. As Patterson and Kim explain, "we guaranteed to the people we interviewed that no one who read their replies would know their identities. . . . They could say whatever they wished—whatever they *really* believed. They had no reason to be hypocritical or to lie. They could unburden themselves and tell the truth" (4).

7. Ibid., 4.

8. Ibid., 18. Here Patterson and Kim draw on Joel Garreau's *The Nine Nations of America* (Boston: Houghton Mifflin, 1981). In addition to the already mentioned Rust Belt, Patterson and Kim's nine moral regions and "capitals" include: (1) New England (the northeastern states, with Boston as the chief city); (2) Metropolis (the New York City–Washington, D.C., corridor, with New York City as the pacesetter); (3) the New South (an area—led by Atlanta—that encompasses Florida, Georgia, and the Carolinas); (4) Old Dixie (Birmingham is crucial in this region, which reaches from East Texas and Louisiana to Alabama, Tennessee, and Kentucky); (5) the Granary (a vast geographical spread—Iowa, Kansas, Minnesota, and Nebraska, to name a few of its states—that pivots around Kansas City); (6) L.A.-Mex (the southwestern sunbelt, stretching from Texas to California and dominated by Los Angeles); (7) the Pac Rim (western parts of Washington and Oregon and northwestern California, an area oriented toward Seattle); and (8) Marlboro Country (Rocky Mountain terrain led by Denver).

The population of the regions varies from about 8 million (3 percent of the American total) in Marlboro Country to a high of about 49 million (20 percent) in the Rust Belt. For our purposes it is worth noting, too, that Patterson and Kim found belief in God highest (96 and 92 percent) in Old Dixie and the Granary, respectively. It is lowest (82 and 81 percent) in Marlboro Country and the Pac Rim, respectively. For more detail, see Patterson and Kim, *Day America Told the Truth*, 11–22, 203, and 255.

9. Patterson and Kim, *Day America Told the Truth*, 245.

10. Ibid., 52.

11. Ibid., 66.

12. Ibid., 71.

13. Quoted in ibid., 84.

14. Ibid., 73, 100.

15. Ibid., 94, 88.

16. See Edward O. Laumann, *Social Organization of Sexuality: Sexual Practices in the United States* (Chicago: University of Chicago Press, 1994).

17. Patterson and Kim, *Day America Told the Truth*, 125.

18. Ibid., 120.

19. Ibid., 132.

20. Ibid., 120.

21. Ibid., 123. In the 1996 national election campaigns, Republican and Democratic candidates alike were critical of television and film violence, urging greater

responsibility from the American entertainment industry. In late 1996 the television industry responded by unveiling a TV ratings system. Evaluating television programs for their levels of sexual content, violence, or foul language, it calls for on-screen labels at the beginning of programs. The program ratings will also be available for listings in magazines and newspapers. The intention is to help parents decide what their children should see, but numerous advocacy groups for children have condemned the system as inadequate. Meanwhile, Congress has mandated that the so-called V-chip, a device that allows parents to block objectionable shows from home television sets, must be available by 1998.

It should also be noted that pornography on the Internet raises additional concerns about censorship, freedom of speech, and the common good. Among other things, all of the debates about television, film, and cyberspace indicate that the boundaries between "private" and "public" are not absolute. Increasingly, these always-related and interactive dimensions of our experience are influenced by and inseparable from one another.

22. Ibid., 133.

23. Ibid., 155. These figures should be compared and contrasted to Gallup poll findings from September 1995, which found that about 95 percent of Americans described themselves as "very happy" or "somewhat happy." See Golay and Rollyson, *Where America Stands, 1996*, 1.

24. Patterson and Kim, *Day America Told the Truth*, 155, 146.

25. Ibid., 51.

26. Ibid., 45.

27. Ibid., 49.

28. For the details, see ibid., 216. The findings reported by Patterson and Kim concentrate on percentages of people who have "a great deal" of confidence in the various institutions. Their findings correlate well with a March 1993 poll that was reported in the *Los Angeles Times*, 29 May 1993, B5. Based on telephone interviews with 1,003 people aged 18 or older, the 1993 survey found that the American military is the institution most trusted by Americans. About two-thirds (67 percent) reported either "a great deal" or "quite a lot" of confidence in the military, compared to 53 percent who expressed that opinion about the church. On this occasion, 29 percent indicated a great deal of confidence in the church, 24 percent quite a lot of confidence. Overall the church nudged out the police, who received a 52 percent approval rating.

These institutions were the only three to inspire confidence in a majority of the American people. Least favored among the institutions the survey asked participants to evaluate were the criminal justice system and Congress, which received 17 and 19 percent approval ratings, respectively. A decade earlier, in 1983, the church received an approval rating of 62 percent. That result put the church in first place, ahead of the military, whose rating at that time was 53 percent, the same as the church received in 1993.

That no American institution obtained an approval rating higher than 67 percent in these two polls is hardly a cause for rejoicing. The same is true of a June 1993 *Los Angeles Times* poll that interviewed 1,474 adults nationwide. It found that only 2 percent and 12 percent of the respondents answered "always" or "most of the time," respectively, when the question was "How much of the time do you think you can trust the government in Washington to do what is right?" The other two choices — "some of the time" and "hardly ever" — got 54 percent and 31 percent, respectively. See the *Los Angeles Times,* 1 July 1993, A1, A18. Despite the budget conflicts between the Congress and the White House that the American people experienced in late 1995 and early 1996, some improvement in the government's mid-decade ratings could be found. See Golay and Rollyson, *Where America Stands, 1996,* 33–45.

Gallup polls taken in 1995 showed that the American people have somewhat greater confidence in the police, organized religion, and the presidency than they did the year before, but in the 1990s the American people have lost at least some confidence in nearly all the major public institutions in American life — the Supreme Court, news media, big business, and public schools among them. Only the military's credibility has been maintained, and it has continued to enjoy the most favorable ratings. As far as respect for the professions is concerned, only car salesmen were regarded as having lower ethical standards than congressmen, while the list of those receiving highest approval included pharmacists, clergy, dentists, college teachers, engineers, medical doctors, and policemen. See Golay and Rollyson, *Where America Stands, 1996,* 176–77.

29. Patterson and Kim, *Day America Told the Truth,* 171. To add some perspective to these figures, it should be noted that American philanthropy, most of it provided by individuals, raises a huge amount of money annually. In addition, some 80 million Americans, including 31 million who volunteer in their churches or synagogues, are engaged in unpaid caring activities. Granted, membership in organized religion is hardly a sufficient condition for authentic, transforming religious faith, but the fact remains that, compared with all other groups, the rates of involvement among the active, dedicated members of religious institutions rise substantially where the giving of time and money is concerned. Involvement in religious organizations fosters help for those who need it. For more detail, see George H. Gallup Jr. and Timothy Jones, *The Saints among Us* (Harrisburg, Pa.: Morehouse Publishing, 1992), 68–69. In particular, they cite an Independent Sector, Inc./Gallup organization survey from early in the 1990s. It showed that those who attended religious services each week "were clearly the most generous givers of both time and money, compared to all other groups" (69).

The data cited above compare and contrast in significant ways with Robert Wuthnow's findings in *God and Mammon in America* (New York: Free Press, 1994). Thirty-nine percent of weekly churchgoers, Wuthnow found, say that they are involved in charity or social service activities, compared with one-quarter of all the respondents in a group of 2,013 working adults that his survey polled in 1992.

On the whole, however, Wuthnow found that Americans are preoccupied with their own economic security. Four out of five Americans do consider selfishness and the condition of the poor to be serious national problems, but a similar percentage regarded having a beautiful home, a new car, and other nice things as essential or important to them. In most cases, though by no means all, Wuthnow found that religion is more a therapeutic device that helps people feel good about themselves than a force that challenges them to think critically about their lifestyles. Yet Wuthnow also detected a yearning among Americans for a more consistent and solid set of values. American religious institutions, he argues, need to do a better job of cultivating and channeling that yearning.

30. Patterson and Kim, *Day America Told the Truth*, 180–81.

31. Ibid., 183–84.

32. See Golay and Rollyson, *Where America Stands, 1996*, 1.

33. For further detail on the data cited in this paragraph, see Patterson and Kim, *Day America Told the Truth*, 213–17, and Golay and Rollyson, *Where America Stands, 1996*, 1. Robert J. Samuelson's 1995 discussion of American assumptions and aspirations is also important in this context. A well-informed columnist for *Newsweek* and the *Washington Post,* Samuelson focuses on the American economy. In *The Good Life and Its Discontents: The American Dream in the Age of Entitlement, 1945-1995* (New York: Times Books, 1995), he analyzes why Americans tend to be pessimistic about the country's future. He concludes that post–World War II Americans have been too optimistic about solving all social problems and in thinking that personal happiness could be virtually ensured for everyone. In sum, this version of the American Dream destined us for disappointment because human institutions—government and the economy, to name only two—are incapable of delivering such goods in the quantity and quality we have grown to expect. Americans have accomplished a great deal. As a people we have reason to be happier than we sometimes say we are, but insofar as we have expected too much, Americans are likely to be disillusioned and dismayed because we feel that the country has not lived up to its promises. Samuelson suggests that we must modify our expectations. He does not say much about religion's role in the creation of the unintended pessimism that has resulted from our excessive expectation or in the modification of our attitudes that he urges. Both of those topics, however, are worthy of consideration as far as talk about religion in America is concerned.

34. Patterson and Kim, *Day America Told the Truth*, 202.

35. Ibid., 231. Gallup poll findings at mid-decade indicated that 63 percent of the American people would describe themselves as "environmentalists," 62 percent favor environmental protection over economic growth, and 83 percent want the country to take "some additional actions" to protect the environment. See Golay and Rollyson, *Where America Stands, 1996*, 5. Concern about the quality of education in the United States is reflected in a January 1996 poll that found 43 percent of Americans claiming that the quality of their local public schools had declined in the past three years. See *Time*, 5 Feb. 1996, 30.

36. Patterson and Kim, *Day America Told the Truth*, 233.

37. Ibid., 199. American belief in angels is also widespread. According to a 1993 *Time* magazine survey, 69 percent of Americans believe in the existence of angels, 46 percent say they have a guardian angel, and 32 percent report feeling an angelic presence in their lives. What Americans mean when they speak of angels ranges from "higher spiritual beings created by God with special powers to act as God's agents on earth" (55 percent) to "the spirits of people who have died" (15 percent). See Nancy Gibbs, "Angels among Us," *Time*, 27 Dec. 1993, 56–65.

38. See Golay and Rollyson, *Where America Stands, 1996*, 185.

39. Heaven has become a topic of widespread interest to Americans in the 1990s. Roy Rivenburg, "Heaven," *Los Angeles Times*, 2 Dec. 1994, E1, E4, states that nearly 80 percent of Americans believe in it. *Embraced by the Light* and *Life after Life*—books with such titles have achieved bestseller status. Scholars have discovered heaven and the considerable variety of images that human minds have constructed about it. See, for example, Colleen McDannell and Bernhard Lang, *Heaven: A History* (New Haven: Yale University Press, 1988); Peter J. Kreeft, *Everything You Ever Wanted to Know about Heaven . . . But Never Dreamed of Asking* (San Francisco: Ignatius, 1990); and Jeffrey Burton Russell, *A History of Heaven* (Princeton: Princeton University Press, 1997). According to Mally Cox-Chapman's book *The Case for Heaven* (New York: Putnam, 1995), recently reported "near-death" experiences number in the millions, and many of them offer visions more reassuring than theology or philosophy typically provide.

40. According to the *Newsweek* poll, belief in the Devil's existence has a wide range of meanings. For example, about 25 percent of the Americans who accept the Devil's existence regard Satan as a symbol of man's inhumanity to man, but many others speak of the Devil as someone more than human who tempts and even controls human life. Commenting on *Newsweek*'s findings, sociologist Robert Wuthnow sees social class at work. Affluent and well-educated Americans are the mostly likely to be skeptical of the Devil's existence. See Kenneth L. Woodward, "Do We Need Satan?" *Newsweek*, 13 Nov. 1995, 48–54.

The question raised in the title of Woodward's *Newsweek* article is discussed by Andrew Delbanco, *The Death of Satan* (New York: Farrar, Straus and Giroux, 1995). Delbanco rejects literal belief in Satan, but his book argues that Americans need to talk about evil more openly if we are to address the moral and political needs facing the United States as the twenty-first century approaches. Delbanco's point is well taken as part of our national need to talk more and better about the public roles of religion in American life.

41. This finding does not mean, however, that Americans—individually and collectively—believe that religion should not be involved in and influence politics. A 1996 report from the Pew Research Center for the People and the Press, Washington, D.C., found that 54 percent of the American people believe that religious institutions should express political views, while 43 percent said they should not.

Those percentages were reversed when a Gallup poll raised a similar question in 1968. The Pew survey also found that, regardless of their religion or denomination, the most religiously active Americans tend also to be politically conservative. My information about the Pew report was obtained from an Internet release from the U.S. Information Service, dated June 26, 1996.

42. The sociologists Barry A. Kosmin and Seymour P. Lachman cite figures for the 1990s indicating that about 80 million Americans attend weekly worship services. See their *One Nation Under God* (New York: Harmony Books, 1993), 1. William Bennett notes that although more than 85 percent of the country's people identify themselves as either Protestant or Catholic, sociological findings show that only 20 percent of Protestants and 28 percent of Catholics are in church during any given week in the 1990s, figures that are considerably lower than more optimistic studies have obtained. See Bennett's *Index of Leading Cultural Indicators: Facts and Figures on the State of American Society* (New York: Simon & Schuster, 1994), 116. The findings of Kosmin, Lachman, and Bennett jibe well with Patterson and Kim's.

43. Golay and Rollyson, *Where America Stands, 1996*, 192.

44. Patterson and Kim, *Day America Told the Truth*, 201.

45. Gallup and Jones, *Saints among Us*, 11, 14.

46. Gallup and Jones reprint the complete set of questions they used in their survey as well as another series of worthwhile questions that invite further reflection on their book's findings. See ibid., 41, 123, and 125–34.

47. Ibid., 19, 21, 35, 36. The figures cited by Gallup and Jones sometimes differ from those reported by Patterson and Kim. Nevertheless, those differences are usually small enough that the findings of both teams tend to be more in agreement than in disagreement with each other.

In the 1990s, debate has swirled around the rates of church attendance in the United States. A 1992 Gallup poll found that 45 percent of Protestants and 51 percent of Catholics attend religious services weekly. These figures balance with data that for decades have shown weekly church attendance to be approximately 40 percent for all denominations. Sociologists of religion such as Kirk Hadaway, Penny Long Marler, and Mark Chaves claim, however, that these figures over-report behavior that people perceive to be socially desirable. These scholars contend that only about 20 percent of Protestants and 28 percent of Catholics attend church on a weekly basis. How to obtain the most accurate picture about this matter is a problem that social scientists will continue to explore and debate. See "Number of Attendees Disputed in Study," *Los Angeles Times*, 18 Sept. 1993, B4–B5.

48. See Golay and Rollyson, *Where America Stands, 1996*, 185–91. In March 1957, a high-water mark of 82 percent of the American people affirmed that religion could remedy most, if not all, of the nation's problems. As far as the history of public opinion polling about religion is concerned, Golay and Rollyson point out that the positive attitudes about religion got their highest marks in the 1950s.

49. Gallup and Jones, *Saints among Us*, 15.

50. Gallup and Jones reprint both of their questionnaires. See ibid., 41 and 123.

51. In this context, Gallup and Jones cite additional polling data gathered and analyzed by Robert Wuthnow. See ibid., 67. Wuthnow asked people to rank how important religious beliefs were in teaching them to be "kind and caring." He reports that "a majority (57 percent) said this was a major reason for them to be kind and caring. Another 26 percent selected it as a minor reason. Only 14 percent said it was not a reason for them to be kind and caring." See Robert Wuthnow, *Acts of Compassion* (Princeton, N.J.: Princeton University Press, 1991), 51.

52. Gallup and Jones, *Saints among Us,* 22.

53. William James, *The Varieties of Religious Experience* (New York: Doubleday Image Books, 1978), 261.

54. Ibid., 272–73.

55. Ibid., 368.

56. For important examples of related topics that need to be addressed, see Thomas C. Reeves, *The Empty Church: The Suicide of Liberal Christianity* (New York: Free Press, 1996). An active Episcopalian, Reeves wonders whether the so-called mainline churches really matter much anymore. He identifies these "seven sisters" of American Protestantism as the American Baptist Churches in the USA, the Christian Church (Disciples of Christ), the Episcopal Church, the Evangelical Lutheran Church in America, the Presbyterian Church (USA), the United Church of Christ, and the United Methodist Church. Concerned to revive these institutions and traditions, which are still the spiritual homes for millions of Americans, he offers an informed diagnosis of the mainline churches' decline and constructive prescriptions for their renewal. The success of his approach depends on improved talk in public about religion—specifically discourse about Protestant Christianity—which can, in turn, strengthen the practice of religion and the quality of American life.

57. Gallup and Jones, *Saints among Us,* 29.

CHAPTER FIVE

Religion Matters

We should talk . . . Gotta run . . . Let's have lunch . . .
—ANDREW LLOYD WEBBER, *Sunset Boulevard*

Census data and polling statistics give information that should help to focus talk about religion in the United States. What that discussion says, however, also needs to maintain contact with the fact that every American has personal stories to tell about our memories, our dreams, our lives. Different though those stories may be, they are likely to contain more in common than we might think at first. The common ground will indicate that we often care deep down about similar things.

By sharing some American stories, this chapter shows that when we look carefully, the things we care about deep down pivot around our yearning to make sense of what is happening to us, our desire to discern what is good and right, and our need for meaningful goals to which we can commit ourselves wholeheartedly. Such yearnings, desires, and needs show how our private and public lives intersect and depend upon each other. They also connect to issues that religion raises and to which it responds. Those issues, which always have overlapping social and personal dimensions, involve our sense of the whole, our understandings about what deserves to be called sacred, and our loyalties to the ideals that those senses and understandings emphasize.

A Hollywood Parable

The stories I have in mind begin with *Sunset Boulevard*. That 1990s mega-musical drama is the creation of Andrew Lloyd Webber,[1] whose exceptional talent and distinguished career have included ways to talk about religious themes on stage through classics such as *Joseph and the Amazing Technicolor Dreamcoat*, *Jesus Christ Superstar*, and *The Phantom of the Opera*.

As it tells a Hollywood story set in the Los Angeles of 1949–50, *Sunset Boulevard* seems to offer a plot more melodramatic than profound. Initially the basic story line says little, if anything, about religion and American culture, for at first glance, *Sunset Boulevard* simply narrates the demise of an aging movie queen named Norma Desmond. First glances, however, only begin to tell this story. As one looks again, the plot thickens and, at least indirectly, the story has much to suggest about religion in American life.

Though a dazzling star during the days of silent films, Norma Desmond has been displaced by the sound and light of a new era typified by Cecil B. DeMille's epic productions. They include the biblical story of Samson and Delilah, the film DeMille is shooting as the action of *Sunset Boulevard* unfolds. As she approaches fifty, Norma insists, "I will never bend . . . I'll fight on to the end," but she also lives in a bygone world, that of the silent screen when she was seventeen and an American idol for the twenties.[2] Refusing to admit that time has passed her by, Norma's delusions include the fantasy that she can script a new film—perhaps it will be silent—to bring her stardom back.

DeMille's Paramount studio does call, but Desmond's hopes rise only to be dashed when Joe Gillis, the struggling young screenwriter who has been living with her, tells Norma that Paramount has no interest in her script. The studio wants only the car, as outdated as it is elegant, that helps Norma keep alive the dream that she remains "the greatest star of all." Still refusing to concede that time has passed her by, Norma kills Joe, the messenger who is the youth she loves but cannot have.

If things did not work out, Gillis had said, he would be writing obituaries. He ends up the subject of an obituary instead. With day breaking over the murder house, the Los Angeles police arrive to take Norma Desmond away. A reporter broadcasts that "Norma Desmond, famed star of yesteryear, is in a state of complete mental shock." Bewildered and disoriented, she descends the staircase to her arrest. Living in a world that does not exist, Norma will not, cannot, yield to reality. "I can't tell you," she says as the flash bulbs pop, "how wonderful it is to be back in the studio making a picture."

Thanks to the book and lyrics by Don Black and Christopher Hampton and the production's staging, as well as to Webber's music, *Sunset Boulevard* avoids the temptations of melodrama and turns out to be much more than a musical. It is really a parable, a story that uses the directness of its particularity to point out indirectly the directions that our lives need to take or avoid. As a parable, *Sunset Boulevard* studies crucial relationships between speech and silence, hope and despair, delusion and lucidity, success and failure. The experiences it recounts, the questions it raises, the feelings it evokes—they can be perceived, each and all, as matters of the spirit that show how much spirit matters. Those matters matter largely because they connect with religion's defining themes: senses of the whole, concerns about what deserves to be called sacred, and loyalties to the highest ideals we can identify. *Sunset Boulevard* is an important part of the dialogue that we need about those themes because the drama's very American address is a street of dreams.

As *Sunset Boulevard* makes clear, the captivating power of the movies and of Norma Desmond's stardom in particular existed because, as she puts it, "we gave the world new ways to dream." Those ways to dream included aspirations to be "discovered" at Schwab's drug store, to make it big in Hollywood, to write the next blockbuster screenplay, to achieve the celebrity, glamour, and glitter that stardom brings. So Americans headed west, as they have done so often, flocking to Los Angeles and the movie studios, everybody on the make even if not making out.

"How's it hanging?" *Sunset Boulevard*'s dreamers-in-a-hurry ask—Joe Gillis among them—as they hustle their ambitious ways toward the top. "We should talk," they insist. "Gotta run," they go instead. "Let's have lunch," they promise as a way to avoid saying they never will. *Sunset Boulevard* is a place where appearance and reality do not—must not—meet, at least not always, and yet they do.

What We Need to Know

Norma Desmond's genius was that her alluring beauty could make people dream without her saying a word. In the silent world of her silver screen, no words were needed to tell the stories her eyes could tell, for "with one look," she sings, "I can break your heart. With one look I play every part. . . . With one look you'll know all you need to know." *Sunset Boulevard* talks about religious themes in public, indirectly perhaps but really none-theless, because it is an extended meditation on what we need to know.

What do we need to know, especially in a world touched so often and so deeply by Hollywood dreams? They tantalize with visions like the ones that *Sunset Boulevard*'s young hopefuls resolve to make good on New Year's Eve 1949: "By this time next year / . . . we'll have nothing to fear / contracts all signed / three-picture deal / yellow brick road career."

Norma Desmond also celebrates New Year's Eve 1949. At her declining estate on Sunset Boulevard, she plans a lavish party reminiscent of her hey-day with yesterday's Clara Bows and Rudolf Valentinos. Although no one but Joe comes to her party, still Norma's "hopes are high" as she dances "one year in" and kisses "one goodbye." With "another chance / another start / so many dreams / to tease the heart," she hopes with Joe to "embrace the perfect year."

Next year, Norma Desmond hoped, would be the perfect year. But that was not to be in 1950 or in any other year. Perfect years do not exist. One reason is *Sunset Boulevard*'s cue that "no one ever leaves a star." Norma Desmond says those words as she fires her revolver to kill her love, Joe Gillis, who has told her "something you ought to know," namely, that her script is hopeless, her audience vanished, her fan mail an illusion created by the fidelity of her former director-husband Max, who made her a star and now tries against all odds to keep Norma's dreams, her life—and per-haps his own—from being destroyed. "Nothing's wrong with being fifty," Joe tells her in words she may understand but to which she cannot surren-der, "unless you're acting twenty."

It is too late for Norma to learn what she needs to know. As though enacting the story that her hoped-for script had told—it is her version of a biblical tale about Salome, who wants but cannot have John the Bap-tist and thus has him beheaded instead—Norma kills Joe Gillis. "No one," says Norma, "could play [Salome's life] like I can" because "no one ever leaves a star"—not John the Baptist, not Salome, not Joe Gillis, and not Norma Desmond, either. And yet there is truth in her judgment that she is "the greatest star of all," for her tragic story is a cautionary tale in which we can share and see ourselves and our country.

Norma Desmond would not, could not, surrender her dreams. She would not give up either the conviction that she had been somebody and done magnificent things—"without me there wouldn't be any Paramount studio"—or the hope that she would be that way again. Norma is as appeal-ing and magnificent as she is seductive and destructive. In that respect she is like the biblical Delilah who entices Samson, taking vision and strength from him in the process. As Norma Desmond lived her impossible convictions, she embodied an endearing pugnacity, courage, and rebellion, but those virtues also contained deception, destruction, and death. As Joe says, knowing that Paramount is not Paradise, "in those dreams were hidden dragons."

"I'll be back / where I was born to be," Norma Desmond proclaims as the curtain falls, "with one look I'll be me." However appealing the sound of those lines may once have been, the silence between them now says they are not true. Given or received, the look, whatever its energizing effect may once have been, has become one of madness. The tragedy of *Sunset Boulevard* lives in the fact that Norma Desmond is fatally trapped by the mixing of truth and falsity and the ways their riddles give the world to dream. In that respect her "me" is like America's "we," for what we need to know is how to cope with those ambiguities.

"With one look you'll know / all you need to know." There is no look like that, given or received, but Norma Desmond is right when she says that "no words can tell / the stories my eyes tell." Our lives, including the ambiguity they contain, are too much for words, and thus speech and song and silence must intermingle as they do in *Sunset Boulevard* to say what can and cannot be said, what must and must not be done.

"When I look your way," Norma Desmond sings, "you'll hear what I say." Like Joe Gillis, we "can't help being / touched by her folly." The street called Sunset Boulevard tempts and twists; its turns are frenzied and brutal, ruthless and lethal. What one comes to hear and know as a result is that in the sharing of this story people may have been moved to feel more deeply, to question what is going on, to think more carefully, to look more searchingly, and to speak with greater sensitivity. For Norma Desmond's story—silent, spoken, played, and sung—is about our deepest private needs, our most public selves, and the relations among them. Leading us to wonder and to see, even if we cannot say exactly, what life is all about, part of the magic in the making of *Sunset Boulevard* is that as Norma Desmond "returned at last / to my people in the dark / still out there in the dark," her story sheds light on why we are here and what we need to know.

"Let's get a look at you." With that exclamation, Hog-eye, an old hand who knew Norma Desmond during her best days at Paramount, bathes her in a spotlight when she returns to the set of DeMille's *Samson and Delilah*, still believing that she will be a star again. In one of *Sunset Boulevard*'s most wistful scenes, as she basks for a moment in nostalgia's limelight, Norma shares her feelings honestly: "I don't want to be alone . . . Has there ever been a moment / with so much to live for? . . . So much to say / not just today / but always." Filling her mind, finding expression in her voice, those feelings are ours as well, and we need ways to express them. Those private needs make us public selves, and if we let them, all of those realities have power to suggest how talk about religious matters can be evoked, carried on in public, and revealed as palpably important even when we least expect it. If they work that way, *Sunset Boulevard*'s sentiments can indeed teach the world new ways to dream.

Sharing Interpretations

Sunset Boulevard is worth talking about. That conviction grew after I saw Glenn Close in her Los Angeles starring role in the summer of 1994. As my thoughts about the religious significance of the show took shape, I knew that not everyone would agree with my interpretation. Agreement, however, is not the point I have in mind. More important is the sharing of varied interpretations of this very personal and public story, which is so full of philosophical questions and religious themes. That impression became even stronger and more persuasive as I reflected on three activities that engaged me immediately before and after roaming *Sunset Boulevard.*

In the ten days before I saw *Sunset Boulevard,* I worked with two gifted teachers, Murray Schwartz, dean of the Claremont Graduate School, and Martha Andresen, professor of English at Pomona College, to lead the annual Bradshaw Seminar for Young Professionals and the Humanities, which the three of us have done for several years. Each June the seminar brings fifteen young and distinguished leaders to Claremont, California. They hail from diverse professions—business, health, journalism, law, to name a few—and from all over the United States. The ethnic and cultural mix is diverse as well, as are the points of view. We come together to study and talk. What focuses our study and talk are shared books, questions, and concerns, which always discuss senses of the whole, what deserves to be called sacred, and loyalties to the highest ideals people have identified. The 1994 study list included Shakespeare's *Hamlet* and the novel and film versions of *Schindler's List* by Thomas Keneally and Steven Spielberg, respectively.

When the Bradshaw Seminar focuses on "the humanities," the task is to explore what it means to be human. Those explorations use history, literature, philosophy, and the study of religion to engage what the California Council for the Humanities aptly calls "our most vital inheritance: the wisdom of our cultures, the experience of remarkable individuals, and the values that define and guide our lives as persons and as a people. The humanities invite us to life-long learning, to continuing conversation about what matters to each and all of us."[3] That definition of the humanities also helps to define what talking about religion in public should be about. At its best, such talk, which has its place in the humanities, engages our most vital inheritances as it explores what it means to be human. The Bradshaw Seminar builds on such insights about and from the humanities and, as a consequence, it also illustrates how such building can facilitate constructive talk about religion in public.

Talking about religion in public is not one of the Bradshaw Seminar's stated purposes. Yet almost unavoidably, religion does come up when people get around to conversation about what matters most to each and all of us. Such sharing happens every year in the seminar. It happens in space that is safe and secure for people to say what they think and feel, to disagree and differ, and yet to appreciate and learn from each other. Each year the group is small, but still it is public, and the impact of the discussions has the potential to reach far beyond the close circle that virtually complete strangers form in the short time that they work together. It has that potential because each seminar member is not only an individual with private needs but also a public self whose commitments emphasize engagement with the major social issues of the day. Directly and indirectly, small groups such as the Bradshaw Seminar make a modest but very significant contribution to the common good Americans need to pursue. There is no doubt that the Bradshaw Seminar does so in part because the sharing it encourages allows people to talk critically and constructively about religion in public.[4]

The day the 1994 Bradshaw Seminar ended, I saw *Sunset Boulevard* and then headed for Highlands, North Carolina. Located in the far western part of that state, it is the lovely village in the Great Smoky Mountains where another small group meets annually for continuing conversation about what matters to each and all of us. Its name is HIART, which stands for the Highlands Institute for American Religious Thought. HIART's mixture of Americans also arrives from all over the country. Most, but not all, of them are academics. HIART does focus explicitly on religion and American culture, but again the purpose is to study and learn through discussion and debate in which inquiry and questioning are the vehicles for increasing understanding.

In 1994 the HIART meeting talked about a significant book, *The Reli-*

gious Critic in American Culture, by an important American thinker named William Dean. His book argues that American life needs more public intellectuals, as he calls them.[5] Such people are committed to criticism and reconstruction of the nation's spiritual culture, which, according to Dean, consists of "the myths, rituals, narratives, traditions, and theories that inform and mold a society's deepest purposes."[6]

To a considerable degree, Dean holds, the United States presently lacks enough of these public intellectuals, particularly in their role as religious critics, because the nation has been deeply affected by a pessimism that has robbed us Americans of an earlier self-confidence. Though necessary, the disillusionment has gone too far, but that trend is scarcely surprising because American pessimism has been intensified by multiple factors. They range from a decline of the nation's international political-economic hegemony and the country's increasing ethnic and religious pluralism to the relativizing and deconstructing effects of recent philosophical theories.

Confidence that Americans do or even can agree that we hold any truths to be "self-evident" has been profoundly shaken, Dean believes. Among the results of this shaking of the foundations have been a privatizing of religious expression and the retreat of intellectuals into the confining safety of specialized professional scholarship that is housed in the academy and carried out within disciplines that correspond poorly to the stress, strain, and strife of public life. We Americans, says Dean, need religious critics who can help us to relocate our "sense of the whole of the world" and of ourselves in that world. Even more specifically, he urges, we need to relocate the sacred, which Dean identifies with "whatever is ultimately important within 'the whole.' "[7] Without efforts of this kind, Dean asserts, "the public is jeopardized."[8]

William Dean's HIART colleagues did not agree with everything he said, but the conversation about his book showed that open debate about religion can do things that are much needed in American life. Done well, it can build bridges between different and differing points of view. It can help us to locate and tell, recollect and revise, the stories that make up the story of our nation, the histories that comprise the history of our people. Through speech and silence, dialogue and listening, criticism and insight can be fostered to enhance shared appreciation and action for what matters to each and all of us.

One of the things that matters to each and all of us is that we Americans come from and identify with different traditions in political, cultural, ethnic, religious, and family life. So it was fitting that I made another stop before I returned from Highlands, North Carolina, to my home in Claremont, California. This time my destination was Baltimore, Maryland, a city with a special place in the American story because of a fort named McHenry and a poet named Key.

In September 1814, during the War of 1812, British troops invaded Washington, D.C., and torched much of the city. Baltimore was their next objective. As events unfolded, Francis Scott Key, a Maryland attorney, was trying to obtain the release of an elderly friend from British captivity. His negotiations took him aboard a British ship that was part of the fleet targeting Baltimore. So it was that Key witnessed the bombardment of Fort McHenry during the night of September 13–14, 1814. Dimly, through the smoke and haze, he could see the tattered American flag flying from the fort's ramparts. "By the dawn's early light," as the poem Key was inspired to write would put it, he saw that "our flag was still there."

Upon his release by the British, Key finished the poem in a Baltimore hotel room on the evening of September 16. At first it was called "Defence of Fort McHenry." Within a few weeks, however, its name had changed to "The Star-Spangled Banner." With the words set to an English drinking song called "To Anacreon in Heaven," Key's poem was first sung publicly at the Baltimore Theater on October 19, 1814. Its popularity grew during the nineteenth century. Only on March 3, 1931, however, did President Herbert Hoover sign the bill that officially made "The Star-Spangled Banner" our national anthem.[9]

Although Americans usually know only the first verse of "The Star-Spangled Banner," Francis Scott Key wrote three more. All four speak about the United States as "the land of the free, and the home of the brave," but the last one goes on to emphasize religious themes. For instance, it describes American ground as "heaven-rescued," exhorts that our motto should be "in God is our trust," and urges the people to "praise the power that hath made and preserved us as a nation."

My Baltimore visit did not echo the triumphal notes of the national anthem. Definitely, however, that visit was an occasion for reflection about freedom and preservation, about trust, rescue, and God. It made me realize increasingly that promoting and caring about public religious discourse is not only an essential right but also a basic responsibility that must be met if Americans are to be loyal to the ideal that the United States should be a land of the free.

Specifically, I went to Baltimore to participate in a conference called "Faith for the Future." It was sponsored by the Institute for Christian and

Jewish Studies (ICJS), whose mission statement emphasizes the institute's intention to address "the contemporary challenges of religious pluralism by helping to shape a new relationship between Christians and Jews."

For nearly two thousand years, the religious traditions of Christianity and Judaism have lived with distortions and misconceptions about each other. That tragedy was not sufficient to cause the Holocaust, but the anti-Jewish feeling fostered by Christianity contributed decisively to that catastrophe. Aiming to make a contribution to mending the world, ICJS provides occasions for careful study of the sacred writings and traditions of Judaism and Christianity. More than that, the Institute looks for new ways to dream by encouraging Christians and Jews "to reexamine the meaning of their religious assumptions, particularly about one another; to question the theological distortions and misconceptions which have contributed to historical conflict between Christians and Jews; [and] to develop the resources within their respective communities which inspire both Christians and Jews to appreciate the legitimacy and distinctiveness of each religion."

"Faith for the Future" fitted that description. Designed especially for clergy and laypersons from Lutheran and Presbyterian churches, it provided safe and open spaces where people could meet and explore how the particularity of our traditions affects what it means to be human. There were small group sessions and panel discussions, as well as plenary presentations and curriculum materials, that brought Christians and Jews together not by seeking bland, lowest common denominators of agreement but by affirming differences, challenging exclusivism, rediscovering how important a thoughtful humility can be, and locating in the midst of disagreement common ground that can help to make the whole world more a land of the free.

These explorations were not without moments of painful recognition—many of them grasped in the silence of careful listening—especially for Christians like me who still have much to do to overcome the harm that the Christian tradition has inflicted on Jews. So steps in good directions were taken in Baltimore. They would not have taken place if people had been unwilling to take the risks and to assume the responsibilities of listening and talking in public about religion. Equally important, these voluntary discussions—like the ones in the Bradshaw Seminar and at HIART—occurred because they were supported by institutions and communities, although in these cases not necessarily by ones that we associate most obviously with religious life.

In Baltimore a coalition of Christians and Jews from varied communities has worked for years to develop the Institute for Christian Jewish Studies. In Highlands another voluntary group has organized itself to promote on a regular basis public inquiry about religion and American life. In Claremont the Bradshaw Seminar finds support from the Claremont Graduate School but also, significantly, from corporate sources as well. And then there is the theater and *Sunset Boulevard,* which turn out to be not at all the unlikely venues they may seem at first to be when talk about religion in public is on our minds and getting under way.

We should talk . . . Gotta run . . . Let's have lunch . . . *We should talk*— and if we do, looking for all we need to know, then we might move next to consider how one thing leads to another, how one place takes us to another, and how finding new ways to dream reveals, as *Sunset Boulevard* shows, "so many roads still unexplored." So let this chapter's narrative add one more story by returning to Baltimore words such as ICJS's concern to address "the contemporary challenges of religious pluralism" and Francis Scott Key's insistence that our flag must wave "o'er the land of the free."

The Art of Being Free

In early November 1831, a public intellectual and religious critic named Alexis de Tocqueville, the astute French author of that classic *Democracy in America,* traveled in Maryland, a state with deep-seated Roman Catholic origins. One of his stops was a call on James Carroll, who at the time was not only a Catholic but also ninety-five years old, probably the richest man in America—his Maryland estate reportedly contained 13,000 acres of land worked by 300 slaves—and the last surviving signer of the Declaration of Independence. On his way, Tocqueville stopped in Baltimore. A Bostonian had told Tocqueville that it was "the most democratic town in the Union." [10] The reason, Tocqueville heard, was that Catholics, a religious minority looking for freedom of religious expression in the young republic, "always vote for the most democratic party." [11]

Whether Tocqueville accepted the Bostonian's appraisal of Baltimore is unknown, but he did find that the state of Maryland was "the first to proclaim universal suffrage and introduced the most democratic procedures throughout its government." [12] What is even easier to document is Tocqueville's emphasis that "the religious atmosphere of the country was the first thing that struck me on arrival in the United States." [13] Religion's importance in the United States, he underscored, was that it did so much to teach Americans what Tocqueville called "the art of being free." [14]

More than a century and a half after Tocqueville visited Baltimore and published *Democracy in America*, another public intellectual and religious critic, Stephen L. Carter, who is a leading legal scholar at Yale University, talked about religion in public and amplified key parts of Tocqueville's understanding of religion's role in the United States. As expressed in *The Culture of Disbelief: How American Law and Politics Trivializes Religious Devotion*, Carter's insight helps to focus more new ways for Americans to dream and act.

American religion, Carter affirmed, still has much to teach about "the art of being free," but the religious atmosphere of the United States tends to hinder that instruction. It does so because the atmosphere is dominated by a political and legal culture that leans toward trivializing religious devotion. If that trend continues, Carter fears that the result will be, as his book's title suggests, a culture of disbelief. Such a culture will undercut the diversity of religious commitment and perspective that helps to ensure the vitality of democratic life.

Carter believes that the dominant legal and political forces in contemporary American life have interpreted the U.S. Constitution's First Amendment in ways that rob religious belief of its importance. Determined to safeguard the wall of separation between religion and the state, those forces have placed too little emphasis on the fact that the First Amendment's primary purpose is to provide protection for the "free exercise" of religious life. In Carter's judgment, the effect of First Amendment interpretations has too often promoted indifference, if not hostility, toward religion.

The "free exercise" of religion has been needlessly restricted, Carter argues, and the country is worse, not better, for it. Those philosophical views do not mean that Carter ends up with predictable public policy positions that reflect conventional conservative or liberal outlooks. He does think that the courts have properly proscribed formal prayer in the schools, and he is opposed to capital punishment. Although he would not deny women the right to abortion, he has strong "pro-life" sympathies as well. But his book is primarily an inquiry—not a set of public policy pronouncements—that reasons its way to views that he wants to be part of a wide-ranging national conversation about the state of the nation's union and religion's place within it.

Carter's judgments are informed not only by his study of the law but also by his religious commitments and his ethnic heritage. A dedicated Christian of Episcopalian persuasion, Carter is also an African-American who firmly believes that the free exercise of religion had much to do with civil rights advances in American society. He knows, of course, that religion has never been an unmitigated force for justice. Many of history's most destructive chapters have been written in blood spilled by and for religiously inspired causes. Even in the United States the "free exercise" of religion is rightly checked and balanced by sound legal restraints to ensure that it does not become an instrument of oppression. Nevertheless, Carter affirms, religion remains overall a great force for good. "In recent history," he writes, "we have seen religious witness against oppression around the world, which tyrannical governments have often met with antireligious slaughter. In America, we have seen religious witness against slavery and segregation, against the war in Vietnam, and against poverty. Witness of this kind will be most effective in a nation that truly celebrates its diverse religious traditions, valuing them instead of trying to hide them." [15]

Carter judges the quality of American religious life. He carries no brief for every religious belief and practice, but he is deeply sympathetic when American religion plays a resisting, independent, minority role. When religious expressions work in that way, Carter insists, they "promote freedom and reduce the likelihood of democratic tyranny by splitting the allegiance of citizens and pressing on their members points of view that are often radically different from the preferences of the state" (37).

A key strength of religion is its power to dissent not only from state power but from the tyranny that cultural conformity and other forms of "majority rule" are tempted to enforce. Following Tocqueville, then, Carter upholds a tradition affirming the importance of religion as a source of moral understanding that checks the tendencies of a secular state and culture to dominate tyrannically. Religion's proclivity to be unfashionable, its refusal to go along with what most people may find expedient, politically correct, or even rational — in short, the very dissenting aspect of religion that many of its critics most fear — is precisely religion's great strength and gift to a democratic republic.

Contemporary American society, however, is in danger of diminishing religion's strength, if not of rejecting its gift outright. Irony permeates that prospect because an overwhelming majority of Americans identify themselves as religious. Citing polls like the ones mentioned in previous chapters of this book, Carter notes that nine out of ten Americans believe in God and four out of five pray regularly. Americans are much more likely to attend worship services regularly than any other people in the Western world. Overwhelming numbers of them also report that religious faith is a crucial factor in their moral decisions. Granted, not all of these reportedly religious Americans take religion very seriously, but in Carter's view that fact has much to do with what he calls the trivialization of religious devotion. Religion has been trivialized in the United States not only because many people fail to take it seriously but also because secular authority — especially in our legal interpretations — often makes it impossible for religion to be, in Carter's words, little more than a private hobby that neither governs an individual's life decisively nor intrudes on anyone else's.

To see more of what Carter means, recall again that the United States is one of the most religious nations on earth, at least in the sense of having a deeply religious citizenry, but Americans are also wary when people are too zealous about their religious commitments.[16] In particular, Americans are vigilant about guarding public institutions against explicit religious control. That vigilance certainly has its place, for religion is not without oppressive tendencies, and if any religious tradition dominates public institutional life, the outcome can be tyrannical. In contemporary American life, however, Carter finds that this vigilance has lost its balance. A legitimate concern has reached too far and turned punitive toward religious influence on public life. Public expressions of religion are silenced, even punished, and the religiously devout are disabled "from working seriously in the realm of policy" (21). One effect of this imbalance is that it is fine to be religious in private, but religion is cast in a far more dubious light when private beliefs are publicly expressed and become the basis for public action.

There are, of course, exceptions to this rule. When restricted to the confines of generally accepted, official places of worship, religion is no bother. When its voice simply echoes sentiments or values held by the dominant culture, religion is no threat. But when religion reaches beyond these boundaries, cries about imposing religious values or undue political involvement are bound to be heard. The law may even come down on religious folks when their practices conflict with culturally dominant senses of economic gain, political necessity, or social progress.

"Our public culture," writes Carter, "more and more prefers religion as something without political significance, less an independent moral force than a quietly irrelevant moralizer, never heard, rarely seen" (9). In zealously preventing the imposition of religion, Carter believes, Americans have silenced the public expression of religion too much for their own good. It is wrong, he argues, to think that religious impulses to public action should be prejudged as oppressive or even wicked. History, especially American history, cannot sustain such judgments. In history's long run, at least in the West, religion has had a liberalizing, democratizing effect that has undergirded human freedom and equality and has resisted their enemies. Nor, according to Carter, can such restrictive attitudes toward religion in contemporary American life do justice to what religion actually is and entails, a point that should not be overlooked in a nation with such a long-standing commitment to defend religious liberty.

Carter's emphases are not always the same as mine. My understanding of religion makes it a broader category than his. But that does not mean that his understanding of religion is at odds with mine. On the contrary, I take his understanding to be fully compatible with and complementary to my own. I agree that religion typically finds its primary location in traditions of group worship. I would only underscore that those locations are by no means religion's only homes. I agree, too, that religion is essentially a social and public activity, not just a private and an individualistic matter, but I would add that religion's range and importance will be underestimated if its deeply personal dimensions are not emphasized as well. I concur with Carter that religion assumes the existence of a reality—most, but not all, Americans would call that reality God—which is more than human, but what "more than human" means is an idea that admits of wide and varied interpretation. In Carter's view and in mine, this reality is not bounded by the observed principles and limits of natural science, but I think it can be interpreted and understood naturalistically as well as in supernatural categories. Of greatest importance, we agree that religion makes moral demands on its adherents, and those demands themselves have to be evaluated and judged. Overall, religion's effect on human life has been good, but much of its influence has not. The difference is found in the degree to which a religion promotes freedom and justice for all.

Religious belief and practice require acting in some ways and not in others; they entail convictions about right and wrong, good and evil, that must find public expression. Those convictions must do so because no person's life is ever a purely private affair—we all live in public—and because the demands that religion enjoins are rarely, if ever, purely private matters, either. Thus, Carter fears trends that he sees: Americans endanger both religion and the ideal of democratic liberty to the extent that their suspicions about imposing religion escalate into positions that restrict American religion from informing and influencing the public dialogue on which the health of democracy depends.

Naturally, Carter's concerns direct his attention to the U.S. Constitution and its central role in establishing boundaries and protections for American expressions of religion. Although the historical accuracy of his judgment is debatable, Carter's jurisprudence emphasizes that "the metaphorical separation of church and state originated in an effort to protect religion from the state, not the state from religion. The religion clauses of the First Amendment were crafted to permit maximum freedom to the religious" (105–6).

The American government can neither require sectarian observances nor favor one religion over another. But Carter holds that other considerations are equally valid: the American government cannot bring sanctions against anyone's religious persuasion without a compelling reason to do so. Neither is it the government's place to ban religiously motivated people from influencing public policy. Nor is the government banned from listening to and being affected by such voices.

"The principal task of the separation of church and state," says Carter, "is to secure religious liberty" (107). Thus, the state properly forbids the imposition of religious belief. But *imposing* religious belief must not be confused, and certainly not equated, with *acting* from religious motivation. Granted, the practices and programs that are advocated when people act from religious motivations may rightly be found wanting, but Carter's position is that it will not do to discriminate against them simply because those practices and programs arise from religious motivations. Instead, as Carter celebrates the separation of church and state as one of the greatest insights that American political philosophy has given to the world, he stresses that the state must avoid imposing religious belief so that people are free to express themselves religiously in public as well as in private.

But there is the rub: in contemporary American culture the difference between imposing religious belief and acting from religious motivation is not discerned clearly enough. Carter is concerned that American culture too readily equates the latter with the former, ignoring a crucial difference in the process. If people say publicly that they must do this or refrain from that, or that they advocate this and deplore that, because their religious persuasion requires it, they may be regarded as odd, irrational, scary, or worse—especially if their religious persuasion dissents from what the majority of society believes is right. According to Carter, however, religion's tendency to "thumb its nose at what the rest of the society believes is right" is invaluable for democratic life (35). To be sure, a society may need to protect itself from dissent that goes well beyond nose-thumbing, but Carter contends that the autonomy of religion should be upheld unless the reasons to check it are truly clear and compelling.

Taking different paths from those of the dominant culture is at the heart of religious life that affirms "the authority of God as *superior to* the authority of the state" (38). Such autonomy for religion can help the nation to think more deeply, critically, sensitively, freely, and fairly about what is good, right, and just. A healthy democracy, Carter concludes, will not want religion to control or impose its particular values on society. But it should want religion to influence public life because that is how religion serves democracy and helps to teach the art of being free.

Supporting Roles

Mapping traces of America from coast to coast—*Sunset Boulevard* to Fort McHenry with stops at places such as Claremont, Highlands, and Yale along the way—this chapter's mural illustrates that the art of being free entails new ways to dream that see beyond the years. It shows, moreover, that new ways to dream in American life are never far removed from the concerns and varieties of religious experience. That claim holds because life is so deeply moved by commitment, hope, and what to do next when commitment breaks down and hope is lost. Wherever ingredients like those are found, religion is close by because they are the elements that make and sustain it.

Returning to *Sunset Boulevard* for a moment more as this chapter's sketches end, it is worth noting that Norma Desmond and Joe Gillis are only two of the Americans featured in that story. A young woman named Betty Schaefer plays an important supporting role, too.

Betty is the third generation of her family to work in the movies that give people new ways to dream. None of the Schaefers, however, has been a star. Electricians, wardrobe specialists, stunt persons—their parts have mostly been behind the scenes. Betty's family groomed her for something bigger and brighter, but the crucial screen test did not go well. So Betty evaluates and edits manuscripts for Sheldrake, a Hollywood agent. Her work is not glamorous, but it has one crucial advantage: it alerts her to the differences between good scripts and poor ones, between stories that probe and inquire deeply and those that promise and answer superficially. She yearns to write something of her own.

Betty's work for Sheldrake leads to her meeting Joe Gillis. At first she is unimpressed. "Bases Loaded," a baseball story that Joe wrote and Sheldrake pitches for production, strikes out with her. "It doesn't have to be so mindless," she tells Joe about his writing. "You should write from your experience / give us something really moving, / something true." Joe is not sure anyone wants true or moving—"moving means starving," he contends, "and true means holes in your shoe." Betty disagrees.

Despite their rocky start, the two figure out that Betty has read and liked an earlier story of Joe's. Called "Blind Windows," it is about a teacher. They decide to work on it together. One thing leads to another, and they fall in love, too. Unfortunately, neither their script nor their love work out easily. Joe ends up dead, his murder by Norma Desmond provoked by her jealous discovery that Joe's love for Betty will prevail over Norma's love for him. As for the script, Betty and Joe could not agree about what to say. Off and on again, they tried. Sometimes their writing together went well, sometimes not. Finally Betty finished the script—alone.

"I can't write it on my own," she had insisted, and she was right. Strictly speaking, no one can write or talk alone about what matters to each and all of us, for our selves are public, and it is our living and dying together that make our private needs so intense and the stories they evoke so compelling. *Sunset Boulevard* ends without our knowing what Betty Schaefer's script contains. Maybe it was her response to questions that humanity—and perhaps divinity—kept asking her: "How should I feel? / What should I look for? / . . . Please can you tell me what's happening?" Maybe Betty Schaefer wrote her version of *Sunset Boulevard* in reply.

American life raises her questions from coast to coast. They are ours. With our lives each of us scripts our own responses to them, but even if we can try to write that script alone, we can write it better together. As we look for new ways to dream, we should talk. We should talk about what matters. When we do that, we will be talking, one way or another, about religion in public.

NOTES

1. Andrew Lloyd Webber borrows heavily from Billy Wilder's great 1950 movie *Sunset Boulevard,* which starred Gloria Swanson as Norma Desmond.

2. This quotation and others that follow from *Sunset Boulevard* are taken from the libretto booklet that accompanies the show's world premiere compact disc recording on Really Useful Records.

3. Here it is worth noting that leaders across the nation's political spectrum—including Bill Clinton and William J. Bennett, to name but two—have raised their voices to say that a "great crisis of the spirit . . . is gripping America today" (Clinton) and that "the real crisis of our time is spiritual" (Bennett). See Ronald Brownstein, "Administration Tackles 'Great Crisis of the Spirit' in America," *Los Angeles Times,* 22 Dec. 1993, A5.

Agreeing that sound responses to the nation's problems depend on more than economic policies and legislative acts, Sheldon Hackney, then chairman of the National Endowment for the Humanities, called for "a national conversation." Its purpose, he argued, should be to examine "what unites us as a country" and to discuss "what we share as common American values in a nation comprised of so many divergent groups and beliefs." (The quotations are from a National Endowment for the Humanities news release, which contains the text of Sheldon Hackney's speech, "Beyond the Culture Wars," which was delivered at the National Press Club, Washington, D.C., on November 10, 1993.)

Such a conversation could fulfill Hackney's objectives only to the extent that public discussion of religion's place in American democracy has a prominent place within it.

4. As two studies by Robert Wuthnow show, small groups—some of them far removed from the Bradshaw Seminar, some of them more closely akin to it—are flourishing in the United States. See his *Sharing the Journey: Support Groups and America's New Quest for Community* (New York: Free Press, 1994) and *"I Come Away Stronger": How Small Groups Are Shaping American Religion* (Grand Rapids, Mich.: Eerdmans, 1994).

Over a three-year period, Wuthnow headed a team of fifteen scholars who studied the burgeoning American appeal of small groups such as book discussion clubs, political or civic groups, Bible studies, prayer fellowships, self-help groups, twelve-step gatherings, therapy sessions, and recovery groups. The results of this study show that there are some three million of these groups in the United States in the 1990s. Not only are two-thirds of them connected to churches or synagogues, but also 40 percent of the American people belong to at least one small, organized group whose regular meetings and networks provide care, support, and an opportunity for people to talk about things that matter.

Wuthnow finds that the proliferation of these groups reflects an ongoing fluidity in American life and in American religious experience particularly. He observes, for example, that our early national history included the disestablishment of state churches that the colonists imported from Europe. Denominational pluralism was protected by the Constitution's separation of church and state, and eventually even the hegemony of a few Protestant denominations was undermined as the nation's religious life became more varied and democratic. The proliferation of small groups indicates that the religious vitality of the nation still runs high, but it also shows that the ways in which that vitality finds expression are continuing to change.

Wuthnow appraises this change with a mixture of enthusiasm and caution. He is cautious about the fact that "the small group movement is currently playing a major role in *adapting* American religion to the main currents of secular culture that have surfaced at the end of the twentieth century" (*Sharing the Journey*, 7). His concern is that this adapting "encourages a safe, domesticated version of the sacred" that focuses too much on private needs and ignores our public selves and their relationship to God and the most pressing moral problems of our times (7).

But the small group phenomenon reflects something else as well. It demonstrates, says Wuthnow, "our continuing desire for community. We want others with whom we can share our journeys. Its appeal extends even beyond this desire, tapping into our quest for the sacred itself" (5).

Wuthnow's studies are important not only because they document the importance of the talk about religion that goes on in small groups but also because they show how important it is for talk about religion in public to include critical and constructive discussion about what small groups can and cannot do. As Wuthnow sums up his analysis, the small group movement is both "a distinct product of our times" and "a resource. If deployed effectively, it can encourage deeper reflection about ourselves and our relationship to the sacred. It can motivate its members to engage in volunteer activities and in public service. It can probably be prompted to take a greater role in working for peace, justice, and other social reforms. It can also prompt us to think harder about what kind of community we seek, and how to attain it" (365–66).

5. Related themes are explored by Michael Lerner, *The Politics of Meaning: Restoring Hope and Possibility in an Age of Cynicism* (Reading, Mass: Addison-Wesley, 1996), and Michael J. Sandel, *Democracy's Discontent: America in Search of a Public Philosophy* (Cambridge, Mass.: Harvard University Press, 1996).

6. William Dean, *The Religious Critic in American Culture* (Albany: State University of New York Press, 1994), xiv.

7. Ibid., xvi and ix.

8. Ibid., x.

9. I am indebted to Diane Ravitch, ed., *The American Reader: Words That Moved a Nation* (New York: HarperCollins, 1991), 44–46, for information about "The Star-Spangled Banner."

10. Alexis de Tocqueville, *Journey to America,* trans. George Lawrence, ed. J. P. Mayer (Garden City, N.Y.: Anchor Books, 1971), 48. This book consists of the notebooks that Tocqueville kept during his travels in the United States. They were key sources for *Democracy in America.*

11. Ibid.

12. Alexis de Tocqueville, *Democracy in America,* 2 vols., ed. J. P. Mayer, trans. George Lawrence (Garden City, N.Y.: Anchor Books, 1969), 1:59. The two volumes of *Democracy in America* were published originally in 1835 and 1840.

13. Ibid., 1:295.

14. Ibid., 1:290.

15. Stephen L. Carter, *The Culture of Disbelief: How American Law and Politics Trivialize Religious Devotion* (New York: Basic Books, 1993), 85. Subsequent page references are given parenthetically in the text.

16. When individuals or groups are being "too zealous" religiously is, of course, a bone of American contention in itself. To cite but one example, press coverage in the summer of 1994 included several stories about deteriorating relationships

between the Clinton administration and conservatives who are both religious and Republican. The latter have been intensely critical of President Clinton and his administration almost from the beginning of his time in office. Provoked especially by the Rev. Jerry Falwell and conservative commentator Rush Limbaugh in the late spring and early summer of 1994, Clinton and other prominent Democrats—including then Surgeon General Joycelyn Elders and Representative Vic Fazio of California, who chaired the Democrats' Congressional Campaign Committee—launched a counteroffensive attacking religious right activists for going too far in trying to impose their agendas. In response, eighty-seven House Republicans called for Elders's resignation, and forty-four Senate Republicans petitioned Clinton to denounce the "religious bigotry" they attributed to Fazio's remarks.

This acrimonious debate was a sad and discouraging form of talk about religion in public, and the accusatory climate that produced it is precisely the one that better public religious discourse should aim to improve. Meanwhile, the Equal Employment Opportunity Commission was deluged at about the same time with some 56,000 protesting letters from people who feared that the EEOC was trying to stifle religious discussion. The controversy began when the EEOC issued guidelines against harassment in the workplace. Those guidelines included references to religion.

In sum, the EEOC guidelines made it possible for a person to claim protection against "religious harassment." Originating primarily from people who do not want to be evangelized, preached at, or denigrated for their religious beliefs or the lack of them, relatively few religion-based complaints have been filed with the EEOC—for example, 1,386 out of 72,120 in the 1992 fiscal year and 1,449 out of 87,887 in 1993. Still, the potential for lawsuits was real enough to make at least one labor lawyer advise his clients that the only sure way to avoid them would be to eliminate all religious expression in the workplace. As word about that interpretation spread, reaction against the EEOC rulings erupted. EEOC spokesman Reginald Welch denied that the religious harassment guidelines had any intention to abridge the free exercise of religion in the workplace. Not everyone, however, was reassured. Legislation was introduced into both the House and the Senate to remove religion from the EEOC's harassment guidelines.

Apparently Americans will have to talk about how to talk about religion, if at all, in the public space of the workplace. If it can be done with a civility that precludes lawsuits—a challenge we Americans need to accept and work on—such talk would be good for us because it would put us in closer touch with what matters to each and all of us.

For more detail on these matters, see "Democrats Begin to Counterattack the Religious Right" and "Plan to Extend Job Harassment Rule to Religion Draws Fire," *Los Angeles Times*, 2 July 1994, B4–5.

CHAPTER SIX

Getting Along in America:
How Talk about Religion
Can Help

Can we get along?
—RODNEY KING

Although the stories of our lives touch common ground, we Americans do not have an easy time getting along with each other. Unfortunately, religion has often intensified the divisions among us, but as we look for good ways to cope with the differences that divide us, the right kind of talk about religion can help us to get along. Using more case studies from the 1990s, this chapter focuses attention on ways in which discourse about religion can foster that goal by increasing sensitivity about the interdependence of our lives. Specifically, it does so by exploring upheavals that have rocked Los Angeles, a city of dream and nightmare that has often foreshadowed the nation's destiny.

Come to L.A.

The American novelist Nathanael West was killed in a California highway accident on December 22, 1940. Several years earlier, his American dream had taken him to Hollywood, where he hoped to get along as a scriptwriter during the Great Depression. That experience led him to write *The Day of the Locust*. Not much noticed when it appeared in 1939, that novel is now at least a minor classic.

In a major way, *The Day of the Locust* makes one wonder about getting along in L.A., for it is a story that ends with the City of Angels ablaze, a figurative and literal image that has been all too real in the Los Angeles of the 1990s. West's fictional inferno is ignited by a riot. Although the riot is provoked by "the world premiere of a new picture" at Kahn's Persian Palace Theater, its real causes run deeper.[1] They consist of the amassed disappointment, resentment, and boredom, the accumulated sense of fraud and betrayal that people drawn west by new ways to dream have felt through disillusioning discoveries that Southern California's calls of fame and fortune produce no perfect years. As *The Day of the Locust* describes it, Los Angeles is anything but paradise on earth. Instead L.A. appears to be a "dream dump" where "the sun is a joke" (128, 192).

The novel's narrator, Tod Hackett, a young artist from the Yale School of Fine Arts, has been lured to set and costume design by a Hollywood talent scout. Hackett's journeys around Sunset Boulevard, his work at the movie studios, and his observations of life in Los Angeles convince him that people have "come to California to die" (23).

West leaves Tod's fate unresolved, but throughout the story the artist works on a huge painting called "The Burning of Los Angeles." The novel describes Hackett's picture as follows:

Across the top, parallel with the frame, he had drawn the burning city, a great bonfire of architectural styles, ranging from Egyptian to Cape Cod colonial. Through the center, winding from left to right, was a long hill street and down it, spilling into the middle foreground, came the mob carrying baseball bats and torches. For the faces of its members, he was using the innumerable sketches he had made of the people who come to California to die; the cultists of all sorts, economic as well as religious, the wave, airplane, funeral and preview watchers—all those poor devils who can only be stirred by the promise of miracles and then only to violence. (200–201)

As the story ends, Tod Hackett's picture has become reality, and West's novel has become one of judgment about how we Americans get along, not only in L.A. but perhaps with that city as a prism through which the importance of talking about religion in public can be discerned more clearly.

Significantly, the title West chose for his novel has biblical roots. Locusts are found, for example, in the New Testament's book of Revelation: "Then from the smoke came locusts on the earth, and they were given authority like the authority of scorpions of the earth. They were told not to damage the grass of the earth or any green growth or any tree, but only those people who do not have the seal of God on their foreheads."[2] In the

Hebrew Bible's Exodus story, God instructs Moses to tell Pharaoh, "If you refuse to let my people go, tomorrow I will bring locusts into your country. They shall cover the surface of the land, so that no one will be able to see the land." [3] The biblical story says that when Pharaoh did not comply, the locusts arrived with a vengeance.

The biblical locusts that wreaked havoc on Egypt were only one of ten plagues that Pharaoh faced. Had he been interviewed on some ancient equivalent of America's popular talk show "Larry King Live," as Los Angeles mayor Richard Riordan was on June 23, 1994, Pharaoh surely would have shared the feeling when the mayor remarked that he hoped God would not send L.A. another such interesting year. Riordan's comment came on the eve of his first anniversary as the leader of Los Angeles, a city with cultures so diverse that some ninety languages are spoken in its public schools and 125 on its streets. Although the city may not have had ten biblical plagues during Riordan's administration, the question of who, if anyone, has God's seal on their forehead in that place may come to mind nevertheless, for in many ways the 1990s have produced disruptions that make getting along in L.A. problematic too much of the time.

What can and should be made of those upheavals? Although that question invites talk about religion, it should not do so primarily in terms of accusing judgment. More to the point is the lingering plea that Rodney King made on May 1, 1992, when, in the aftermath of a real burning of Los Angeles, he asked, "Can we get along?" Talk about religion needs to focus on how the answer to that question can be yes. In fact, without such discourse, the answer to King's question is more likely to be no. Reflection on four misfortunes that have afflicted Los Angeles during the 1990s suggest how talk about religion could help us Americans to get along.

Pray for O. J.

"Pray for O.J." Not long after O. J. Simpson, the popular ex-football star, sports commentator, Hertz ad man, bit-part movie actor, and multimillionaire became a murder suspect in the June 12, 1994, nighttime stabbing of his former wife, Nicole Brown Simpson, and her friend Ron Goldman, that message could be seen on bumper stickers, T-shirts, and signs outside of Los Angeles jail and courtroom scenes as well as at Rockingham, Simpson's Brentwood estate.

Christian ministers Billy Graham and Roosevelt Greer made a point of contacting O.J. soon after his arrest on June 17. Prayer about the case could be heard in the U.S. Senate when its chaplain at the time, the Rev. Richard C. Halverson, opened one session by intoning words about O.J. that said, "Whether he is innocent or guilty rests with our system of justice, but our hearts go out to him in his profound loss." Critics complained that Halverson barely mentioned the murder victims or the Simpson children.[4]

On October 3, 1995, 474 days after O.J.'s arrest, what many Americans called "the trial of the century" came to its climax. The trial included 133 days of testimony and brought 126 witnesses to the stand. It lasted nine months, but while 150 million Americans watched on television, it took just four hours for the jury to reach a decision and only ten minutes for the twelve jurists—ten women and two men; nine blacks, one Hispanic, and two whites—to enter the courtroom one last time and for their verdict to be read: "We, the jury in the above entitled action, find the defendant, Orenthal James Simpson, not guilty of the crime of murder."

Summing up his attack on the prosecution's evidence, Simpson's most effective attorney, Johnnie Cochran, had borrowed a preacher's cadence to rap his best line to the jury, "If it doesn't fit, you must acquit." Reports of the post-trial celebration at Rockingham indicated that O.J. and Cochran sang "Amazing grace—/How sweet the sound—/That saved a wretch like me!/I once was lost, but now am found/Was blind, but now I see."

No one could see or say how many prayers have been made for O.J., or for the murder victims and the Simpson children, or for the city and country that have been so deeply affected by this American tragedy. No one knows how much ink has been spilled—or will be—to write the O. J. Simpson story. No one can tell how much Americans talked—and will continue to talk—about the murder trial and its verdict. Nor is there much clarity yet about the trial's long-term impact on the integrity of American law enforcement, the trust that we place in the jury system, and most important, the quality of race relations in the United States.

Much about this case, including whether Simpson committed murder, will never be public knowledge, but the trial riveted the nation's attention as few things in recent memory have done. Multiple reasons accounted for that interest. First, the trial provided a vintage Southern California story: a triangle of trendy but troubled people from a tony neighborhood, plus a cast of other fascinating characters, including Judge Lance A. Ito, prosecutors Marcia Clark and Christopher Darden, problematic LAPD detectives Philip Vannatter, Tom Lange, and the apparently racist Mark Fuhrman, O.J.'s dream—but ultimately bickering—defense team of Johnnie Cochran, Robert Shapiro, F. Lee Bailey, Alan Dershowitz, and Gerald F. Uelmen. A high-profile, big-stakes whodunit, this murder mystery was worthy of the best Hollywood movie studio except that this drama was far more real than any screenplay.

The media hyped the story, and why not? How could one expect them to promote less than the feeding frenzy that captivated most of us Americans, at least off and on? Deeper than those elements, however, there was the fall of a celebrity, not to say hero, for despite the "not guilty" verdict, the story involved the shattering of O.J.'s American dream. There were also the factors of race, class, and status. How far did O.J.'s fame and fortune work to his advantage? In a case as charged with racial tensions as this one inevitably turned out to be, to what extent could Americans agree that justice was done? When the disagreement about the verdict broke predictably along racial lines, we Americans had to wonder how we would get along?[5]

On February 4, 1997, sixteen months after Simpson was acquitted of murder, the jury in another trial involving O.J. ended its deliberations. This case involved the wrongful-death and battery lawsuits that had been brought against Simpson by the families of Ron Goldman and Nicole Brown Simpson. At 7:12 P.M. on that Tuesday night, the verdict returned by the mostly white jury was read while television networks nationwide cut away from the final lines of President Bill Clinton's 1997 state of the union address in Washington, D.C., to cover the drama in Los Angeles. Quoting a biblical verse from Isaiah 58, "you shall be called the repairer of the breach, the restorer of streets to live in"—a text brought to the president's attention by the Rev. Robert Schuller, pastor of the Crystal Cathedral in Orange County, California—Clinton's optimistic speech had emphasized that America is "the most powerful idea in the history of nations." The nation's diversity, he proclaimed, is our greatest strength. In a world "torn asunder by racial, ethnic, and religious conflicts that fuel fanaticism and terror," he said, we can "show that it is possible to live and advance together across those kinds of differences."

With the validity of those interrupted words hanging in the breach, the civil jury found O. J. Simpson liable for the deaths of Nicole Brown Simpson and Ronald Goldman. Although Simpson owes compensatory and punitive damages that total $8.5 million and $25 million, respectively, the divisive "not guilty" verdict in the criminal case still stands. So when Ron Goldman's sister, Kim, shouted in the courtroom, "Oh my God, you're a murderer," O. J. Simpson may not have moved, but the nation was racked again by divisions, many of them located along racial lines. Justice had been done, said some Americans. Payback time, concluded others. Such judgments were often colored white and black. On the night of the civil jury's decision, Los Angeles police chief Willie L. Williams reported that "the city is extremely quiet." No more than Clinton's optimism, however, could Williams's relief assume that America is headed where it needs to go in the twenty-first century.[6]

"Pray for O.J.?" In his case, should the call to pray be disregarded, not taken seriously, dismissed as one more part of the circus atmosphere that surrounded the criminal trial? Or is the Simpson saga one that should make us Americans pray? If so, how should we pray, what should we pray for, and to whom? What would happen if we Americans talked more about such questions? Here are some possibilities.

Not all Americans pray, but most of us do—at least from time to time—and so we know that prayer can take many forms and include different moods and expressions. At its most profound, however, prayer involves intense concentration and yearning about what deserves to matter most to us. Often prayer is private. It expresses our deepest personal needs and hopes, and so we may pray for strength or deliverance, courage or health, as we face our individual problems.

But prayer is also public. In certain times and places, people gather together to pray. Sometimes people do so to express gratitude. Perhaps even more often people do so in times of shared loss or social crisis. In prayer, we reach out to one another, connect and share with one another, in ways that nothing else can do. Even when prayer is most personal, it often focuses on relationships and loyalties to others. As we pray for ourselves, we often pray for others—our family and friends, our country and our world, even at times for our enemies. What we pray for is as much social as it is personal, too. When prayers are said for justice, peace, freedom, for relief from hunger, homelessness, disease, addiction, racism, violence, and war, we can recognize how interdependent and interrelated we are, and how our private needs and public selves are intertwined.

It is easy to be skeptical, even cynical, about prayer. People ask and do not receive. Or they ask, expecting to receive just what they ask for, and when such prayer goes "unanswered," they conclude that prayer does not "work." These experiences are significant because they invite us to consider how prayer may and may not work, and what we ought to do in those circumstances.

Reports vary from person to person and from group to group, but usually prayer involves quieting and opening ourselves in recognition that life involves power that transcends our own and value that extends beyond the boundaries of our finite years. What follows—and it is a kind of answer to our needs and petitions—is that we may be encouraged to keep trying and working toward goals that prayer itself has helped us to identify as aims that are ultimately worthy of the best and most that we can give.

In moments when our prayer is motivated by the deepest needs that we may feel, our humanity achieves some of its greatest intensity. Thus, the talk about religion that we need in the United States today ought to include public sharing about what we pray for, individually and collectively. Specifically, if we think and talk about what it could and should mean to "pray for O.J." there is much worth praying about—not only O.J., Nicole Simpson, Ron Goldman, and their families but also Los Angeles, our country, and ourselves because the trail of blood that began at Nicole Simpson's townhouse did not end at any single doorstep. It has become part of a map that reaches beyond Brentwood and Los Angeles; it has become part of the map of our country. We should pray that its trail shows us not only where we have been but also where we ought to be going. Talk about what we do pray for and what we should pray about can help Americans to focus those needs. Prayer itself can encourage us to pursue what we discern.

A Taste of Paradise

During the O. J. Simpson criminal trial many arguments were heard and much time was spent clarifying precisely when Nicole Simpson and Ronald Goldman were murdered. Six months earlier, on Monday, January 17, 1994, it was no problem to determine when a second destructive event took place in Los Angeles, but assessment of the damage was another matter. At 4:31 that morning, L.A. shook as the 270 seismometers located throughout Southern California measured the most devastating earthquake in the city's recorded history.[7]

Originally pegged at 6.6 on the Richter scale, a magnitude later upgraded to 6.7, the quake started ten miles underground in the heart of the San Fernando Valley. Officially it was over in about ten seconds, but that was long enough to black out most of the city, derail trains, flatten buildings, destroy freeways, and ignite raging fires. Frightening aftershocks, more than 2,500 of them within a week, did more damage—psychological as well as physical—for months to come.

The quake's long-lasting toll, including American dreams that could not be resurrected from the rubble, eluded clocked time. For some people, its toll will never go away: fifty-seven persons perished, one of them, Howard Lee, a fourteen-year-old boy who wanted to be a priest. Thousands were injured, and thousands more found themselves homeless. Damage calculations soared toward $30 billion, a huge hit for a Southern California economy still mired in recession at the time. Relatively few people had earthquake insurance. Deciding that pursuit of the American Dream in California was no longer worth the cost, many people left the area. But most did not. Los Angeles was their city, Southern California their place. They would stay and rebuild. One woman, a transplanted New Englander who had arrived in 1989, expressed her feelings about leaving Los Angeles with a defiant "Hell, no! We've suffered through the worst L.A. has to offer. I'm not leaving till I get a taste of paradise. Southern California owes us!" [8]

For millennia, earthquakes have happened in this region. Long before it became known as Southern California, fault lines honeycombed this part of the earth. Temblors go with the territory. Those who choose to live in and around L.A.—I am one—stay with the realization and the danger that we never know when the earth will quake again. When it does, the experience is as humbling as it is terrifying. One feels very small, trembling, and insignificant when the ground is no longer solid and the foundations shake. Our perspectives are sobered further when we consider that the Los Angeles quake of 1994 was not the "Big One" we have been warned to expect in the not-too-distant future. We would rather not think about that probability, hoping instead that we have not come to California to die in a disaster—human or natural. Yet there is more than a chance that such a fate awaits us.

One of the most gripping pictures from the 1994 L.A. quake was taken by the *Los Angeles Times* photographer Al Seib. It showed Sharon Adams's twenty-seven-foot motor home, Nick Nichols's sixty-five-foot truck, and Dave Farley's pickup marooned on an island of concrete in the Santa Clarita Valley, where the Golden State Freeway had been sheared off at both ends. That stretch became known as the Freeway to Nowhere. When the quake shook the freeway apart, the three of them narrowly escaped. Later some ingenious engineering rescued their vehicles. Scarcely a scratch was on them. Unlike others who were in nearly the same place at the same time, these were three very lucky Americans.

Still stranded far from their Oregon and Nevada homes, Nichols and Adams were taken in by Danny and Jeannie Scoggin, who were headed north to their Portland home when the quake hit. Still operational, their motor home became a haven. As *Times* reporter Amy Wallace wrote about these strangers who had never intended to meet, "They passed the time telling stories." Nichols, a truck driver, told her, "I'm not a religious man, but I think I'm going to start carrying some religious tapes to listen to."[9]

Did Nick Nichols follow through, or was that part of his story soon forgotten? The point of that question is not so much him in particular as us in general. What are we Americans listening to—religiously or otherwise—in the midst and aftermath of quaking earth, repeated narrow escapes, luck that may not last, collapses of one kind or another, and trips on so-called freeways that turn out to be toll roads exacting the price of going nowhere?

Among the tapes that Nick Nichols might hear could be one that speaks of earthquakes as acts of God. Insurance policies read that way sometimes, using a reference to God to convey that no man or woman intended or caused disaster. In that sense, acts of God simply mean that we were in the way when a natural process beyond our control unleashed power that resulted in destruction. Religiously speaking, however, that tape would be far less beneficial than another that might talk about how people courageously rescued the living and retrieved the dead during the emergency, how they grieved with each other, worked to bind up each other's wounds, cleaned up the wreckage, and rebuilt from the ruins.

L.A. is not a dream dump where the sun is a joke—at least that is far from the whole story—and neither is the United States. Stories of help— Nick Nichols's among them—could fill enough tapes for unending transcontinental trips in his rig. Could we hear them containing acts of God in human form, or are we better off dispensing with acts of God altogether? Could our telling of stories of help become one important way of talking about religion in public, or are we better off refusing to think of them in that way altogether? Tapes that talk about questions like those would be important to make and hear because they can help to keep people in touch about what is most important and deserving of our loyalty. Keep in touch— "After something like this, that's what you do," Nick Nichols told Jeannie Scoggin when it was time for them to go their separate ways.[10]

Voices in the Fire

Jim Neumann might have been talking about the 1994 Los Angeles earthquake, but he was not when he said, "We're asking for trouble—this is going to happen every year."[11] A California state forestry agent, Neumann had another calamity on his mind, one unleashed by the desolating wildfires that roared over Southern California's mountains and through its canyons from Ojai to the Mexican border in late October and early November 1993.

Abundant rain in the winter of 1992–93 spurred plant growth, but summer heat dried the grasses, adding to the tinderbox conditions produced by six prior years of Southern California drought. Those conditions became treacherous in the autumn when the desert winds called Santa Anas began to blow as they always do. Generated by high pressure systems over Utah and Nevada, the Santa Ana winds push dry air toward California. Gaining heat as they pass over the Mojave Desert, the winds reach speeds of up to 100 miles per hour as they funnel their ways through narrow mountain passes. Such mountain passes are not safe for human settlement.

As *Los Angeles Times* writer Al Martinez tells the story, the 1993 firestorm started at 2:00 A.M. on October 26 when a Santa Ana took down a power line near a town called Escondido. The Escondido blaze, unfortunately, was only the beginning of a multifire inferno. Before it ended a month later, seventeen major fires—nine of them attributed to arson—had scorched 200,000 acres in six huge Southern California counties. Arriving from all over the country, some 3,500 firefighters had battled the wildfires. Loss of human life was miraculously small—the same could not be said for wildlife—but 1,200 homes were consumed by flames that reached heat levels of 2,000 degrees and produced financial losses approaching $1 billion.

Laguna Beach, Altadena, Thousand Oaks, Yucaipa—the names of those Southern California places became familiar as television beamed nationwide the eerie pictures of out-of-control flames. Almost surrounded by a ring of fire, Los Angeles became more than that when the flames broke out in Malibu and Topanga Canyon, too. The topography of the City of Angels is one of the factors that makes it such a distinctive and dangerous place. It is not only a city of freeways and immense urban sprawl but one of mountain canyons and narrow winding roads that lead to houses—many, but not all of them lavish—perched precariously in conditions so ominously dry that Richard Minnich, a fire researcher at the University of California, Riverside, says they are equivalent to "a lake of gasoline."

Nature, it has been said, uses fire to start over again. Long before human life appeared in this part of the world, fire's ways of stimulating, cleansing, and rejuvenating have kept the natural life cycle moving. Such recognitions help to explain why fire, which can be so awesome in its power to give and take, has long been a feature of religion, a symbol for the sacred and even for God in particular.[12] When people encounter fire—there are now some nineteen million of them located in a narrow coastal strip between Santa Barbara and San Diego who could literally have to do so again in Southern California—they may also have to start again, if they can survive and muster the strength to try after being burned out.

How do people find such strength? What are its sources? "I have lost my past," said one 1993 survivor as he pondered the ashes that remained of so much that he had worked and cared for. "I will never be the same again." What keeps people going when they have lost their pasts and know they will never be the same again? In such circumstances, most people do keep trying to go on as long and as well as they can. We often help each other, in the most impressive and sacrificial ways, to do so. The courage of the firefighters during the Southern California wildfires bore witness to that. Against odds that could not always be beaten, they risked everything to save anything they could. One unit rescued a home for people they did not know and might never meet. They asked nothing for this gift, but on the dusty top of a grand piano they simply left behind their message: "Saved by Engine Company 57."

Do firestorms and our reactions to them make us wonder? How could they not? Is there anything in these experiences to make us talk about religion in public? What if the answer is no? What if it is yes? If we let them, conversations about such questions can make us Americans more sensitive, more caring about our need for one another. They can help us to get along as we face the threats of firestorm and burnout—figurative and literal—that are so much with us, not only in Los Angeles and Southern California but all across our country.

Starting Over

Just as infernos come in different degrees and earthquakes in varied magnitudes, they may manifest themselves in diverse ways. Not all of the temblors are geological, not all of the flames are restricted to fire. At least metaphorically, their characteristics and effects fit "earthquakes" and "firestorms" that are social and political as well. "Big Ones" of that kind struck Los Angeles on Wednesday, April 29, 1992. On that date, four Los Angeles policemen—Sergeant Stacey C. Koon and Officers Theodore J. Briseno, Laurence M. Powell, and Timothy E. Wind—won acquittals in their trial for the beating of an African-American named Rodney King.[13] What followed was an outbreak of frustration and violence that even the vivid imagination of a Nathanael West could scarcely have envisioned.

The Rodney King quake had foreshocks; anticipations of its firestorm could be felt by listening to L.A.'s winds. One of them occurred on the night of March 3, 1991. After a high-speed chase, King was apprehended by Los Angeles policemen. What ensued was witnessed by a man named George Holliday, who happened to be in the area with his video recorder. Holliday distributed his eighty-one-second clip to CNN and other stations. Soon screening around the world, it surely has been seen by more people than any other piece of amateur filmmaking. Holliday captured a scene that was to create jolts and rumbles, the inflaming and burning of Los Angeles. In L.A. the divisions were so great that people could not agree on what to call it. Was the event a riot? An uprising? A rebellion? In any case, it was a major upheaval whose aftershocks and smoldering embers provided a problematic context and counterpoint for the O. J. Simpson trial.

Writhing on the ground that March night in 1991, Rodney King had been kicked, stunned, and struck with nightsticks fifty-six times. Once it was made public, George Holliday's videotaped evidence of the beating required official investigation. The white officers were arraigned on felony charges on March 15, 1991. Not until a year later, on March 4, 1992, were the first arguments heard in the King trial, whose venue had become not Los Angeles but Simi Valley in Ventura County. On April 29, the jury—ten whites, one Asian, one Hispanic—brought in not-guilty verdicts on all counts except one of excessive force against Officer Powell. On that count, a mistrial was declared. Television carried live coverage of the verdicts. Within hours L.A. was not getting along but exploding. In particular, disbelief in South Central Los Angeles turned into rage as protesters and opportunistic looters, many but not all of them black and Hispanic, took to the streets. Burning, robbing, the beating of the truck driver Reginald O. Denny at the intersection of Florence and Normandie (broadcast "live" by a television station's airborne camera crew)—mayhem and death ripped a social fabric that was already frayed by L.A.'s long history of racism and police brutality against people of color, flawed by poverty and unemployment, fragmented by gang wars, and frustrated by deteriorating social services and decaying public education. To restore uneasy order, National Guard troops had to augment a Los Angeles police force that was ill-led by its since-departed Chief Daryl Gates and overwhelmed by the spreading lawlessness.

On April 30, as looting and burning spread from South Central Los Angeles to other parts of the city and beyond, the federal Department of Justice announced that it would investigate possible civil rights violations in the King beating. Meanwhile, President George Bush declared Los Angeles a disaster area, and the following day, May 3, the *Los Angeles Times* reported the following toll: 58 deaths; 2,383 injuries; more than 7,000 fire responses; 12,111 arrests; and 3,100 businesses damaged. At least on the surface, L.A. gradually calmed down, but the peace was uneasy at best. On April 17, 1993, verdicts in the federal King civil rights trial found Sergeant Koon and Officer Powell guilty of violating King's civil rights. Subsequently they were given thirty-month prison terms. Officers Briseno and Wind were acquitted. Eventually, in the summer of 1994, Rodney King received a $3.8 million dollar settlement from the city of Los Angeles for injuries he suffered in the 1991 beating. Most of that money went to lawyers, doctors, and investigators who billed King for their work on his case.

Meanwhile, on August 19, 1993, the Reginald Denny trial got under way. Many acquittals followed in that case, too, but on December 7, Damian Williams, who was charged with attempted murder, was sentenced to a maximum of ten years in prison for his attacks on Denny. Convicted of one felony count of firing a shotgun into an unoccupied vehicle, the last criminal defendant in the Denny case was sentenced to three years probation on July 8, 1994. Asked why he was crying after he heard the sentence, Lance Jerome Parker said, "It was just. . . . We had to go back over two years of pain. I'm just glad everything is over with. Now I can go back to work, to church, to plan my life." [14]

On multiple fronts, the quake of the King verdict and the ensuing firestorm produced aftershocks and ashes of discouraging disillusionment. Some Korean students on my Claremont McKenna College campus, for example, expressed fear for the lives of their Los Angeles families as animosity flared between African-Americans and Korean-Americans. [15] "We've got to start all over in our assumptions about ourselves," I heard one woman say at a public meeting. Her comment, she explained, was prompted when a white friend of hers—someone she previously could not have imagined doing such things—joined the looters. Rodney King summed up the dilemma on May 1, 1992, when he appeared on Friday afternoon television. His voice quaking with emotion, he made a plaintive, sometimes barely audible plea: "Can we get along? . . . We've just got to, just got to. We're all stuck here for a while. . . . Let's try to work it out. Let's try to work it out." [16]

Rodney King's question is the right one for L.A.—and by extension for the United States and the entire world—because the individuals and communities that comprise Los Angeles speak many languages. Literally and symbolically, they do so because their expectations and memories, their joys and sorrows, their senses of justice and fairness are sufficiently diverse to render understanding difficult. But difficult need not, must not mean impossible if we Americans keep working to create ways to listen carefully and to speak thoughtfully about the things that matter most to us, things that in one way or another involve us in talking about religion in public.

Twilight Moments

To see further how that talk might unfold and what success it might enjoy, it is worth noticing the kind of listening and speaking that has been encouraged by Anna Deavere Smith's inspired "documentary theater." Playwright and actress, Smith is a professor of drama at Stanford University. For more than a decade she has created gripping solo performances based on actual events. Forming a series she calls *On the Road: A Search for American Character,* they show—symbolically and even literally—how one person's story is infused with another's and how one person's identity is understandable only in relationship to the other people who form the social circumstances under which individual experiences take place. So, she explains, "in May 1992 I was commissioned by Gordon Davidson, artistic director/producer of the Mark Taper Forum in Los Angeles, to create a one-woman performance piece about the civil disturbances in that city in April 1992."[17] She spent nine months interviewing more than two hundred people who experienced the riots. The result was *Twilight: Los Angeles, 1992,* which premiered in Los Angeles on May 23, 1993. A month later I was fortunate enough to see this deeply disturbing, immensely moving production in which Smith became a multitude of individual persons, speaking verbatim—with the right accents and dialects—the words they gave her.

"Theater," says Smith, "can mirror society" (xxi). When Smith interprets what she means, her words can also help to explain what talking about religion in public might mean. Consider some of them in that light. First, to make *Twilight*'s reflections illuminating, Smith had to listen "with an ear that was trained to hear stories for the specific purpose of repeating them with the elements of character intact" (xxiv). Only in that way could she amplify and connect L.A.'s diverse and often dissonant voices in ways that would make them heard as never before. In such hearing one could find eloquence, poetry, and concerns about common ground and the common good that could help people to get along. When talking about religion in public is done well, these ingredients will be present both as causes and as effects.

Fearing that "my own history, which is a history of race as a black and white struggle, would make the work narrower than it should be," Smith created a team of multitalented, multiethnic dramaturges. A dramaturge, she explains, "is a person who assists in the preparation of the text of a play and can offer an outside perspective to those who are more active in the process of staging the play" (xxii). They helped her to enlarge the play's perspectives and to ensure that the effect of the whole production would be greater than the sum of its parts. Effective public discourse about religion requires the recognition that we need each other to help broaden our individual perspectives and horizons.

"Words," Smith emphasizes, "are not an end in themselves. They are a means to evoking the character of the person who spoke them" (xxiii–xxiv). Her listening and speaking, acting and evoking are not solutions to social problems, she goes on to say, but are ways to look at "the *processes* of the problems* (xxiv). When it works well, that is what talking about religion in public can accomplish, too. What Smith says about her acting— it is, she says, "a constant process of becoming something"—can also be applied to talking about religion in public and what it can do when it is at its best. Indeed, when Smith does what she does so well, she is talking about religion in public because she is looking so deeply and intently for what she calls "the humanness inside the problems, or the crises" (xxiv). Consider talking about religion in public while following more of what she has to say about that:

The spoken word is evidence of the humanness. Perhaps the conclusions come somewhere further down the road. I see the work as a call. I played *Twilight* in Los Angeles as a call to the community. I performed it at a time when the community had not yet resolved the problems. I wanted to be a part of their examination of the problems. I believe that solutions to these problems will call for the participation of large and eclectic groups of people. I also believe that we are at a stage where we must first break the silence about race and encourage many more people to participate in the dialogue. (xxiv)

Reginald Denny is one of the people in the dialogue that Smith enacts in *Twilight*. As with all the voices she embodies, Smith speaks and writes their words in the free-verse style that her ear found in their original expression. Thereby she alerts us to something important, namely, that ordinary, everyday talk has distinctive rhythms, cadences, and inflections that enrich and convey its meanings. Smith teaches us Americans to be better listeners, ones who can hear each other as possessing everyday voices that are full of poetry. Such voices brim with humanity because they cry out in pain, yearn for healing, and hope for the connections that can make sense out of chaos. Because those cries, yearnings, and hopes are so fundamental, so much an expression of what we take to be ultimately important and sacred, their presence makes it possible to see *Twilight* as a public expression of religion in America.

Full of poetry and therefore brimming with humanity, snatches of Denny's broken silence can be heard as public expressions of religion because they say,

> How does one say that
> someone
> saved
> my life?
> How does a person,
> how do I
> express enough
> thanks
> for someone risking their
> neck?
>
> . . .
>
> There was a weird common thread in our lives
>
> . . .
>
> I don't know what I want.
> I just want people to wake up.
> It's not a color, it's a person.
>
> . . .
>
> One day,
> Lord
> willing, it'll happen.   (107–8, 112)

The same is true when Smith becomes Peter Sellars, director of the Los Angeles Festival, whose words are almost in tears when they say,

> We may have a good GNP
> but not a family to come home to.
> Can't live in our own house.
> That's what the LA riots is about.
> We can't live,

> our own house burning.
> This isn't somebody else's house,
> it's our own house.
> This is the city we are living in.
> It's our house.
> We all live in the same house. . . . (200)

Katie Miller, a bookkeeper and accountant, spoke with Smith in South Central L.A. in September 1992. On stage, Smith says for her,

> I think this thing
> about the Koreans and the Blacks . . .
> that wasn't altogether true,
> and I think that the Korean stores
> that got burned in the Black neighborhood that were Korean-owned,
> it was due to lack of
> gettin' to know
> the people that come to your store —
> that's what it is.   (129)

Anna Deavere Smith also becomes Cornel West, a leading African-American philosopher and theologian, who tells her:

> The best we can do
> is hold up
> a bloodstained banner
> of a black struggle that is rooted in moral vision
> and yet
> acknowledging the fact
> that a power struggle
> will be fundamental for any change, so you don't wanna be naive
> and on the other hand you don't also wanna just become
> amoral at the same time
> or give up
> on
> the broader possibilities of hu*mann*
> beings engaging in interaction that accents our humanness,
> more than simply our, uh,
> our delusory foundations,
> race or gender or whatever.   (45)[18]

Partly Persian, Homi Bhabha is a literary critic. He shares his perspective on the riots by phone from England: "This twilight moment," he says,

is an in-between moment.
It's the moment of dusk.
It's the moment of ambivalence
and ambiguity.
The inclarity,
the enigma,
the ambivalences,
in what happened in the L.A.
uprisings
are precisely what we want to get hold of. (232)

Smith's *Twilight* did not take its name from a moment or an image but from a person, Twilight Bey, an ex-gang member who helped to organize a truce among those warring tribes. She plays him in the Denny's restaurant where they talked in February 1993:

I see the light as knowledge and the wisdom of the world and
understanding others,
and in order for me to be a, to be a true human being,
I can't forever dwell in darkness,
I can't forever dwell in the idea,
of just identifying with people like me and understanding me and mine.
(255)

Expressions of thanks . . . common threads in our lives . . . burning homes . . . gettin' to know the people . . . in-between moments . . . being neither naive nor amoral . . . becoming a true human being. As *Twilight* searches for, finds, expresses, and reveals American character with voices such as those, Smith's repertoire is not exhausted. Anger, rage, cynicism, insensitivity, racism, and much, much more can be heard during *Twilight* in L.A. Smith reports that she was frequently asked whether she had found any one voice that could speak for the entire city. The expectation that such a voice could be found, let alone that there could be one that would unify L.A. or even the United States, surprised her because the diversity of the American people is so pronounced. But Smith's surprise about the expectation of unity did not mean that she despaired about the possibility that Americans could come closer together in sharing and understanding. Steps in that direction could be made if we all learned better how to follow Twilight Bey's lead, which suggests that getting along means getting beyond "just identifying with people like me and understanding me and mine."

At its best, public discourse about religion can encourage significant steps in that direction. It can do so by reminding us that no person or group has a corner on truth and insight. We have to stir and move each other. It can also do so by emphasizing that we need to be self-critical, which takes not only the courage of conviction but also the courage to question conviction. In addition, the right kind of talking about religion in public shows that empathy with others is essential for getting along. It shows, too, that even as we share a tragic history, hope may still be found to resist odds that no simple "optimism" can ever overcome. Talking like that requires us to take careful turns at listening and speaking. When that listening and speaking involve the things that deserve to be the most important to us, such turns are tuned religiously. Then identifications expand, constructive changes of mind occur, insight emerges, respect grows, and beneficial actions can follow.

The Urge to Do More

April 29, 1992, the day that the verdicts in the Rodney King case came down, was a Wednesday. As the burning of Los Angeles raged into the weekend, leaders of the city's religious communities could not take the months that Anna Deavere Smith had to prepare for *Twilight*. They had to speak to their people, their congregations, in a matter of days, if not minutes, and often they did so with an eloquent authority that matched any theater's power to mirror reality. One of their number, Ignacio Castuera, the pastor of Hollywood United Methodist Church, preserved those spoken words in an inspiring book called *Dreams on Fire/Embers of Hope*.

As Castuera tells the story of this book's origins, he recalls that on April 29, he received word that his San Diego friend, David Jessup, would succumb to AIDS within a few hours. The family would have his memorial service on May 9. Some time before, Castuera had said that he would preside at the memorial, a promise that required him to cancel plans to attend the General Conference of the United Methodist Church in Louisville, Kentucky, on May 5. As he thought about his friend on that day and about what had ensued in Los Angeles, Castuera explains, "I began to feel the urge to do more about the riots than I had already done." [19] Some members of his congregation had urged him to share with the larger community the sermon he had preached on Sunday, May 3. It occurred to Castuera that other religious leaders must have received similar requests. Checking with some of his clerical colleagues, he became convinced that words preached from Los Angeles pulpits in the midst of the city's burning deserved to be shared as widely as possible. Publication followed, with the agreement that all royalties from the book would go to a reconciliation fund administered by the Interreligious Council of Southern California.

Whether those royalties have amounted to much, I do not know. What is clear is that the black, white, Hispanic, Asian, male, female, Catholic, Protestant, Jewish, and Buddhist voices raised in churches, synagogues, mosques, and temples from Watts to Hollywood and contained in the pages of Castuera's book make a fitting complement to the ones that Anna Deavere Smith lifted up in *Twilight*. The religious traditions and spiritual perspectives expressed through those voices may have differed in many ways, but taken together, their diversity spoke with shared intent words that Americans need to hear, words to breathe life into embers of hope. Scrapping earlier ideas, throwing previously prepared sermon notes to the winds, L.A.'s spiritual leaders spoke from their hearts and souls, from Scripture and from experience, as they responded to what Rabbi Steven Jacobs aptly called "a defining moment in American history" (67). Consider what some of their public expressions of religion contained.

At the time, Linnea Juanita Pearson guided the First Unitarian Church of Los Angeles. It stands in the heart of the city's Koreatown. "This morning," she said on Sunday, May 3, 1992, "we come together with ashes in our mouths. We come with anger in our hearts. We come with aching in our bodies. We come with bitterness and mourning. Come, let us gather together, out of despair, desolation, and death. Out of darkness, desperation, and doom. Out of loneliness, separation, and alienation. Out of agony and fear, let us come together in our tears and in our pain. Come, let us gather together again. Let us gather up the ashes, and blow upon the embers until a fresh spark ignites to give light to the life that is yet to come, that we might gather around this new fire of hope and warm ourselves" (29).

For many years, Cecil L. "Chip" Murray has led the First African Methodist Episcopal Church in Los Angeles. Several thousand strong, it is L.A.'s largest African-American congregation. On May 3, Murray said he would "like to make a distinction to America this morning—the difference between setting a fire and starting a fire. We set some of those fires, but we didn't start any of those fires. Those fires were started when some men of influence decided that this nation can indeed exist half slave and half free. Those fires were started when some men poured gasoline on the Constitution of the United States of America" (13).

The L.A. riots led to a police curfew that restricted activities in the city after dark. So it was that Rabbi John L. Rosove, the spiritual leader of

Temple Israel in Hollywood, had to cancel his congregation's annual observance of Yom Hashoah (Holocaust Memorial Day) on Friday, May 1. On Sunday, May 3, however, he and seventy-five members of Temple Israel attended Messiah Baptist Church in South Central L.A. His public expression of religion on that occasion included the following statement:

> I must tell you that only since getting to know you folks at Messiah have I begun to understand what your lives are about, about your dreams and about the nature of your community. I have grown to appreciate who you are and respect you as I had never known before. . . . If better conditions, better lives, and greater understanding come as a consequence of these riots, then we can say "dayenu" (it will have been enough!). But much work needs to be done in the months and years ahead. We need political leaders with courage and community leaders who speak the truth. We need the effort of every black, white, and Asian person living in this community. And we need goodwill and the willingness to take risks and make sacrifices for the common good. For purposes of enlightened self-interest, this is a necessity. In the interest of God's will, it is mandatory. (26–27)

As for Ignacio Castuera, his Methodist sermon emphasized that "we have a great challenge in this city, but we are not going to leave. [As Rodney King said], we are all 'stuck here,' caught in this net, the net of the church, the net of the City of Angels, the net of a geography that is a gift of God, of a weather that is the envy of most of the world, and of a city that can be and will be a human and humane city 'undimmed by human tears' as 'America the Beautiful' so wonderfully states. But, also in 'America the Beautiful,' we have this prayer: 'America, America, God mend thine every flaw.' And God, do we have flaws to mend!" (77). To those sentiments, Havanpola Ratanassra, then president of the American Buddhist Congress and Buddhist Sangha Council of Southern California, would have added words from the address that he delivered at Kwan Um Sa Temple, a Korean Buddhist Temple on Third Street in L.A.: "Let us seize the moment to work out problems between our ethnic and religious groups. Let us rebuild our city *properly*, to be a place of prosperity, where our children can grow up in a true multiethnic community, a community based on understanding, tolerance, and peace" (100).

In *The Day of the Locust,* Nathanael West spoke of possibilities that become probabilities and wind up as inevitabilities (164). Talking about religion in public figures into such logic, and the quality of that talking goes far to determine whether West's logic entails good or ill. If our American talking about religion in public stays akin to the kind found in *Twilight, Dreams on Fire/Embers of Hope,* and other sources explored in this chapter, then it will make more and more sense. Getting along is not very likely to happen well unless we Americans do more talking like that. But then, of course, we will have to heed the words that are spoken and heard. We will need to practice what is preached so that Rodney King's question—Can we get along?—does not end with possibilities that turn into the probability and then the inevitability that people will keep coming to California to die as the burning of Los Angeles blazes all over again.

NOTES

1. Nathanael West, *The Day of the Locust* (New York: New American Library, 1983), 189. Subsequent page references are to this edition and are given parenthetically in the text.

2. Revelation 9:3-4.

3. Exodus 10:1-20.

4. See the *Los Angeles Times,* 30 June, 1994, A5.

5. A *Newsweek* poll conducted October 4-6, 1995, found that 85 percent of American blacks agreed with the jury's verdict and 80 percent believed the jury was fair and impartial. Only 32 percent of the whites polled agreed with the verdict and 50 percent thought the jury was fair and impartial.

6. My account of the civil case against O. J. Simpson relies on the *Los Angeles Times,* 5 Feb. 1997, section A.

7. For information on the January 1994 earthquake in Los Angeles, I am indebted to the staff of the *Los Angeles Times,* who produced a detailed and brilliantly illustrated book about the event. Its contents, an editorial note explains, are essentially the same essays that appeared in the newspaper around the time that the quake happened. See *4:31: Images of the 1994 Los Angeles Earthquake* (Los Angeles: Los Angeles Times Syndicate, 1994).

8. Quoted from Patt Morrison, "We Can Take It," in *4:31,* 91.

9. Amy Wallace, "Reunited on I-5," in *4:31,* 76.

10. Ibid., 78.

11. The quotation is from *Newsweek*'s November 8, 1993, cover story, "Inferno: Fighting the California Firestorm." See "Earth, Wind and Wildfire," 37. My account of the Southern California wildfires is indebted to *Newsweek*'s coverage and also to the script that *Los Angeles Times* columnist Al Martinez prepared for *Fire in the Wind: The Southern California Wildfires,* a documentary video produced by the *Los Angeles Times* media lab.

12. In his foreword to *Dreams on Fire/Embers of Hope: From the Pulpits of Los Angeles after the Riots,* ed. Ignacio Castuera (St. Louis: Chalice Press, 1992), Harvey Cox observes that "for people whose lives are shaped by the biblical narratives, . . . fire can mean many different things. Flame signifies destruction and judgment, the

kind that fell upon the cities of Sodom and Gomorrah. It can also mean purification or—as in the case of Shadrach, Meshach, and Abednego—an occasion for the testing of faith. It can mean divine guidance, like the pillar of fire that led the Hebrews through the wilderness at night. Tongues of flame can become bearers of the Holy Spirit descending with power, as it did on the occasion of Pentecost in the Acts of the Apostles."

13. My interpretation of the Rodney King trial and its aftermath is indebted to the staff of the *Los Angeles Times,* which prepared *Understanding the Riots: Los Angeles before and after the Rodney King Case* (Los Angeles: Los Angeles Times, 1992).

14. See Eric Malnic, "Last Defendant in Denny Case Gets Probation," *Los Angeles Times,* 9 July 1994, B3.

15. Strained for some time, relations between the African-American and Korean communities in Los Angeles were strongly exacerbated by the Latasha Harlins case. On March 16, 1991, less than two weeks after the Rodney King beating, a security camera at the Korean-owned Empire Liquor Market Deli in South Los Angeles recorded the fatal shooting of the fifteen-year-old black girl. Accused of stealing orange juice, Harlins had been shot in the back of the head as she left the store. Seven months later, on October 11, 1991, a jury found Harlins's killer, Soon Ja Du, guilty of voluntary manslaughter. On November 15, 1991, Compton Superior Court Judge Joyce A. Karlin sentenced her to five years probation, four hundred hours of community service, and a $500 fine. The resentment caused by the Harlins case in South Central was considerable and volatile.

16. *Understanding the Riots,* 98.

17. Anna Deavere Smith, *Twilight: Los Angeles, 1992—On the Road: A Search for American Character* (New York: Anchor Books, 1994), xvii. Subsequent page references are given parenthetically in the text. This book contains the interviews Smith performed in Los Angeles and New York but also additional interviews and introductory explanations by Smith that were not included in those stage productions.

18. West has much more to say about what happened in Los Angeles in April 1992, and about many other aspects of racism in the United States. See, in particular, *Race Matters* (Boston: Beacon Press, 1993). In this book, West expresses special concern about *nihilism* in American culture and in the nation's black communities in particular. He identifies nihilism as "the lived experience of coping with a life of horrifying meaninglessness, hopelessness, and (most important) lovelessness" (14). Arguments and analyses, he insists, are totally inadequate for overcoming this kind of outlook, which destroys individuals and communities alike. To start a sound response to American nihilism, West argues, "one must talk about some kind of *politics of conversion*" (18). Its chief ingredients must include love and care, the common good, and our common history. West's politics of conversion and the talking about religion in public that I am advocating have much to do with each other. West has also spoken effectively about religion in public in his dialogues with Michael Lerner,

a leading Jewish thinker in the United States. See Michael Lerner and Cornel West, *Jews and Blacks: Let the Healing Begin* (New York: G. P. Putnam's Sons, 1995).

Less optimistic than West, another leading African-American thinker in the 1990s, Derrick Bell, contends that far from being a "curable aberration," racism in America is "permanent." See his *Faces at the Bottom of the Well: The Permanence of Racism* (New York: Basic Books, 1992), x. Recognizing that his thesis is hard for blacks and whites alike to accept, Bell states that "what I want to achieve is a revival of discussion about the sources of racial problems, and why, though as old as our nation, they grow more intractable with time" (xii).

Refusing to succumb to the despair that his argument seems to invite, Bell insists that the struggle against racism is more, not less, important than ever. To explain what he means, Bell talks about religion in public, turning to the spiritual traditions of African-American song and religion. Even when, indeed precisely when, action seems most futile, those traditions communicate "the unalterable conviction that something must be done, that action must be taken" (199).

The spirituals that were sung by enslaved African-Americans, Bell reminds us, "have become the foundation of American music, and their stories are an important component of the nation's folklore" (xi). The persistence and courage of those who sang their hopeful notes in the midst of such hopeless conditions commit Bell to continue their story, which is, he says, "a story less of success than of survival through an unremitting struggle that leaves no room for giving up" (200). Using words from "When the Saints Go Marching In" to identify the protesting slave singers, Bell says, "I want to be in their number." Hoping perhaps against hope, he listens for other Americans—white, black, every color—to sing that way, too. Bell amplifies similar themes in *Gospel Choir: Psalms of Survival for an Alien Land Called Home* (New York: Basic Books, 1996).

19. Castuera, *Dreams on Fire/Embers of Hope,* 6. Subsequent page references are given parenthetically in the text.

CHAPTER SEVEN

Things Unspoken:
Religion and Human Rights

You mustn't believe in your own religion; I don't believe
in mine.

—SWAMI MUKTANANDA OF GANESHPURI

When Rodney King asked, "Can we get along?" Los Angeles and its
troubles were on his mind. His question, however, pertains to much more
than that, for the violence people do to one another respects no city limits.
Thus, no reflection on public expressions of religion in the United States
could begin to be adequate unless it addresses relations between religion
and the human proclivity to unleash the suffering and mass death that have
characterized so much of twentieth-century life in particular.

How has talk about religion in public contributed to this century's immense destruction, and how should religious discourse be affected by those
catastrophes? How might public expressions of religion in America help
to check the divisions and hatreds that inflict needless pain and death?
From my perspective, no event raises those questions more sharply than
the Holocaust. So this chapter's case study examines how reflection on that
disaster can provide additional ways to understand what good talk about
religion in public ought to mean.

Holocaust Years

Calling their regime the Third Reich, Adolf Hitler and his Nazi party ruled Germany from 1933 to 1945. The Holocaust happened during those years. It was Nazi Germany's planned total destruction of the European Jews and the actual murder of nearly six million of them, including one-and-a-half million children under the age of fifteen. That genocidal campaign—the most systematic, bureaucratic, and unrelenting the world has seen—also destroyed millions of non-Jewish civilians. They included Roma (Gypsies), Slavs, Jehovah's Witnesses, Freemasons, homosexuals, and the mentally retarded, physically handicapped, and insane. Those people, the Nazis believed, posed a threat to the Third Reich's racial purity that approached, though it could never equal, the one posed by Jews.

In the German language, this unprecedented destruction process became known euphemistically as *die Endlösung*—the Final Solution. The Hebrew word *Shoah,* which means catastrophe, also names it, but the term *Holocaust* most commonly signifies the event. That word has biblical roots. In the Septuagint, a Greek translation of the Hebrew Bible, the Hebrew word *olah* is translated as *holokauston*. In context, *olah* means that which is offered up. It refers to a sacrifice, often specifically to "an offering made by fire unto the Lord." Such connotations make *Holocaust* a problematic title for the devastation it designates. The word's religious implications seem inappropriate, even repulsive, to many people, including many Jews. Still, *Holocaust* remains the name most widely used.

Nazi Germany's system of concentration camps, ghettos, murder squadrons, and killing centers took more than twelve million defenseless human lives. Although not every Nazi victim was Jewish, the Nazi intent was to rid Europe, if not the world, of Jews. Hitler went far toward achieving that goal. The biggest group of the Jewish victims came from Poland, where the German annihilation took 90 percent of that country's three million Jews. Located in Poland, Auschwitz was the largest Nazi killing center. More than one million Jews were gassed there. Although Europe's Jews resisted the onslaught as best they could, by the time Germany surrendered in early May 1945, two-thirds of the European Jews—and about one-third of the Jews worldwide—were dead.

Apart from saying that events affect people differently, we can scarcely anticipate what aspects of the past will affect us decisively or how their impact will be most strongly felt. The Holocaust did not touch me or any of my immediate family directly. But when I weigh how my identity depends on the interdependence of private needs and public selves, I can neither talk about religion in public without thinking about the Holocaust nor think about the Holocaust without talking about religion in public. Being the son of a Presbyterian minister, the husband of a dedicated schoolteacher, and the father of two children as well as an active Protestant Christian, American, and professor of philosophy, I find that the Holocaust has kept provoking me to revise my life, not just my ideas and values, ever since I began studying that event intensively more than twenty-five years ago. My American experience in this regard is particular but not isolated. Especially in the 1990s, millions of Americans have encountered the Holocaust by viewing films such as *Schindler's List,* by visiting museums such as the U.S. Holocaust Memorial Museum in Washington, D.C., or the Museum of Tolerance at the Simon Wiesenthal Center in Los Angeles, or by studying the Holocaust in universities, colleges, and schools all around the United States. Unavoidably, such encounters drive home the point that the quality of a society's religious expressions can become quite literally a matter of life and death. The wrong kinds of religious discourse helped to cause the Holocaust. The right kinds could have prevented it.

After Auschwitz

My convictions about public expressions of religion were deepened during a meeting that took place on May 21, 1993. Returning to the United States only the day before, one of my closest friends had been in the former Yugoslavia. He went there to do research on a forthcoming book called *Holy War and Ethnic Cleansing.* It deals not only with the genocidal, ethnic-religious conflict in the Balkans but with turmoil between Muslims and Hindus in India as well as Palestinians and Israelis in the Middle East.

My friend emphasized how his contacts in Belgrade, Zagreb, and other sites of tension and tragedy in Serbia, Croatia, and Bosnia made him aware of what he called "things unspoken." For example, although relatively few people in those troubled places admitted this to him, it was no secret that a crucial fact loomed large, and it will continue to shadow the prospects for peace long after the Dayton Accords and the NATO troop deployment in late 1995, which included thousands of American soldiers, brought a respite from war in the Balkans: Absent a unifying cultural tradition—including religion—that helps people to live harmoniously because ethnic, racial, and religious differences do not eclipse shared memories, ideals, and hopes, life's diversity can pit individuals and groups against each other in genocidal violence.

As that fact loomed large, "ethnic cleansing" showed its "rationality." For it was also my friend's discovery that another of the "things unspoken" was the answer—"Members only of my particular ethnic or religious group"—when the logical question "Whom can I trust?" became understandably more pronounced.

Governed by the perspective of this book, parts of which I was then drafting, my listening told me that my friend was sketching a mural. It showed how the odds favoring a nightmare could be enhanced any time people of different traditions fail to talk well about religion's public importance. So I wondered: Could my friend's mural become a map of our country?

This mural is sketched by my friend Richard L. Rubenstein. For decades, this author of many important books has been a leader when it comes to talking about religion in public. Advancing ideas that are as significant as they are controversial, all of his writings talk about religion, exploring both the dark sides of public expressions of religion and the irreplaceable ways in which religion meets private needs and gives meaning to public selves.[1] We Americans might prefer to ignore or dismiss them, but to disregard Rubenstein's insights and their implications is to live at our peril.

I did not become well acquainted with Rubenstein until 1976, but he had influenced me well before our initial meeting and eventual collaboration on a number of writing projects.[2] He did so first through *After Auschwitz: Radical Theology and Contemporary Judaism,* a work first published in 1966 and thoroughly updated and revised in 1992.[3] Particularly in the United States, the book's sustained impact has rightly been considerable in Jewish circles and on many gentile audiences as well. Rubenstein's reflections were among the first by any American to probe publicly and systematically the significance of Auschwitz for post-Holocaust religious life. More important, Rubenstein's analysis sparked debate that will continue well into the future. That debate has much to do with speaking about religion in public, because it challenges a belief that many Americans have long held dear. After Auschwitz, Rubenstein contends, belief in a redeeming God—one who is active in history and who will bring an end to the vicissitudes of the human condition—is no longer credible.

In the late 1960s, the stir caused by *After Auschwitz* linked Rubenstein to a group of young American Protestant thinkers—Thomas Altizer, William

Hamilton, and Paul van Buren among them—who were dubbed "death-of-God theologians."[4] The popular media, including *Time*'s cover, picked up the story, and the movement ignited public discussion for some time. Although the spotlight eventually moved on, the contributions of these thinkers—at least Rubenstein's—were not a passing fad. The testimony this outlook contained, the questions it raised, remain too fundamental for that. Yet neither the labeling nor the clustering of these thinkers was entirely apt. None was atheistic in any simple sense of the word. Nor were their perspectives, methods, and moods identical. What they loosely shared was the feeling that talk about God did not—indeed could not—mean what it apparently had meant in the past. In that respect, the term "radical theology," which was sometimes applied to their work, made more sense. Prompting breaks with the past and discontinuities within traditions, they ventured to talk about experiences that were widely shared even though most people lacked the words or the encouragement to say so in public.

At the time, the three American Protestants hailed the "death of God" with considerable enthusiasm. They concurred that secularization—manifested especially in an expanding consciousness of human freedom, technological power, and responsibility—called into question the need for, or even the possibility of a traditional, transcendent God who exercised providential care over human history by episodic intervention in it. In good American-Christian fashion, these heralds were future-oriented. A new beginning, they proclaimed, ought to leave the past behind so that autonomous men and women could flourish.

As young theologians, none of the three Protestants emphasized the importance of memory. As we Americans are prone to say, they wanted to "put the past behind us." So when the question was "Where do you see it from?" their answer emphasized cultural moods more than actual historical events. Later, van Buren would concentrate on the Holocaust as he rejected his earlier positions and developed a Christian theology that is deeply sensitive to Jewish tradition, but the Holocaust did not explicitly inform the early discourse of these "radical" Christian theologians. On the contrary, the young Altizer, Hamilton, and van Buren were, on the whole, quite optimistic about the human prospect. They celebrated the liberation that men and women—perhaps Americans especially—could experience if they moved beyond an outmoded theological past to see that the whole world was no longer in God's hands but in ours alone.

Rubenstein's outlook differed in important ways. If he was not alone among those thinkers in denying that he literally believed "God is dead,"

Rubenstein made clearer than most his view that "the ultimate relevance of theology is anthropological," a perspective reflected in his long-standing use of psychoanalytic insights when he speaks about religion (*After Auschwitz*, 250). What Rubenstein meant was that whenever we speak about God we are talking about what we believe about God, which is not the same as talking about God directly. Thus, it can make sense to say, as Rubenstein did and still does, that "we live in the time of the death of God," but, he explained further, we cannot say whether "the death of God" is more than an event within human culture (250).[5]

Nor should it be expected, Rubenstein would add, that living in the time of the death of God will mean the end of religion. On the contrary, it may be precisely in such a time that important upsurges of religion, new and old, will appear. Far from being paradoxical, such expressions of religion are understandable because people seek meaning for their lives, and they may do so most intently when meaning is uncertain. Religion is not going away anytime soon. Revitalized in surprising ways, it may manifest itself in new forms or in the reaffirmation of old ones, even—indeed perhaps especially—in the time of the death of God.

In the time of the death of God, what kinds of religion will there be, how will they meet private needs, and how will they express themselves in public? Talk about those questions needs to include the view that whatever is ultimate, sacred, or divine eludes full disclosure in our experience. Religious traditions try to give expression to fundamental human yearnings and hopes for meaning. As they seek to nurture the divine-human encounter, those traditions channel our yearnings and hopes in distinctive and important ways. But each and all of the world's religious practices involve finite perspectives, limited interpretations, and fallible claims. Some of those practices are biased, blind, even corrupt in ways that show religions to be far from immune to the sin and fallenness about which they say so much. Yet those facts do not mean that religious traditions fail altogether to relate us meaningfully to the reality in which we live and move and have our being. On the contrary, especially when they are at their best, religious traditions are essential for helping to locate ourselves in the world and to give us as meaningful a sense of the whole as possible. Even if only by rejection of them, they are vital for meeting the profound need—public and private—to know ourselves. In any case, however, all expressions of religion, private or public, say more about *us* and about what we regard as sacred than about any reality external to us that they purport to reveal.

Rubenstein's emphasis on what he calls the anthropological dimensions of theological discourse did not mean—then or now—that he was indifferent to the nature of ultimate reality. One place, for example, where he parted company with the Christian radical theologians involved his impression that with very little regret, they " 'willed' the death of the theistic God" (*After Auschwitz*, 248). By contrast, as he found himself unwillingly forced to conclude that the idea of a God of history lacked credibility after Auschwitz, Rubenstein reports being saddened. He recognized that history had shattered—at least for him—a system of religious meaning that had sustained people, especially Jews and Christians, for millennia. For him, the destruction of such a pattern of meaning was no cause for celebration.

It would not be his final word on this dilemma, but on one occasion Rubenstein summed up his melancholy as follows:

> If the God of history does not exist, then the Cosmos is ultimately absurd in origin and meaningless in purpose. We have been thrust into the world in which life proliferates, has its hour, only to disappear amidst the further proliferation of life. As human beings we are divided by historical and geographical accident into the tribes of mankind, to no ultimate reason or purpose. We simply are there for but a moment only to disappear into the midnight silence of Eternal Chaos.[6]

Seeking an alternative perspective that could work for him and for others who might share his outlook, Rubenstein went on to write movingly and much more positively about his vision of "God after the Death of God."[7] Instead of "faith in the radically transcendent Creator God of biblical religion, who bestows a covenant upon Israel for His own utterly inscrutable reasons," Rubenstein holds that "an understanding of God which gives priority to the indwelling immanence of the Divine may be more credible in our era" (*After Auschwitz*, 295–96).

Drawing on both Eastern and Western mystical traditions, including key strands within his own Jewish heritage, Rubenstein speaks of God as the Holy Nothingness. Submitting that "omnipotent Nothingness is Lord of all creation," he uses that concept to refer to "the ground, content, and final destiny of all things," adding that "God as the 'Nothing' . . . is not a thing" but "no-thing." Beyond distinctions between the masculine and the feminine or human understandings of good and evil, Rubenstein's Holy Nothingness is not the "absence of being, but a superfluity of being . . . a *plenum* so rich that all existence derives therefrom" (298, 305). The best metaphor for this concept, Rubenstein suggests, is that "God is the ocean and we the waves. Each wave has its moment when it is identifiable as a somewhat separate entity. Nevertheless, no wave is entirely distinct from the ocean, which is its substantial ground" (299).

The advantages of this perspective, says Rubenstein, include "a judgment on the overly individualistic conception of the self which has predominated in the Western world" (302). Emphasizing the interdependence of all things, Rubenstein insists that "the world of the death of the biblical God need not be a place of gloom or despair. One need not live forever for life to be worth living. Creation, however impermanent, is full of promise. Those who affirm the inseparability of the creative and the destructive in the divine activity thereby affirm their understanding of the necessity to pay in full measure with their own return to the Holy Nothingness for the gift of life" (306).

There is much more to Rubenstein's constructive theological vision. For our purposes, however, it must suffice to say that, if omnipotent Nothingness is Lord of all creation, we can ask but never really answer the question "Why is there something rather than nothing?" Far from reducing, to say nothing of legitimating, the horror of "ethnic cleansing" and the Holocaust, that outcome may make human life more tragic than ever. But it does remove the theological "problem of evil" that intrudes when such devastations are interpreted as part of a world created and sustained by a powerful biblical God of history whose providential purposes are supposedly governed by goodness, justice, and love.

The concerns that drove Rubenstein to reject the traditional God of history, however, were never directed by unsatisfactory attempts to solve a dilemma whose dissonance had been reduced to the abstract question, "If there is radical evil in the world, how can God be omnipotent and completely good?" His issue was far more concrete, particular, and historical than that. With Auschwitz as the place where he "saw it from," what sense could be made of a Jewish tradition of covenant and election, a perspective in which Jews interpreted themselves to be specially chosen by God, bound to God in a covenant that entailed God's blessing for faithfulness and God's judgment against infidelity? Common to that tradition's self-understanding was the belief that "radical communal misfortune," as Rubenstein calls it, was a sign either that God found the Chosen People wanting and dispensed punishment accordingly, or that God called upon the innocent to suffer sacrificially for the guilty, or that an indispensable prelude for the messianic climax of Jewish history was under way, or some combination of such outlooks. In any case, the Holocaust, an event in which Nazi Germany was hell-bent on destroying Jewish life root and branch, made Rubenstein collide head on with the biblical tradition of covenant and election, which seemed to him to lead consistently to a positive answer to the question: "Did God use Adolf Hitler and the Nazis as his agents to inflict terrible sufferings and death upon six million Jews, including more than one million children?" (*After Auschwitz*, 162).

Rubenstein had to decide whether to affirm the existence of a God who inflicts Auschwitz on his people. Finding that affirmation obscene, he had to look elsewhere to make sense of his Jewish identity.

What about the rest of us? If Auschwitz is where we "see it from"—and it ought to be at least one of those places—where do we look to make sense of our identities? Christians, for example, are not untouched by Rubenstein's dilemma, because his rejection of the God of history attacks a fundamental premise of all biblical faith. Insofar as American identity rests on that premise—"In God We Trust"—it, too, requires us Americans to confront how we think of ourselves after Auschwitz.[8] So it is worth contemplating that Rubenstein's developing religious perspective led him to emphasize nothing like a God who can be counted on to bless "America the beautiful." His sense of the whole and of the sacred within it is far more awesome than that, for "creation and destruction," he affirms, "are part of an indivisible process. Each wave in the ocean of God's Nothingness has its moment, but it must inevitably give way to other waves. We are not, like Job, destined to receive back everything twofold" (*After Auschwitz*, 306).

Far from appealing to God to legitimate and guarantee the American Dream or any other human cause, Rubenstein finds that "a demonic aspect to reality and divinity must be accepted as an inescapable concomitant of life and existence." Momentarily human virtue may overcome life's negativities and savor the goodness that makes our lives the best that they can be. But, Rubenstein hastens to add, "life is thrust forward in divinity's ceaseless project to enjoy its hour and then to become the consumed substance of other life. Such a view of divinity makes tragedy and destruction inescapable and ineradicable" (208, 306).

As Rubenstein sees it, birth throws us into existence. No one is consulted about genes or gender, race or nationality, historical location, socioeconomic circumstance, or religious situation, to mention only some of the factors that identify us. Yet we also have considerable freedom to direct the journey we take during our limited time on earth. Rubenstein's distinctive journey began with *After Auschwitz*. Decades later it returned to that place as he looked back on his early work and saw that "no person writing about the religious significance of contemporary history can rest content with what he or she has written at a particular moment in time. As history is an ongoing process, so too is theological writing concerning history" (xi). As the second edition of *After Auschwitz* makes clear, however, Rubenstein has consistently followed his conviction that "the ultimate relevance of theology is anthropological." Thus, the accent of his work has fallen increasingly on history, politics, economics, and sociology—always, to be sure, with reference to religious thought and practice but with the emphasis on the conditions that produce human conflict and the safeguards that must be shored up to limit that conflict's destructiveness.

Deeply concerned about history and its symptoms concerning the future, Rubenstein has focused specifically on the ways in which state-sponsored programs of population elimination, often through mass murder, have been brought on by modernity, whose essence was captured early in the twentieth century by the German sociologist Max Weber when he spoke of the "disenchantment of the world." To Weber, and Rubenstein often builds on his point, that disenchantment was both cause and effect of a powerful but problematic human sensibility that "there are no mysterious incalculable forces that come into play, but rather that one can, in principle, master all things by calculation."[9] Yet, because of his concerns about history, and especially the state-sponsored programs of mass extermination that modernity has produced, Rubenstein finds it vital to keep talking about religion in public. As he does so, his work in two Holocaust-related areas is especially significant for us Americans. The first pertains to individual human rights, the second to the fact that more people exist than anyone needs.

Human Rights

Short but hardly sweet, Rubenstein's book *The Cunning of History* hits even harder than *After Auschwitz*, for there Rubenstein has written, "The Holocaust bears witness to *the advance of civilization*."[10] To see how that proposition is charged with ominous portents, return to Chicago, an American place where we have been before. In 1933, the year in which Hitler came to power, the Chicago World's Fair celebrated what its promoters optimistically hailed as "A Century of Progress." As Rubenstein points out in *The Cunning of History*, the fair's theme was expressed in a slogan: "Science Explores; Technology Executes; Mankind Conforms" (78). Cast in those terms, the Holocaust not only bears witness to the tragically cunning and ironic elements of "progress" but also delivers a warning about what could—but ought not—lie ahead for humanity.

The Final Solution was symptomatic of the modern state's perennial temptation to destroy people who are regarded as undesirable, superfluous, or unwanted because of their religion, race, politics, ethnicity, or economic redundancy. The Nazis identified what they took to be a practical problem: the need to eliminate the Jews and other so-called racial inferiors from their midst. Then they moved to solve it. Consequently, the Holocaust did not result from spontaneous, irrational outbursts of random violence. Nor was the Final Solution a bizarre historical anomaly. It was instead a state-sponsored program of population riddance made possible by modern technology and planned by contemporary political organization.

Significantly, the Holocaust did not occur until the mid-twentieth century, but conditions necessary, though not sufficient, to produce it were forming centuries before.[11] Decisive in that process was Christian anti-Judaism and its demonization of the Jew. For example, Rubenstein appraises the Christian New Testament correctly when he writes that "no other religion is as horribly defamed in the classic literature of a rival tradition as is Judaism" (*After Auschwitz,* 131). The reason for that defamation was the Christian belief that the Jews were, as Rubenstein puts it, "the God-bearing and the God-murdering people *par excellence*" (131). Jesus, the incarnation of God according to Christian tradition, was one of the Jewish people, but the Christian telling of this story depicted the Jews as collectively responsible for his crucifixion and thus for rejecting God through deicide, the most heinous crime of all. Christian contempt for Jews was advanced further by the belief that the dispersion of the Jews from their traditional homeland after the Judeo-Roman War and the fall of Jerusalem in 70 C.E. — and perhaps all of their subsequent misfortune — was God's punishment for their failure to see the light. The effect of this centuries-old tradition was, as Rubenstein says, "to cast them [the Jews] out of any common universe of moral obligation with the Christians among whom they were domiciled. In times of acute social stress, it had the practical effect of decriminalizing any assault visited upon them" (132). Building on a long history that went beyond religious to racist antisemitism, the assaults reached their zenith when Nazi Germany became a genocidal state.

The Nazis' antisemitic racism eventually entailed a destruction process that required and received cooperation from every sector of German society. Moreover, the killers and those who aided and abetted them directly — or indirectly as bystanders — were civilized people from a society that was scientifically advanced, technologically competent, culturally sophisticated, efficiently organized, and even religiously devout. Those people were, as the Holocaust scholar Michael Berenbaum cogently observes, "both ordinary and extraordinary, a cross section of the men and women of Germany, its allies, and their collaborators as well as the best and the brightest."[12]

Many Germans and members of populations allied with the Nazis resisted Hitler and would not belong in the following catalog, but they were still only exceptions that prove the rule that the Nazi-inspired intersection of private needs and public selves produced catastrophic destruction. There were, for example, pastors and priests who led their churches in welcoming nazification and the segregation of Jews it entailed. In addition, teachers and writers helped to till the soil where Hitler's racist antisemitism took root. Their students and readers reaped the wasteful harvest. Lawyers drafted and judges enforced the laws that isolated Jews and set them up for the kill. Government and church personnel provided birth records to document who was Jewish and who was not. Other workers entered such information into what were then state-of-the-art data processing machines. University administrators curtailed admissions for Jewish students and dismissed Jewish faculty members. Bureaucrats in the Finance Ministry handled confiscations of Jewish wealth and property. Postal officials delivered mail about definition and expropriation, denaturalization and deportation.

Driven by their biomedical visions, physicians were among the first to experiment with the gassing of *lebensunwertes Leben* (lives unworthy of life). Scientists performed research and tested their racial theories on those branded sub- or non-human by German science. Business executives found that Nazi concentration camps could provide cheap labor; they worked people to death, turning the Nazi motto, *Arbeit macht frei* (Work makes one free), into a mocking truth. Stockholders made profits from firms that supplied Zyklon B to gas people and from companies that built crematoriums to burn the corpses. Radio performers were joined by artists such as the gifted film director, Leni Reifenstahl, to broadcast and screen the polished propaganda that made Hitler's policies persuasive to so many. Engineers drove the trains that transported Jews to death, while other officials took charge of the billing arrangements for this service. Factory workers modified trucks so that they became deadly gas vans; city policemen became members of squadrons that made mass murder of Jews their specialty. As the list went on, Nazi Germany's fatal interdependence of private needs and public selves led to the destruction of the European Jews.

Short of Germany's military defeat by the Allies, no other constraints—social or political, moral or religious—were sufficient to stop the Final

Solution. That fact led Rubenstein to write *The Cunning of History*. It also made him wonder about truths whose status is far more fragile and precarious than Thomas Jefferson assumed when he taught us Americans to hold them as "self-evident." None of those truths is more crucial to the American Dream than the claim that persons are "endowed by their Creator with certain unalienable Rights." Those rights, Jefferson believed, are not merely legal privileges that people grant to each other as they please. Rather, his philosophy held, reason—rightly used—shows that such rights are "natural." Part and parcel of what is meant by *human* existence, they belong equally to all humanity and presumably cannot be violated with impunity. Nonetheless, the sense in which rights are unalienable—inviolable, absolute, unassailable, inherent—is an elusive part of Jefferson's Declaration, for it also states that "to secure these rights, Governments are instituted among Men." Apparently unalienable rights are not invulnerable; but if they are not invulnerable, then in what way are they unalienable?

One answer could be that what *is* and what *ought to be* are often not the same, and reason can make the distinction. To speak of unalienable rights, therefore, is to speak of conditions of existence so basic that they ought never to be abrogated. Persuasive though it may be, such reasoning may still give too little comfort. Rights to life, liberty, and the pursuit of happiness are qualified repeatedly, even by governments that seek to secure them. But even more radically, Auschwitz questions the *functional* status of unalienable rights. In Rubenstein's words, the Holocaust, genocide, and related instances of state-sponsored population elimination suggest that "there are absolutely no limits to the degradation and assault the managers and technicians of violence can inflict upon men and women who lack the power of effective resistance" (*Cunning*, 90).

True, nearly everyone says that certain rights must not be usurped. Still, if those rights are violated completely and all too often with impunity—and they are—how can they convincingly be called "natural" or "unalienable"? Is that not one more idealistic illusion, another instance of how the American Dream obscures reality? Rubenstein's proposition is debatable—it should be on the agenda when we Americans talk about religion in public and about God-given rights in particular—but he contends that greater credibility is found when one concludes that "*rights do not belong to men by nature*. To the extent that men have rights, they have them only as members of the polis, the political community. . . . Outside of the polis there are no inborn restraints on the human exercise of destructive power" (89).

A man named Hans Maier knew too well whereof Richard Rubenstein speaks. Born on October 31, 1912, the only child of a Catholic mother and a Jewish father, more than anything else he thought of himself as Austrian, not least because his father's family had lived in that country since the seventeenth century. Hans Maier, however, lived in the twentieth century, and so it was that in the autumn of 1935 he studied a newspaper in a Viennese coffeehouse. The Nuremberg Laws had just been promulgated in Nazi Germany. Maier's reading made him see—unmistakably—the fatal interdependence of all human actions. Even if he did not think of himself as Jewish, the Nazis' definitions meant that the cunning of history had given him that identity nonetheless. By identifying him as a Jew, Maier would write later on, Nazi power made him "a dead man on leave, someone to be murdered, who only by chance was not yet where he properly belonged."[13]

When Nazi Germany occupied Austria in March 1938, Maier drew his conclusions. Fleeing his native land for Belgium, he joined the Resistance after that country fell to the Third Reich in 1940. Arrested by Nazi police in 1943, Maier was sent to Auschwitz and then to Bergen-Belsen where he was liberated in 1945. Eventually taking the name Jean Améry, by which he is remembered, this philosopher waited twenty years before breaking his silence about the Holocaust. When Améry did decide to write, the result was a series of remarkable essays about his experience. In English they appear in a volume entitled *At the Mind's Limits: Contemplations by a Survivor on Auschwitz and Its Realities*. One is simply entitled "Torture."

Torture drove Améry to the following observation: "The expectation of help, the certainty of help," he wrote, "is indeed one of the fundamental experiences of human beings." Thus, the gravest loss produced by the Holocaust, Améry went on to suggest, was that it destroyed what he called "trust in the world, . . . the certainty that by reason of written or unwritten social contracts the other person will spare me—more precisely stated, that he will respect my physical, and with it also my metaphysical, being" (28).

Jean Améry would wonder about the American Dream, its affirmations about unalienable rights bestowed by God, and its hope for new beginnings. "Every morning when I get up," he tells his reader, "I can read the Auschwitz number on my forearm. . . . Every day anew I lose my trust in the world. . . . Declarations of human rights, democratic constitutions, the free world and the free press, nothing," he went on to say, "can again lull me into the slumber of security from which I awoke in 1935" (94–95).

Far from scorning the human dignity that those institutions claim to honor, Améry yearned for the right to live, which he equated with dignity itself. His experiences, however, taught him that "it is certainly true that dignity can be bestowed only by society, whether it be the dignity of some office, a professional or, very generally speaking, civil dignity; and the merely individual, subjective claim ('I am a human being and as such I have my dignity, no matter what you may do or say!') is an empty academic game, or madness" (89).

Lucidity, believed Améry, demanded the recognition of this reality, but lucidity did not end there. "What happened, happened," he wrote. "But *that* it happened cannot be so easily accepted" (xi). So lucidity also entailed rebellion against power that would make anyone "a dead man on leave." Unfortunately, it must also be acknowledged that Améry's hopes for such protest were less than optimistic. On October 17, 1978, he took leave and became a dead man by his own hand.

Améry's testimony questions assumptions that have long been at the heart of the American Dream and its religious underpinnings. They include beliefs that the most basic human rights are a gift of God and that nature and reason testify to a universal moral structure that underwrites them. But what if we live in the time of the death of God? What if Rubenstein's omnipotent Nothingness is Lord of all Creation? What if there is no God, not even omnipotent Nothingness? What if nature is amoral? Granting that reason can make critical distinctions between what *is* and what *ought to be,* what if reason also insists that the most telling truth of all is that history is what Hegel, the nineteenth-century German philosopher, called it: a slaughter bench, a realm where unalienable rights are hardly worth the paper they are written on — unless political might ensures them.

Such questions have crossed American minds in the past, but in a post-Holocaust age they cross-examine American optimism and our religious discourse more severely than before. For it is no longer clear that anything but human power does secure a person's rights, and if rights depend on human power alone, then they may well be natural and unalienable in name only. In such circumstances, to call rights unalienable may still be a legitimate rhetorical device, perhaps buttressed by religious discourse, to muster consensus that certain privileges and prerogatives must not be taken away. No doubt the idea of unalienable rights functions — and will continue to do so — precisely in that way as an ingredient in the American Dream. But ideas do not necessarily correspond to facts any more than dreams do to waking life. It appears increasingly that rights are functionally unalienable — which may be what counts most in the long and short of it — only within a state that will successfully defend and honor them as such.

Rubenstein's perspective urges us Americans to consider how our views about human rights can and should connect to public expressions of religion. Those expressions will not serve us well to the extent that they exclusively identify and divisively invoke some "God of history" as being only on the side of one party, one position, one group, one race, one religion, or one nation. When people join the gods of history on those paths, trust is likely to be misplaced, deceptions multiplied, and destructive "cleansings" and "holy" wars of one kind or another are likely to be increased. But public expressions of religion can serve us well to the extent that they move us to reflect inclusively about the common good and then to honor loyally the liberty, mutual respect, and justice without which our private needs go unfulfilled and our public selves are impoverished.

Surplus People

Our senses of the whole and our convictions about what is sacred within it remain important in defining the rights we ought to honor and in keeping the power of the state focused to defend them. Considering further those factors about religion and human rights, Rubenstein also insists that we need to face the fact that more people exist than anyone needs.

Demographic studies in the mid-1990s put the world's population at about 5.7 billion. With such numbers in mind, James Gustav Speth, administrator of the United Nations Development Program (UNDP), released that agency's seventh annual report in the summer of 1996. Its findings showed a world that is more economically polarized than ever, moving in the report's words from a condition that is "inequitable" to one that is "inhuman." Overall the wealth of the world's nations has increased but not equally; more than a quarter of the world's population is worse off than it was fifteen years ago, while the net worth of the 350 richest people is equal to the combined income of the poorest 45 percent of the world's population. According to the UNDP's 1996 report, American trends reflect elements of this same pattern. In the United States, for example, the richest 20 percent of the American population earns ten times more than the poorest 20 percent, and the wealthiest 1 percent of the population increased its share of the nation's total assets from 20 percent to 36 percent between 1975 and 1990.[14] Meanwhile, the rate of the world's population growth is also striking. In 1800, the world's population was about one billion. It took the human species nearly 150,000 years to reach that mark. In the last two hundred years, however, the population has grown to five times that sum. By the middle of the twenty-first century, ten billion human beings may inhabit the earth.[15] Meanwhile, Stanley Meisler had summarized the 1993 findings of the United Nations Fund for Population Activities, which addressed what it called "the human crisis of our age."[16] According to that UN study, Meisler explained, people were migrating from their homelands more than ever before in human history. The migrants' relocation came from necessity more than by choice. Most would have preferred to find life worth living in surroundings that memory, tradition, and human ties make familiar, but poverty, overcrowding, and war were more than hope could bear.

Unfortunately, the extent to which hopes for migration were more realistic remains a serious question. In the early 1990s, uprooted people headed not for the new, underpopulated frontiers that so often provided a demographic safety valve—especially in America—for population redundancy in earlier times. The earth does not have such places anymore. Instead, the displaced people tried to enter space already occupied by others to the point of stress—the cities of North America and Europe, for example.

"Options for successful migration," the UN's 1993 understatement said, "are fewer than ever before."[17] Those words have been backed up by the UN's 1995 follow-up study, "The State of the World's Refugees." It reported that the number of people officially classified as refugees—meaning people displaced outside their home country—declined to 14.4 million in 1995, a significant drop from the 1993 peak of 18.2 million. That fact, however, is much less hopeful than it appears. From 1993 to 1995, the number of people who have been uprooted from their homes by war, atrocities, and persecution has soared from 44 million to a record-high 50 million.[18] As anti-immigration sentiments grow around the world and in the United States in particular, displaced persons increasingly must remain in countries that are scarcely home any more.

Mind-boggling numbers continue to complicate such stories, whose plots are likely to worsen. In the mid-1990s, the world's population is growing at the rate of some ninety-three million people annually. The UN's mid-decade demographic figures showed Tokyo's 26.5 million people topping the list of the world's largest urban areas, with Jakarta, Indonesia, and Bombay, India, showing the fastest rates of growth. Meanwhile, the New York and Los Angeles areas ranked second and seventh with populations of 16.2 and 12.2 million, respectively. Those American cities include many of the 7.4 million legal immigrants who entered the United States in the 1980s, as well as the 10 million estimated by the UN to have immigrated illegally into the United States during that same period. Fears about illegal immigration in California led to a massive victory for a 1994 measure known as Proposition 187, which severely restricts the social services that illegal immigrants can expect to receive in that state. Immigration issues loomed large in the 1996 American elections and are likely to continue to do so in American politics in the foreseeable future.

Three additional factors complicate the immense dimensions of the world's population picture. First, a Worldwatch Institute report has indicated that, exacerbated by declining food production, world population growth is outstripping food availability. According to Worldwatch, if every person in the world in 1993 had received an equal distribution of fish, meat, and grain, everyone would have less to eat than four years earlier.[19] Second, the UN's 1993 findings showed that immigrants from one area tend to cluster together in their new surroundings. If that arrangement provides mutual support, it also makes the newcomers visible, their cultural differences obvious, suspicions about them more severe, and feelings that "they don't belong" more explosive. Third, the immigrants tend to be young people "in the peak years of fertility." They reproduce at rates higher than that of the population as a whole. Although the number of people technically classed as refugees declined in 1995 because there are fewer new places for displaced people to go, the large numbers who do emigrate, and the increasing number who might do so if they could, leave few reasons to believe that the plight of the unwanted and wretched of the earth has been much relieved.

Such conditions do not bode well for domestic tranquility in the United States or elsewhere, a point that is underscored by focusing attention not only on the millions who still do immigrate to other countries each year but also on the fact that the United States continues annually to accept about half of all those who legally immigrate to the world's industrially developed nations. When the UN spoke about "the human crisis of our age," some of the dimensions of that crisis were left in Rubenstein's category of "things unspoken." The crisis runs deeper and beyond the fact that millions have been dislocated—deeper, because of the conditions that cause the dislocation; beyond, because of the reactions that the migrations are likely to produce. With good reason, awareness of the cunning of history arouses suspicion that emigration of the kind described in the UN reports is actually welcomed by those who stand to gain by the departure of people who are surplus, redundant, and unwanted. Often such interests belong to "powers that be" who are simply relieved to be rid of burdensome people. Likewise, when the emigrants head for regions that are already under stress, it is unlikely that all of them will be able to settle there with impunity. On the contrary, many will remain as surplus, redundant, and unwanted as before. When steps are taken to solve that problem—and they will be—chances are those solutions will be less than humane, even deadly. This scenario is no fantasy. It has happened many times before, as Rubenstein points out in *After Auschwitz*.[20] It continues in the 1990s, and far from disappearing, the scenario is likely to worsen in the twenty-first century.

Stressing that genocide is an instrument of state policy, not something done by individuals alone, *The Cunning of History* contains yet another fundamental and controversial thesis derived from the Holocaust: "The Nazi elite," writes Rubenstein, "clearly understood that the Jews were truly a *surplus people* whom nobody wanted and whom they could dispose of as they pleased. . . . In terms of German ideology, the Jews were a *surplus population* because of the kind of society the Germans wanted to create" (18, 83).[21]

Rubenstein would expand those claims in *The Age of Triage,* but already his point was that established interests had for centuries engaged in the riddance of redundant populations. As he saw it, the Nazis' handling of the Jews implemented an extremely calculated procedure for dealing with an old problem. It also involved a host of particular features, which included the blending of ancient strands of Christian anti-Judaism with modern ideologies of nationalism and racism. But in addition to arguing that the Holocaust—though exceptional—was still one of many instances of state-sponsored population elimination, Rubenstein's major claim was that the category of "surplus people" was crucial because it could help us understand not only how the Holocaust was distinctive but also how it is symptomatic of features that may be endemically destructive in our current ways of life.

Lest he be misunderstood, Rubenstein carefully stated that "the concept of a surplus population is not absolute. An underpopulated nation can have a redundant population if it is so organized that a segment of its able-bodied human resources cannot be utilized in any meaningful economic or social role" (*Cunning*, 10). Thus, as he succinctly put the point in *The Age of Triage,* "a surplus or redundant population is one that for any reason can find no viable role in the society in which it is domiciled."[22]

Illustrating those themes, *The Age of Triage* draws out Rubenstein's total vision of our past and future by accenting the importance of religion as well as social scientific realities. To see those connections, note that *triage* is a socioeconomic sorting that saves some ways of life by dispatching others. In modern forms, it shows the ascendancy of a powerfully practical form of human rationality. Casting his point in economic terms, Rubenstein stresses how decisive it has been that people discovered how to produce a surplus. For thereby, he asserts, they also took *"the first step in making themselves superfluous" (Triage, 3)*.[23]

Already we have observed that current concerns about global population find the world containing many more people than anyone needs. Rubenstein recognizes, in turn, that this redundancy exists partly because of sheer numbers but even more because the dominant intentions that energize modern society tend to be governed by the belief that money is the measure of all that is real. More than any other, he claims, that belief drives the modernization process, which has been under way and intensifying over the last five centuries. One effect of this process is that the intrinsic worth of people diminishes. Their worth is evaluated functionally instead. Hence, if persons are targeted as nonuseful—they can be so regarded in any number of ways, depending on how those in power define their terms—a community may find it sensible to eliminate the surplus. In modern times, that action has been facilitated, indeed instigated and promoted, by governmental power. As Rubenstein understands it, then, triage entails state-sponsored programs of population elimination: through eviction, compulsory resettlement, expulsion, warfare, and outright extermination—roughly in that order. This winnowing process, more or less extreme in its violence, enables a society to drive out what it does not want and to keep what it desires for itself.

Persistently intrigued by history's continuity as well as by its cunning, Rubenstein links modernization and mass death in a study that encompasses such *apparently* diverse events as the enclosure movement in England during the Enlightenment, the nineteenth-century famine years in Ireland, and a variety of twentieth-century events—a nonexhaustive list includes the Armenian genocide, the slaughter of Soviet citizens under Stalin, and the devastation of Cambodia, as well as the destruction of the European Jews. No doubt Rubenstein would include "ethnic cleansing" in the former Yugoslavia and the genocide in Rwanda among his historical examples, too. Nor would he overlook the ways in which American perspectives, especially in times of acute social stress, may identify unwanted people—illegal immigrants, the poor who depend on welfare, criminals, drug addicts, gang members, the elderly, gays, AIDS victims, certain racial, ethnic or religious groups—who might become tempting targets for one kind of population riddance or another because their presence "costs too much."

Rubenstein's views on these matters were developed long before Charles

Murray and the late Richard J. Herrnstein published their controversial 845-page study *The Bell Curve: Intelligence and Class Structure in American Life* in 1994.[24] Nevertheless Rubenstein would easily recognize that Herrnstein and Murray are implicitly urging Americans to inaugurate an age of triage.[25] Advancing the questionable proposition that IQ is largely destiny, the authors hold that most low-IQ people are doomed to a life of poverty and possibly crime. They link IQ to race—as a racial group, blacks are less intelligent than whites, the authors contend—and thus to poverty, which they believe low intelligence increases. In addition, Herrnstein and Murray claim that the United States' intellectual health is dropping because low-IQ people have more babies than the "cognitive elite," and because current immigrants have lower IQs than those who came before them. In sum, *The Bell Curve* implies that the United States has a surplus population that should not be wanted, and it advocates public policies that act accordingly.

Religion in the Age of Triage

Returning to Rubenstein, who would be skeptical of *The Bell Curve*'s analysis to say the least, his sociopolitical outlook is telling enough, but his interpretation becomes even more perceptive because of the ways in which it shows that an age of triage makes consideration of the public expression of religion more critical than ever. Explicitly and implicitly, for example, God is both absent and present in *The Age of Triage*. Historically, Rubenstein argues, Western monotheism desacralized the world, leaving human power free to exploit nature and to kill far too much with impunity. Ironically, the same God found in the public religious expressions that were instrumental in unleashing the modernizing process has also been its victim, eclipsed by an advancing civilization that has produced in tandem benefit and destruction—both in unprecedented abundance. Yet, looking toward the future, Rubenstein hints at—even yearns for—a religious revival that might transmute humanity's propensity to waste life and convert us so that we are "born again as men and women blessed with the capacity to care for each other here and now" (*Triage*, 240).

Religion's place in an age of triage deserves attention, not least because religions—even in the time of the death of God—are such potent forces for both unity and division and can be destructive as well as constructive on either count. Consider, then, four of Rubenstein's fundamental propositions. Each merits a governing role in late twentieth-century conversation about religion in the United States.

"Modern civilization is largely the unintended consequence of a religious revolution" (*Triage*, 230).[26] Western monotheism, contends Rubenstein, replaced magic and belief in spiritualized nature by insisting that there is one and only one God who is the sovereign creator of heaven and earth. The success of Judaism and Christianity inadvertently paved the way for the secular outlooks that result in triage. True, these traditions affirmed that the earth is the Lord's. Men and women, moreover, were to be obedient to God's will. That will, in turn, would make itself known in time because in history not everything was to be permitted. Bonds of moral obligation, underwritten by God's judging power, were claimed to be in force. Human life, formed in God's image, appeared to be even more sacred than it had been prior to monotheism's eminent domain.

Neither in practice nor in theory, however, does history conform entirely to conscious intention. In spite of and even because of monotheism's moral components, a course unfolded in which nature and even human life itself came to be regarded as subject to the mastery of politics and economics. Religions predicated on revelation within history unleashed reason in ways that transmuted the moral authority of revelation itself. A biblical God inspired a secular consciousness, and at times God disappeared in the process. Providence became Progress. Progress meant the triumph of a calculating, functional rationality whose Golden Rule was *Efficiency*.

Religions and theologies are loaded dice because they always contain more options for development than the limitations of immediate consciousness can comprehend. In an age of triage, we have learned that lesson to our sorrow. Yet Rubenstein's point is that we can be aware of it now. That awareness enjoins a warning, which takes us to a second proposition that deserves attention.

"In a crisis, a secularized equivalent of the division of mankind into the elect and the reprobate could easily become a controlling image" (*Triage*, 216).[27] Western monotheism's emphasis on a God of history has typically included the idea that some groups or persons are specially called. They are linked together and with God in covenantal relations. At their best, these convictions single people out for service, but nearly all of these doctrines of covenant and election have also been extremely volatile. Separating people, they have induced a host of rivalries. Those rivalries and their offspring, Rubenstein attests, have more than a little to do with triage.

Unintended consequences are no less real than those that are consciously desired. The former, in fact, may be the more devastating precisely because their full power remains hidden until the effects are felt. In our American context, a crucial link between religion and triage lurks in the fact that Western monotheism has much to do with socioeconomic versions of divine election and covenant. Within such perspectives, poverty and wealth, for example, may be much more than economic conditions. They may be understood as entailing divine judgment and just deserts. Thus, their driving force can be not one of ministering to the poor but rather of eliminating them so that the position of the elect remains unthreatened.

The theology of covenant and election sketched here sounds perverse. It is. But Rubenstein's point is that it is too simple, too convenient, only to protest that a tradition has been distorted. No doubt distortion exists, but perhaps the more important point is that what we say religiously is often a two-edged sword. That fact holds even with respect to the best examples of public religious expression that we can cite. For the seeds that sprouted into destructive versions of covenant and election were not sowed first by the spiritually bankrupt or by the intellectually corrupt. They are gifts from the giants of Western religion—Moses, Jesus, and Paul, to cite only three. The issue that remains, then, is whether religion can speak publicly in ways that avert the crises that fuel forces bent on triage because they see the world in terms of the elect and the reprobate.

"We are by no means helpless in meeting the challenge confronting us" (*Triage,* 224).[28] Economically, Rubenstein argues, a basic, not to say complete, remedy for triage would be to create a social order that provides a decent job for any person who is willing to work. His optimism is muted, however, because he knows that the implementation of his economic remedy is anything but an economic matter alone. In fact, the forms of practical rationality that govern modern economic thinking tend to militate against policies of full employment. The challenge that confronts us, then, is largely a spiritual one. Unless men and women are resensitized religiously, the resources to avert triage are likely to be hopelessly inadequate.

Rubenstein thinks that we need nothing less than "an inclusive vision appropriate to a global civilization in which Moses and Mohammed, Christ, Buddha, and Confucius all play a role" (*Triage,* 240). To call Rubenstein's vision demanding understates the case. For, their universalizing tendencies notwithstanding, the major religious traditions have themselves been instrumental in "triaging" people "into the working and the workless, the saved and the damned" (240). Rubenstein hopes that a new religious consciousness will build on the inclusive aspects of the major religious traditions, excluding the exclusive features in the process. Yet a further difficulty is that although the thinker and the theorist can point out the needed direction, they cannot manage the achievement of such a vision. It is Rubenstein's conviction that the needed reversal, one that would substantially reduce the prospects of triage, depends on "authentic religious inspiration" (*Triage,* 239). Such inspiration is not absent, but it cannot be called into being at will, least of all by intellectuals. Nor are religion's presently dominant forms characterized chiefly by the inclusiveness that Rubenstein advocates.

"*Theology seeks to foster dissonance-reduction where significant items of information are perceived to be inconsistent with established beliefs, values, and collectively sanctioned modes of behavior*" (*Triage,* 132).[29] Every religious tradition has to cope with disconfirming evidence. Triage itself is a case in point, for the experience of the death of God in our time has everything to do with the mass wasting of human life. Typically, theologians have apologized for God when the problem of evil has taken center stage. Specifically, they attempt to reduce the dissonance that arises when traditional claims about God's power and goodness collide with history.

The pertinent point here, however, is that Rubenstein's description of theology's function is not offered by him as normative. On the contrary, his use of this description helps him to identify meaningful work that must be done by taking religious discourse into the very center of public life. Rubenstein's *Age of Triage* does little to reduce dissonance. Its mood is quite the opposite. By calling attention to the Holocaust, to triage, to the fact that men and women often kill with impunity, and by doing so in a way that questions the functional status of God in the world, Rubenstein's work is an exercise in dissonance production.

At least indirectly, Rubenstein suggests that an age of triage calls for more, not less, of that kind of public religious discourse. Yet a note of caution should intrude, for the dissonance production that is needed today, Rubenstein implies, is not the kind that will intensify individualism, tribalism, and the divisiveness that both usually bring. Rather, it ought to shatter such barriers and extend the boundaries of mutual social obligation. To move in that direction, however, is a task that will tax the best brainpower and spiritual imagination we can muster, for powerful indeed are the drives and interests that find triage tempting because such sorting offers a solution as "rational" as it is final. Political and economic sophistication will need to join hands with religious thought if public expressions of religion carry out dissonance production responsibly.

In sum, Rubenstein sets an agenda for public expressions of religion. It consists of at least four imperatives that ought to direct American talk about religion in public: (1) Deploy the right kinds of dissonance. (2) Deconstruct the ties between Providence and Progress. (3) Destabilize distinctions between the elect and the damned. (4) Discern, as far as thought permits, ways beyond the self-regarding individualism and the socially dividing tribalism that so often fuel propensities toward triage. Talk about religion in public that exhibits these qualities will help people to get along. Public expressions of religion that fail to move in these directions keep humanity in harm's way.

The Swami's Insight

A good place to end this part of our discussion about public expressions of religion is a story that Richard Rubenstein likes to tell about private needs and public selves. It features the late Swami Muktananda of Ganeshpuri. Invited to meet him, Rubenstein has never forgotten the first words that Swami Muktananda spoke to him, for it seemed, says Rubenstein, that the guru knew instinctively what he needed to hear: "You mustn't believe in your own religion," the Swami advised him, "I don't believe in mine. Religions are like the fences that hold young saplings erect. Without the fence the saplings could fall over. When it takes firm root and becomes a tree, the fence is no longer needed. However, most people never lose their need for the fence" (*After Auschwitz*, 293).

Swami Muktananda was a deeply religious man. What did he mean, then, when he said that he did not believe in his own religion, and that Rubenstein ought not to believe in his? Rubenstein found the Swami's advice particularly helpful because he received it at a time when he was feeling "bitterly pessimistic about almost every aspect of the human condition," a mood that included what he acknowledges as an intolerance toward people in his own Jewish tradition who apparently declined to face "the difficulties involved in affirming the traditional God of covenant and election after Auschwitz" (293). What Rubenstein heard the Swami telling him was something that spoke to his private needs and modified his public self in ways that he describes eloquently in the very first paragraph of his revision of *After Auschwitz*:

If I were to characterize the fundamental difference between the spirit infusing the original edition of *After Auschwitz* and that of the current edition, it would be the difference between the spirit of opposition and revolt, which was an almost inevitable consequence of my initial, essentially uncharted attempt to come to terms theologically with the greatest single trauma in all of Jewish history, and the spirit of synthesis and reconciliation which, I trust, can be discerned in the current edition. The fundamental insights of the original have been retained but with a greater degree of empathy for those who have reaffirmed traditional Jewish faith in the face of the Holocaust. (xi)

Swami Muktananda urged Rubenstein not to give up his fundamental insights but to use them to look deeper and to see beyond their limited meanings. The point was not that the place where one stood was unimportant. Nor was it to stress that particular religious traditions are insignificant and undeserving of loyalty. On the contrary, the issue was to draw on what is best in a tradition and to filter out what is not. In this sense, traditions are not inherited but obtained through work that recovers what has been good in what has gone before. Silence about traditions cannot do this work. One has to discuss and analyze them and then act accordingly.

Just as physical and spiritual growth depends on the nurture that only participation in a particular religious tradition can provide, a specific viewpoint is essential, too. Without a place to "see it from," one could see nothing at all. So vision—but better, clearer, more encompassing than before—remains the key. The vision recommended by the swami emphasizes synthesis, reconciliation, and empathy. Those qualities do not exclude opposition, dissonance, or even revolt, for without them how can there be the synthesis, reconciliation, and empathy that look deeper and see beyond? If we look and see that way, having learned to do so at least in part by talking about "things unspoken" in our public expressions of religion, then we may find that in spite of its impermanence and its immense destructiveness, creation is indeed, as Rubenstein insists, full of promise.

N O T E S

1. See, for example, Richard L. Rubenstein, *The Cunning of History: The Holocaust and the American Future* (New York: Harper Colophon Books, 1978) and *The Age of Triage: Fear and Hope in an Overcrowded World* (Boston: Beacon Press, 1983).

2. See, for example, Richard L. Rubenstein and John K. Roth, *Approaches to Auschwitz: The Holocaust and Its Legacy* (Louisville: Westminster/John Knox, 1987), which, to the best of our knowledge, is the first book about the Holocaust coauthored by a Jew and a Christian.

3. See Richard L. Rubenstein, *After Auschwitz: History, Theology, and Contemporary Judaism*, 2d ed. (Baltimore: Johns Hopkins University Press, 1992). This version of *After Auschwitz* is more a new book than a second edition. Nine of the original version's fifteen chapters have been replaced. Those that remain were substantially rewritten. Although earlier versions of them first appeared elsewhere,

there are ten chapters new to *After Auschwitz*. In this chapter, all of the quotations from *After Auschwitz* are from the second edition and are given parenthetically in the text.

4. Of these three Protestant theologians, Altizer remained the most persistent in pursuing the line of thought he developed in the 1960s. Van Buren rejected his earlier views in favor of a systematic effort to reinterpret Christian theology in relation to the continuity of Jewish religious experience since the rise of Christianity. Notable among Hamilton's recent work is *A Quest for the Post-historical Jesus* (New York: Crossroad, 1993), which studies how Jesus has been portrayed in modern fiction, art, film, and poetry. He has been writing a book about Shakespeare as well.

5. Speaking further about living in the time of the death of God, Rubenstein notes that "in spite of the worldwide growth of religious belief and institutions, this is a position I still maintain in 1990" (*After Auschwitz*, 339n8).

6. Richard L. Rubenstein, "Some Perspectives on Religious Faith after Auschwitz," in *Holocaust: Religious and Philosophical Implications,* ed. John K. Roth and Michael Berenbaum (New York: Paragon House, 1989), 355. Rubenstein made these remarks at the first Annual Scholars Conference on the German Church Struggle and the Holocaust, which was organized by Franklin H. Littell, Hubert G. Locke, and others. The conference was held at Wayne State University in 1970. Rubenstein's essay first appeared in Franklin H. Littell and Hubert G. Locke, eds., *The German Church Struggle and the Holocaust* (Detroit: Wayne State University Press, 1974).

7. The final chapter of the revised edition of *After Auschwitz* bears this title. See 293–306.

8. A sidebar in *Time*'s cover story, "One Nation Under God: Has the Separation of Church and State Gone Too Far" (9 Dec. 1991, 60–68) adds some interesting background about the motto, "In God We Trust," which is familiar to most Americans because it has been stamped on our money for well over a century.

The origins of that tradition go back to Francis Scott Key, whose final stanza to "The Star-Spangled Banner" declares, "And this be our motto, 'In God is our Trust.'" It was during Abraham Lincoln's presidency, however, that the mint first put Key's idea, reformulated to say "In God We Trust," on the nation's coinage. In 1907, President Theodore Roosevelt, believing that religion and money ought not to be mixed in that way, tried to have the words removed from newly designed gold coins. A public outcry put that plan aside. In 1955, Congress legislated that the words should appear on all paper currency and a year later officially designated the four words as the nation's motto. From time to time the use of the motto on the nation's money has come under legal attack as a violation of the separation of church and state. Supreme Court Justice William Brennan, for one, was not much worried about a conflict. In 1983 he wrote that slogans such as "In God We Trust" have "lost any true religious significance."

9. Max Weber, "Science as a Vocation," in *From Max Weber: Essays in Soci-*

ology, ed. H. H. Gerth and C. Wright Mills (New York: Oxford University Press, 1946), 139.

10. Rubenstein, *Cunning of History,* 91. Subsequent page references are given parenthetically in the text.

11. Hard-hitting and controversial, Daniel Goldhagen's best-selling appraisal of the history of German antisemitism and its contributions to the Holocaust has re-opened debates that lead to important discourse about the role of religion in public life. See Daniel Jonah Goldhagen, *Hitler's Willing Executioners: Ordinary Germans and the Holocaust* (New York: Alfred A. Knopf, 1996), especially 25–178. In recent Holocaust scholarship, a more nuanced account of this history is provided by John Weiss, *Ideology of Death: Why the Holocaust Happened in Germany* (Chicago: Ivan R. Dee, 1996). Here it should also be noted that, at the time of this writing, Rubenstein is exploring the hypothesis that the Holocaust can also be viewed as a Holy War whose basic aim was to eliminate Jews as a religious, political, cultural, and demographic presence in Christian Europe. See, for example, Richard L. Rubenstein, "A Twentieth-Century Journey," in *From the Unthinkable to the Unavoidable: American Christian and Jewish Scholars Encounter the Holocaust,* ed. Carol Rittner and John K. Roth (Westport, Conn.: Greenwood Press, 1997), 164–69.

12. Michael Berenbaum, *The World Must Know: The History of the Holocaust as Told in the United States Holocaust Memorial Museum,* with photographs edited by Arnold Kramer (Boston: Little, Brown and Company, 1993), 220.

13. Jean Améry, *At the Mind's Limits: Contemplations by a Survivor on Auschwitz and Its Realities,* trans. Sidney Rosenfeld and Stella P. Rosenfeld (New York: Schocken Books, 1986), 86. The book was originally published in 1966. Subsequent page references are to this edition and are given parenthetically in the text.

14. The UNDP report came to my attention via an Internet release, dated July 16, 1996, from the U.S. Information Service, Washington, D.C.

15. See John Skow, "The Land: Less Milk and Honey?" *Time,* 30 Oct. 1995, 52.

16. Stanley Meisler, "Migration Viewed as 'Human Crisis,'" *Los Angeles Times,* 7 July 1993, A4.

17. Ibid.

18. See "A World of People Without Homes," *International Herald Tribune,* 16 Nov. 1995, 7. Often related to these dislocations, the plight of the world's children, in particular, remains critical. Reports sponsored by UNESCO in late 1995, showed that 1.4 billion of the world's children under the age of eighteen are in poverty and one hundred million are homeless. Diseases such as measles, tetanus, and polio still kill hundreds of thousands of children annually, even though vaccinations are widely employed. The same reports estimate that AIDS will kill 850,000 children annually by the year 2010. See the *International Herald Tribune,* 28 Nov. 1995, 7.

19. This report, "Vital Signs 1993: The Trends That Are Shaping Our Future," was discussed in the *Star Tribune* (Minneapolis edition), 18 July 1993, 5A.

20. In *After Auschwitz* see especially Rubenstein's chapters on "The Unmastered Trauma: Interpreting the Holocaust," "Modernization and the Politics of Extermination: Genocide in Historical Context," and "Covenant, Holocaust, and Intifada," which are found in a part called "The Meaning of the Holocaust," 81–153.

21. The italics are Rubenstein's. My discussion of Rubenstein's views about surplus people draws on my essay "Genocide, the Holocaust, and Triage," in *Genocide and the Modern Age: Etiology and Case Studies of Mass Death*, ed. Isidor Wallimann and Michael N. Dobkowski (Westport, Conn.: Greenwood Press, 1987).

22. Rubenstein, *Age of Triage*, 1. Subsequent page references are given parenthetically in the text.

23. The emphasis is Rubenstein's.

24. Richard J. Herrnstein and Charles Murray, *The Bell Curve: Intelligence and Class Structure in American Life* (New York: Free Press, 1994). In a nation that strongly affirms the political proposition that all persons are created equal and the religious faith that human beings are created in the image of God, the *Bell Curve*'s proposals deserve attention on the agenda for talk about religion in America.

25. For a useful analysis and succinct criticism of the ideological tradition and political climate that promoted *The Bell Curve*, see Roger Boesche, "Homeless? Hungry? It's All Your Fault," *Los Angeles Times*, 1 Dec. 1994, B7. Boesche shows how this tradition and climate reflect social Darwinism. Originating in the nineteenth century and championed by William Graham Sumner, Andrew Carnegie, and other American conservatives, this philosophy twisted Charles Darwin's writings to defend a supposedly scientific view that there are laws of natural selection that govern society.

As Boesche sums up the social Darwinist position, such "laws" mean that "poverty is nature's penalty" for everything from laziness to low intelligence and racial inferiority. Those who are "fit" and deserving of survival lack these qualities. Those who are "unfit" deserve neither to reproduce nor to survive. They are a drag on society. Posing as science but "founded on bogus studies," Boesche concludes, "*The Bell Curve* comforts Americans and erases guilt by telling us that poverty is inevitable. Most important, the book claims that African Americans and Latinos are poor largely because God and nature doomed them to a lower IQ."

26. The emphasis is mine.

27. The emphasis is mine.

28. The emphasis is mine.

29. The emphasis is mine.

CHAPTER EIGHT

The Shadow of Birkenau: How to Talk about Religion in Public

To be free is important. To help others to be free is even more important.

—ELIE WIESEL TO OPRAH WINFREY

With the help of Richard Rubenstein, the previous chapter's reflections on the Holocaust highlighted what public religious discourse needs to do and what its content should include. Now, with the help of another Holocaust interpreter, a survivor of Auschwitz named Elie Wiesel, this chapter explores more fully *how* such discussion can occur successfully. What follows is neither a set of rules nor a prescription about the venues where public discourse about religion can best take place. Instead this chapter probes more fundamental issues about the attitudes and values that are essential for good talk about religion in any time or place. In particular, it argues that the necessary attitudes and values include those that can turn religion against itself so that religion emphasizes the very qualities that it often leaves in scarce supply: better listening, more give and take, greater openness, increased sensitivity, and a deeper commitment to reflection about the things that matter most to us, the things that deserve to matter most to us, and the possible differences between those two categories.

A Nation of Talkers

The scene for this part of the inquiry can be set by mentioning that one December, after my college teaching had ended for the semester, I fulfilled a civic obligation by reporting for jury duty. With the winter holidays at hand, the court schedule was light. Periodically panels of potential jurors were summoned to court rooms, but many of us spent two weeks waiting for calls that never came.

While waiting, we found different ways to pass the time. Some of us—often strangers—struck up conversations. Others worked crossword puzzles. Still others played cards, and some of us read whatever was at hand—newspapers, magazines, books, or, in my case, final exams.

The jury waiting room contained a television set. Always on, the entertainment of its soap operas and game shows helped some folks through the day. Then, about three o'clock, I noticed something. Conversations concluded. Readers stopped. Crossword puzzles were set aside. With the sound turned up so everyone could hear, whether they wanted to or not, previously scattered attention in the jury waiting room focused on TV. It was time for the Oprah Winfrey show.

I do not remember who appeared with her or what the topics were on that talk show during those two weeks in December. But I do remember becoming part of the daily gravitation to learn what Oprah Winfrey and her guests would say. That ritual captivates Americans—twenty million strong, day in and day out—because nobody does "the talk show thing" better than Oprah.

As Randall Balmer has pointed out, we Americans can be described as "people who pick up a telephone rather than write a letter, who enjoy the static-borne banter of CB radios, who are addicted to talk of all kinds, including the prattle of commercials and talk shows on radio and television." It would be no exaggeration, he thinks, to call us "a nation of talkers." That perspective probably helps to account for the fact that ours is, as Balmer and others stress, "a media culture—more particularly, a television culture." [1]

If we love to hear ourselves talk, we Americans like to hear other people talk, too. We want to feel involved; we want to be part of the action in the give-and-take. More than that, we like to see who is saying what to whom. The appeal of the television talk show rests in part, then, on the fact that there is a visible, interacting audience. Although Oprah and her counterparts may be thousands of miles away, television can draw you close and make the whole scene seem as though it is happening right in your own living—or jury waiting—room.

A Talk Show Guest

For a week in the summer of 1993, Oprah varied the format of her immensely popular show. The guests were special people, she said, whom she had long wanted to interview face to face. Maya Angelou was among them. On Thursday, July 15, so was Elie Wiesel, the author of more than thirty books, winner of the 1986 Nobel Peace Prize, and a Jewish survivor of Auschwitz.[2]

Oprah wanted to interview Wiesel because she had been deeply moved by reading *Night,* Wiesel's classic memoir about the destruction of his family during Nazi Germany's Final Solution and his survival of Auschwitz and Buchenwald, where he endured the Holocaust from 1944 to 1945. Wiesel accepted Oprah's invitation. The setting for the interview was not, however, the usual television studio but Wiesel's apartment in New York City.

Oprah was not on her own turf in more ways than one. Perhaps the topics she needed to cover made her uncertain. How could they not? Maybe she was not quite sure how to approach a Holocaust survivor like Wiesel. How could she be? In any case, Oprah appeared less self-assured than usual. She seemed unable to draw Wiesel out as she might have thought she could. When, for example, she asked Wiesel to describe how he felt as he saw his mother forever separated from him at Auschwitz, Oprah received a look that she had not anticipated. Wiesel's silence spoke more than words could say.

A captivating storyteller, Wiesel is a charismatic orator and a spellbinding teacher as well. He asks questions as insightfully as he fields them. He talks in public, often about religion in one way or another. But he is not a garrulous man by any means. He respects language too much to waste words in chitchat and small talk. Often dwelling in the silences of memory and meditation, Wiesel seemed an incongruous talk show guest. Yet the reason for Wiesel's appearance on the Oprah Winfrey show was not incongruous at all. For decades—through books, conferences, public lectures, teaching, and humanitarian acts—Wiesel has tried to "tell the tale," as he puts it. Talking and acting in public, he bears witness for the dead and the living as he protests against the wasting of human life, particularly but not only during the Holocaust. He warns especially against the indifference that permits such evil, regarding that indifference as worse than evil itself. Haunted by the fact that humankind seems to have learned so little from the Holocaust, Wiesel refuses to give up despite having, as he told Oprah, "six million reasons" to do so. Instead he strives to expose the anatomy of hate and to give people the courage to care. "To be free is important," he told those who heard the Oprah Winfrey show. "To help others to be free," he explained further, "is even more important."

A conversation with Oprah Winfrey was another way to "tell the tale." Specifically, it was a way to reach a huge audience of daytime television viewers who might not otherwise listen to what Elie Wiesel hopes they will hear. Among that audience, in fact, there probably were people who contributed to a Roper organization poll, whose disturbing results were released by the American Jewish Committee (AJC) just three months earlier.[3] When the pollsters asked American adults, "Does it seem possible or does it seem impossible to you that the Nazi extermination of the Jews never happened?" one-third (34 percent) said either "it seems possible" (22 percent) or "don't know" (12 percent). For American high school students, the poll's results for the same question showed that more than one-third (37 percent) said either "it seems possible" (20 percent) or "don't know" (17 percent). Moreover, as confirmed by the filmed interview segments that Oprah used during her interview with Wiesel, large numbers of American high school students (39 percent, according to the Roper organization's findings) could not identify the historical event that is called the Holocaust. Apparently some of them (10 percent) had never even heard the word.

Although such skepticism and ignorance would be welcome news for the pseudohistorians who deny that the Holocaust happened, it is important to note that two subsequent polls discredited the initial results of the AJC/Roper inquiry. The wording of the original key question—"Does it seem possible or does it seem impossible to you that the Holocaust never happened?"—was less than crystal clear. When the Gallup organization conducted a subsequent poll in January 1994, it used clearer wording— "Do you doubt the Holocaust actually happened or not?"—and found that only 9 percent of the respondents expressed doubt about the Holocaust's happening. Two percent believed that the Holocaust definitely never happened. These results led the AJC to do another Roper survey, one that asked more clearly, "Does it seem possible to you that the Nazi extermination of the Jews never happened, or do you feel certain that it happened?" Analysis of responses to this second survey showed that only 1 percent of Americans believed it was possible that the Holocaust never happened.

An additional 8 percent indicated that they lacked enough knowledge to answer one way or the other.[4]

The follow-up poll results suggest that Holocaust education has had some success, but those findings were unknown when Elie Wiesel appeared on the Oprah Winfrey show. Rightly determined to prevent the manipulation and falsification of history, committed to overcoming ignorance about the Holocaust, "ethnic cleansing," and every other kind of suffering that people inflict on one another, Wiesel talked in public with Oprah, making use of the vast forum that only her show could provide.

Oprah and Wiesel talked about his experiences in "the kingdom of night," as he calls it, a creation that Nazi Germany produced alongside God's. It was hell. Perhaps it was even worse than hell if chaos rules there, said Wiesel, for in Auschwitz there was order. In that place and others like it at Treblinka, Majdanek, and Belzec, to name just a few, things happened as planned, and the plans called for suffering and death to continue until the Final Solution was complete.

As Oprah and Wiesel spoke, questions were raised about God and religion, too. What, she asked him, was the first thing you did after you were liberated? We prayed, Wiesel replied. The Jewish survivors said Kaddish, the prayer for the dead. They did so for the sake of the dead, and perhaps for God's sake as well, but most of all, Wiesel stressed, the survivors prayed to show themselves that they still could pray—that is, to show themselves that they were still fully human.

What about God? Oprah wanted to know. In Auschwitz, Wiesel told her, bread was more important than God. That statement did not mean, however, that God was unimportant. Rather it was a way of saying how much human life was reduced to the pain of an empty stomach. He had not rejected God in Auschwitz, Wiesel disclosed. His religious upbringing was too deep-seated for that. But he had rebelled against God, although most of his dissenting questions, including the anger and inability to understand God, became more focused and intense later on—partly because Wiesel was only fifteen when he arrived at Auschwitz. Laced with protest, his religious questions persist as Wiesel sustains his quarrel with God and with humankind as well.

Their conversation continued. Wiesel and Oprah talked about serious, horrible, and, at times, hopeful things. They did so with civility and respect. Oprah posed her questions and offered her own observations tentatively. Sometimes she struggled for the right words and, faltering, did not always find them. Other times, she sensed that her own experience was inadequate for penetrating Wiesel's world. For his part, Wiesel reassured Oprah by acknowledging the limitations of his own perspectives. He did not know well enough how to describe, let alone to understand, what he had experienced during the Holocaust and continued to experience after Auschwitz in memories, dreams, and reflections.

If the interview was not entirely successful—interrupted by commercials as it was—there were moments when two very different people communicated with each other, allowing their private needs and their public selves to mix and mingle in sensitive and thoughtful ways. In doing so, they reached millions of others who may have extended and elaborated the conversation across the land. Oprah discovered that she was born on the day Wiesel was liberated from Buchenwald. As she talked with him, it became apparent that her encounter with Wiesel affected how she thought of herself. Wiesel spoke of the gratitude that he and other survivors feel when people try to fathom what happened, and when they are moved to be more sensitive in spite or even because of the fact that full comprehension of the Holocaust eludes them.

By talking in public, Wiesel and Oprah touched others in ways that went far beyond the privacy of Wiesel's New York apartment. The next day, for instance, while browsing in a bookstore, I overheard a young woman asking a clerk if the store had any copies of Elie Wiesel's *Night*. The clerk looked and found one. We had quite a few yesterday, he told the woman, and now this is the last one. The day before, Oprah had told her viewers that they should all read *Night*. I am not sure, but I would bet that the young woman in the bookstore had been watching and listening carefully, too.

The Holocaust and the American Dream

At one point in their conversation, Oprah asked Wiesel about the U.S. Holocaust Memorial Museum, which millions of people have visited since it opened officially in Washington, D.C., on Thursday, April 22, 1993. A key leader in its development, Wiesel joined President Bill Clinton and others as featured speakers at the Museum's dedication. Why, Wiesel's remarks kept asking on that occasion, why did the world not do more to save the European Jews during the Holocaust, why didn't American forces seize the opportunities they had to bomb Auschwitz, and, he added, "why was man's silence matched by God's" during that dark chapter of human history? "There are no answers," Wiesel concluded. "This museum is not an answer. It is a question mark."[5]

Some Americans find the Holocaust Museum a question mark, but not in the way that Wiesel intended. Why, they ask, should Washington, D.C., and especially a place so near the "sacred ground" of our nation's capital, be the site for a museum dedicated to the Holocaust? Wasn't that event, after all, something that happened long ago and far away? Why should its gloom and doom shadow Washington's sanctuaries to American values, its temples to our highest ideals?

In the days before the Museum's dedication, Henry Allen, a writer for the *Washington Post,* prepared a story for his paper. It was about those questions. Gathering responses from around the country, he called to see how I would respond to them. Americans share a dream, I told him, and the Holocaust attacked it. The Final Solution's "self-evident truths" were not about rights to life, liberty, and the pursuit of happiness that belong to all human beings equally. Instead, they focused on *lebensunwertes Leben* ("lives unworthy of life") and sought to destroy them to ensure the racial purity of the Nazi state. Auschwitz and Treblinka: those death camps shadow American ground. They warn us never to take the American Dream for granted. Thus, I suggested to Henry Allen, it is altogether fitting that the U.S. Holocaust Memorial Museum has a prominent place in our nation's capital, adjoining the Washington Monument and the National Mall in Washington, D.C. For Elie Wiesel was right when he said: "If we stop remembering, we stop being."[6]

Remembering requires witnesses, just as witnesses remember. Thus, speaking in public, where no visitor should miss them, biblical words from the prophet Isaiah are inscribed on one of the Holocaust Museum's inside walls. "You," they say, "are my witnesses."[7] The museum takes that mandate seriously. Its mission is nothing less than to create witnesses — people informed to testify publicly against those who deny that the Holocaust happened, sensitized to tell about the genocidal implications of religious and racial hatred, and determined to use their information and sensitivity to mend a world that will be scarred forever by Auschwitz and Treblinka.

If the museum works, its desired effect will not occur merely because visitors spend a few hours there. Rather, that impact depends on whether those hours make us Americans, in particular, feel the need to study further, reflect more deeply, and intensify our feeling and determination to become better witnesses against Holocaust-related horrors and for the dream's best hopes. Movement in those directions needs to relate private needs and public selves by talking about religion in public. Wiesel's appearance on the Oprah Winfrey show made a contribution in that direction. So does the

U.S. Holocaust Memorial Museum. In their own ways, both are significant public expressions of religion.

Mending the World

Some additional reflection on Wiesel's ways of thinking can show further how our talking about religion in public might help to mend the world. To move in that direction, I need to speak in a personal way for a moment, drawing on one of Wiesel's early novels as I do so.

My reading of Elie Wiesel began in 1972 at about the time that my second child was born on the Fourth of July. Those coincidences would affect me in lasting ways. My daughter's birthday symbolized to me the fact that the quality of her life and that of our country's are directly related. In a variety of ways—small and large—that relationship conferred responsibilities upon me. In becoming a father in the early morning of July 4, 1972, I also became America's more concerned son. I continue to discover in new ways that the country belongs to me and I to it.

My wife and I named our daughter Sarah. In more ways than one, my entry into Sarah's world coincided with my entry into Elie Wiesel's. For in the latter, I would meet another Sarah, one whose part in *The Accident* led Wiesel to say, "Whoever listens to Sarah and doesn't change, whoever enters Sarah's world and doesn't invent new gods and new religions, deserves death and destruction."[8] Tensions created by the contrast between my joy as Sarah's father and the despair of "Sarah's world" portrayed in that early novel by Wiesel were among the catalysts that have compelled me to respond to his words by my own writing.[9]

The first essay I published in that vein was called "Tears and Elie Wiesel." It began with a reflection: "Lately something has been puzzling me. I do not think of myself as an emotional person, so why do I sometimes find myself about to weep? Nobody notices, but why is it that especially in church on Sunday mornings tears well up in my eyes?"[10]

That experience continues. It is one reason why I still go to church. In writing that initial article twenty-five years ago, I began to understand that my tears were partly a response to Elie Wiesel. Now that awareness is all the more poignant. It takes me back to Sarah's world and beyond. Here is how and why.

Speaking of *Night,* Wiesel has said that "all my subsequent books are built around it."[11] Spare and lean, it starts with a boy who "believed profoundly," but it ends with a reflection prompted by Wiesel's seeing himself in a mirror for the first time after his liberation from Buchenwald: "A corpse gazed back at me," he observed. "The look in his eyes, as they stared into mine, has never left me."[12] In *l'univers concentrationnaire,* as David Rousset, another Holocaust survivor, named it, assumptions treasured and persons loved were stripped away. But the dead left Wiesel to wonder and, thereby, to encounter the living.

That fate could hardly be a happy one. *The Accident* testifies to that. In this story, despite the fact that he has friends and a woman who loves him, Eliezer, another survivor, steps in front of a moving car in New York City. This "accident" is no accident, and so the victim's artist-friend Gyula, whose name means "redemption," has a formidable task as he urges Eliezer to choose life and to put the past behind him.

Part of Gyula's strategy is to paint Eliezer's portrait. Its eyes are searing, since "they belonged to a man who had seen God commit the most unforgivable crime: to kill without a reason." After showing Eliezer the portrait, Gyula symbolizes the end of the past by setting fire to the canvas. Eliezer is moved by Gyula's caring. He will not, indeed cannot, be fully healed by it, however, for the novel's final line states that Gyula departed and forgot "to take along the ashes."[13]

Included among the ashes are visions that Eliezer's eyes did not see directly—"Sarah's world," for example—but he has glimpsed more than enough of them as well. Though she is the namesake of the Jewish people's mother, Sarah knows too much has happened between their biblical genesis and their post-Holocaust survival. In *The Accident,* Sarah's world is that of a Paris prostitute. But as Eliezer relives his encounter with her, he and Sarah are taken back to an earlier time and place. Thus it becomes clear that the foundation of Sarah's world is a question: "Did you ever sleep with a twelve-year-old woman?"[14]

That question was asked and answered with a vengeance in special barracks of Nazi concentration camps, erected for the camp officers' diversion. The despair of Sarah's world intensifies that of Eliezer's even more when Sarah discloses that her purity as a victim is forever compromised. Sometimes, Sarah recalls, she felt pleasure in those barracks. She probably survived because of it.

Who created Sarah's world and the ones akin to it that have existed before and after? Religion and even God have much—too much—to do with that. Elie Wiesel never shies away from that insistence and its implications. Human beings have much—too much—to do with that, too. Wiesel never uses God's responsibility to excuse humankind. To the contrary, his insistence on human responsibility and its implications requires him to move from the general to the specific. Nazi perpetrators, bystanders (whose neutrality, indifference, and passivity aided the killers far more than the victims), even some of the victims themselves—all have a share of responsibility to bear. No apportioning of responsibility, however, can approach completeness without giving the Christian tradition and its adherents the attention they deserve. One way to put Elie Wiesel's point is to argue, as he has rightly done, that "there would have been no Auschwitz if the way had not been prepared by Christian theology."[15] Christianity was not a sufficient condition for the Holocaust, but it was a necessary one. Remove Christianity and Sarah's world would not have been.

What about the United States? Was there any fatal interdependence between its human actions and those of Sarah's world? The answer must be yes. Had America's analysis of the anatomy of hate been more profound, had our country's courage to care run deeper, Sarah's world could still have existed, but at least it might have been very different. While we rightly honor American sacrifices that stopped the Final Solution by bringing the Third Reich to its knees, we also need to debunk the deceptively comforting myth that the Holocaust was something that only happened "over there," far away from American fields of vision and influence. In ways that can catch us Americans off guard and unprepared to accept the disillusionment that truth can bring, historical documentation exists to show how American domestic, foreign, and at times even military policy tended to leave Jews in the lurch.[16] The Holocaust does not issue alarms from afar but warnings close to home. Not only did that disaster deny every good ideal that the American Dream holds dear, but its waste was also compounded because we Americans could have done much more than we did to help those who yearned so deeply to breathe free.

For me, Sarah's world is not only that of Elie Wiesel's Sarah in *The Accident* but also that of my daughter, Sarah, an American citizen and a baptized Christian. As her father, as one responsible for giving her the nationality we bear, as one responsible for initiating her into the Christian tradition we share, I want both that nationality and that tradition to be characterized less by any darkness they have produced and more by the light they can give. Hence, with the hope and confidence that there are others who will understand what I mean, I recall the way I concluded that meditation on tears with which my responses to Elie Wiesel began. "After reading Elie Wiesel," I wrote then and still feel now, "my faith may be less sure of itself, because no one can read his books without being shaken. On the other hand, I think my faith is also more passionate than before. I am grateful to him for moving me, for setting my soul on fire." [17]

When I say that Wiesel moves me and sets my soul on fire, one of the things I keep hearing him say is that the essence of being Jewish is "never to give up—never to yield to despair." [18] Being loyal in that way is anything but easy. Yet if one asks how Wiesel strives to keep his imperative, and then hears what he has to say, some key themes emerge. They can give us Americans firm places to "see it from" when we try to help each other to be free by sharing the memories and needs, hopes and dreams, that most deeply inform our worlds and identify ourselves.

Consider ten of his major insights—two sets of five that focus first on understanding and then on doing. Simple and yet complex, complex and yet simple, each point is central, I believe, to Wiesel's way of thinking and living. None of his insights is an abstract principle; all are forged in fire that threatens to consume. For those reasons, these themes from Wiesel have integrity, credibility, and durability to make them worthy guidelines that show how to talk about religion in public.

Understanding

Wiesel seeks understanding but not too much. Although wanting people to study the Holocaust, he alerts them to the dangers of thinking that they do or can or even should know everything about it. Although wanting people to meet as friends, he cautions that such meetings will be less than honest if differences—including differences of religious persuasion—are glossed over, minimized, or forgotten. Although wanting humankind and God to confront each other, he contends that easy acceptance is at once too much and too little to bear. Wiesel's understanding is neither facile, obvious, nor automatic. Nevertheless, its rhythm can be learned. Five of its movements follow. Each contains insight about how public religious discourse can best take place.

"*The Holocaust demands interrogation and calls everything into question. Traditional ideas and acquired values, philosophical systems and social theories—all must be revised in the shadow of Birkenau.*" [19] Birkenau was the killing center at Auschwitz, and the first lesson Wiesel teaches is that the Holocaust is an unrivaled measure because nothing exceeds its power to evoke the question Why? That authority puts everything else to the test.

Whatever religions, and reflections or criticisms of them, have existed, whatever dreams human minds have produced, they were either inadequate to prevent Auschwitz or, worse, they helped pave the way to that place. The Holocaust shows, therefore, that how we think and act needs revision in the face of those facts, unless one wishes to continue the same blindness that eventuated in the darkness of *Night*. At least in part, the Holocaust happened because there was too little public discussion and especially self-critical debate about religion, about the values it should honor, the lives it should defend, the powers it should resist. Among the powers that public religious discourse most needed to resist then—and still does now—were those that use political ideology, nationalism, racism, and even religion itself to divide people into "us" and "them" in ways that exclude "others," leave them vulnerable, and even target them for violence. Revised in the shadow of Birkenau, public religious discourse will emphasize the needs and concerns, hopes and dreams, that bind us together on common ground.

"The questions remain questions."[20] As the first lesson suggests, Elie Wiesel does not place his greatest confidence in answers. Answers—especially when they take the form of religious certainties and theoretical systems—make him suspicious. No matter how hard people try to resolve the most important issues, questions remain and rightly so. To encounter the Holocaust, to reckon with its disturbing whys—without which our humanity itself is called into question—that is enough to make Wiesel's case.

Typically, however, the human propensity—religion often reinforces it—is to quest for certainty. Wiesel's style of public religious discourse urges resistance against that temptation, especially when it aims to settle things that ought to remain unsettled and unsettling. For if answers aim to settle things, their ironic, even tragic, outcome is often that they produce disagreement, division, and death. Hence, Wiesel wants questions to be forever fundamental.

People are less likely to savage and annihilate each other when their minds are not made up but opened up through questioning. The history of religion confirms that claim. So does the Holocaust: Hitler and his Nazi followers "knew" they were "right." Their "knowing" made them killers. Questioning might have redeemed them and, more important, their victims.

Wiesel's point is not that responses to questions are simply wrong. They have their place; it can be essential, too. Nevertheless questions—especially religious ones that make us reconsider what is good, just, and true—deserve lasting priority because they invite continuing inquiry, further dialogue, shared wonder, and openness. Resisting final solutions, these ingredients can focus concern toward the common good in ways that answers alone rarely can.

"And yet—and yet. This is the key expression in my work."[21] Elie Wiesel's writings, emerging from intensity that is both the burden and the responsibility of Holocaust survivors, aim to put people off guard. Always suspicious of answers but never failing for questions, he lays out problems not for their own sake but to inquire, "What is the next step?" Reaching an apparent conclusion, he moves on because there is always more to consider, more to warrant our concern and care. Such forms of thought reject easy paths in favor of hard ones.

Wiesel's "and yet—and yet" affirms that it is more important to seek than to find, more important to question than to answer, more important to travel than to arrive. Just as it is dishonest not to focus our thinking as self-critically as we can, the point is also that it can be dangerous to believe what we want to believe, deceptive to find things too clear, destructive to cling too tightly to one religious tradition alone, divisive to interpret the American Dream in only one way, and dumbfounding to fail to talk about these matters in public. He cautions that it is insensitive to overlook that there is always more to experience than our theories admit, even though we can never begin to seek comprehension without reasoning and argument. So Elie Wiesel tells his stories, and even their endings resist fixed conclusions. Instead he wants his readers to feel his "and yet—and yet," which provides a hope that people may keep moving to choose life and not to end it.

"There is a link between language and life."[22] The Holocaust was physically brutal. That brutality's origins were partly in "paper violence," which is to say that they depended on words. Laws, decrees, orders, memoranda, even schedules for trains and specifications for gas vans and crematoriums—all of those Holocaust documents underwrite Wiesel's insistence that care must be taken with words, for words can kill.

Wiesel uses words differently. He speaks and writes to rediscover and recreate. His words, including the silences they contain, bring forgotten places and unremembered victims back to life just as they jar the living from complacency. Doing these things, he understands, requires turning language against itself. During the Nazi era language hid too much: Euphemisms masked reality to lull. Rhetoric projected illusions to captivate. Propaganda used lies to control. All of those efforts were hideously successful.

Language and life are linked in more ways than words can say. In our own day, claims abound concerning what the Bible says or does not say, what God requires or does not require, whether this form of religion is good or that one is not. After-Auschwitz priorities nonetheless enjoin that words—particularly those that express religion publicly—need to decode words. Speech must uncover what speech hides. Writing must rewrite and set right what has been written. The goal of such discourse is to keep inquiry going about our sense of the whole, what is taken to be sacred within it, and what is deserving of our deepest loyalty. Such inquiry cannot be done perfectly, once and for all, but the quality of American religious life depends on the quality of our trying. The task is ongoing, but only as it is going on will lives be linked so that "and yet—and yet" expresses hope more than despair.

"Rationalism is a failure and betrayal."[23] Although Elie Wiesel is hardly an enemy of reason and rationality, he does stand with those who believe that one of reason's most important functions is to assess its own limitations. And yet Wiesel's critique of reason is grounded not so much in theory as in practice, in history, and particularly in the Holocaust.

The Holocaust happened because human minds became convinced that they could figure everything out. Those minds "understood" that one religion had superseded another. They "knew" that one—and only one—political party's platform was right. They "comprehended" that one race was superior to every other. They "realized" who deserved to live and who deserved to die. One can argue, of course, that such views undermined rationality, perverted morality, and distorted religion. They did. And yet to say that much is too little, for one must ask about the sources of those outcomes. When that asking takes place, part of its trail leads to humankind's tendency, and by no means is religion above or beyond it, to presume that indeed we can, at least in principle, figure everything out.

With greater authority than any theory can muster, Auschwitz shows where such arrogance can lead. Wiesel's antidote is not irrationalism; his rejection of destructive madness testifies to that. What he seeks instead is the understanding that makes us and our public expressions of religion more human, not less so—understanding that includes tentativeness and awareness of our fallibility, comprehension that looks for error and revises judgment when error is found, realization that knowing is not a matter of fixed conviction but a question of learning through continuing dialogue.

Doing

Elie Wiesel's lessons about understanding urge one not to draw hasty or final conclusions. Rather, his emphasis is on exploration and study. It might be objected that such an outlook tends to encourage indecision and even indifference. On the contrary, however, one of Wiesel's most significant contributions runs in just the opposite direction. Thus, dialogue leads not to indecision but to an informed decisiveness. Tentativeness becomes protest when unjustified conviction asserts itself. Openness results not in indifference but in interdependence that helps all of us to be free. Wiesel's doing is demanding, but it, too, has a rhythm that can be learned. Here are five of its movements that help to show how public religious discourse can best be developed and focused.

"Passivity and indifference and neutrality always favor the killer, not the victim."[24] Elie Wiesel will never fully understand the world's killers. To do so would be to legitimate them by showing that they were part of a perfectly rational scheme. Though for very different reasons, he will not fully understand their victims, either; their silent screams call into question every account of their dying that presents itself as a final solution.

Wiesel insists that understanding should be no less elusive where indifference and its accomplices—passivity and neutrality—prevail. Too often, indifference exists among those who could make a difference, for it can characterize those who stand between killers and victims but aid the former against the latter by doing too little, too late. Where acting is concerned, nothing arouses Wiesel more than motivating the inactive.

Inactivity, indifference, passivity, neutrality—concerned about the places where they can lead, Wiesel's perspective suggests that where public religious discourse is at stake, those traits prevail at our peril. More openly and thoroughly than we do, Americans need to identify, share, and examine the stories and beliefs that define us. Especially where religion is concerned, we need to ask each other and ourselves what we feel and think and why we do so. Such inquiry can take place in so many places if we only let it unfold. In our homes, schools, colleges, universities, community centers, political gatherings, and religious meetings there is room—or should be—for such sharing. If we are passive or indifferent about bringing such discourse to life, we miss opportunities that are important for renewing American life.

"It is given to man to transform divine injustice into human justice and compassion."[25] Abraham and Isaac, Moses, and Job—these "messengers of God," as Wiesel calls them, understood that men and women abuse the freedom to choose that makes life human. They also wrestled with the fact that human existence neither accounts for nor completely sustains itself. Their dearly earned reckoning with that reality led them to a profound restiveness. It revealed, in turn, the awesome injunction that God intends for

humankind to have hard, even impossible, moral work until and through death.

One may not see life the way those biblical messengers saw it. Whatever one's choices in that regard, it is nevertheless as hard as it is inhuman to deny that injustice too often reigns divine and that moral work is given to us indeed. Elie Wiesel presumes neither to identify that work in detail for everyone nor to insist, in particular, where or how one should do it. Those issues, however, are the right ones to inform public expressions of religion, and he wants us to explore them. That exploration, he urges, is not likely to be done better than through Holocaust lenses. Enhancing vision sensitively, including our religious sensitivity and insight, they can help to focus every evil that should be transformed by human justice and compassion.

"If I still shout today, if I still scream, it is to prevent man from ultimately changing me." [26] Although "and yet—and yet" may be the key expression in Wiesel's writings, a close contender could be phrased "because of/in spite of." Here, too, the rhythm insists that, no matter where one dwells, there is and must be more to say and do. On this occasion, though, the context is more specific, for the place where "because of/in spite of" becomes crucial is the place where despair most threatens to win. So because of the odds in favor of despair and against hope, in spite of them, the insistence and need to rebel in favor of life are all the greater. And not to be moved by them is to hasten the end.

As the twenty-first century approaches, Americans can find plenty of reasons for despair about the quality of our nation's life. Our despair may even be deepened by the discovery that we do not even agree about what those reasons are. That outcome can make us wonder how public discourse about religion could mend American experience. Because of and in spite of those feelings, Wiesel's counsel suggests, the attempt can and should be made to turn despair against itself. Otherwise, despair's prophecy is self-fulfilling.

How Wiesel's logic works is reflected in a story that he often tells. A Just Man came to Sodom to save that ill-fated place from sin and destruction. A child, observing the Just Man's care, approached him compassionately:

"Poor stranger, you shout, you scream, don't you see that it is hopeless?"

"Yes, I see."

"Then why do you go on?"

"I'll tell you why. In the beginning, I thought I could change man. Today, I know I cannot. If I still shout today, if I still scream, it is to prevent man from ultimately changing me."

The Just Man's choice is one that others can make as well. Thus, a future still awaits our determination, especially if the rhythm "because of/in spite of" is understood and enacted in our public expressions of religion.

"As a Jew I abide by my tradition. And my tradition allows, and indeed commands, man to take the Almighty to task for what is being done to His people, to His children—and all men are His children—provided the questioner does so on behalf of His children, not against them, from within the community, from within the human condition, and not as an outsider." [27] Some of Elie Wiesel's most forceful writing involves the Jewish tradition known as Hasidism. [28] Many features impress him as he traces this movement from its flowering in the Jewish shtetls of eastern Europe during the eighteenth century, to its presence in the death camps, and to its continuing influence in a world that came close to annihilating Hasidic ways, root and branch. One of the rhythms of understanding and doing stressed by Wiesel derives, at least in part, from a Hasidic awareness of the relationships between "being for/being against."

Hasidism, in particular, combines a genuine awe of God with direct and emotional reactions toward God. It finds God eluding understanding but also as One to whom people can speak. The Hasidic masters argue with God, protest against God, fear, trust, and love God. All of this is done personally and passionately, without compromising God's majesty and beyond fear of contradiction. Levi-Yitzhak of Berditchev, for example, understood his role as that of attorney for the defense, reproaching God for harsh treatment the Jews received. Joining him was Rebbe Israel, Maggid of Kozhenitz, author of one of Wiesel's favorite Hasidic prayers: "Master of the Universe, know that the children of Israel are suffering too much; they deserve redemption, they need it. But if, for reasons unknown to me, You are not willing, not yet, then redeem all the other nations, but do it soon!" [29]

Nahman of Bratzlav holds another special place in Wiesel's heart. Laughter is Nahman's gift: "Laughter that springs from lucid and desperate awareness, a mirthless laughter, laughter of protest against the absurdities of existence, a laughter of revolt against a universe where man, whatever he may do, is condemned in advance. A laughter of compassion for man who cannot escape the ambiguity of his condition and of his faith." [30] And a final example, Menahem-Mendl of Kotzk, embodied a spirit whose intense despair yielded righteous anger and revolt so strong that it was said, "a God whose intentions he would understand could not suit him." [31] This rebel embraced life's contradictions both to destroy and to sustain them. Short of death, he found life without release from suffering. At the same time, he affirmed humanity as precious by living defiantly to the end. Wiesel implies, too, that Mendl hoped for something beyond death. His final words, Wiesel suggests, were: "At last I shall see Him face to face." Wiesel adds, "We don't know—nor will we ever know—whether these words expressed an ancient fear or a renewed defiance." [32]

Anything can be said and done, indeed everything *must* be said and done that is *for* men and women. Wiesel understands this to mean that a stance against God—against religion, too—is sometimes enjoined. But he hastens to add that such a stance needs to be from within a perspective that also affirms God and that respects the importance of religious traditions. Otherwise, we run the risk of being against humankind in other ways all over again. Those ways include succumbing to dehumanizing temptations which conclude that only human might makes right, that there is human history as we know it presently and nothing more, and that, as far as the Holocaust's victims are concerned, Hitler was victorious.

For/against: that rhythm involves taking stands. Spiritually, this means to be against God and against religion when "being for" would put one against humankind. Spiritually, this also means to be for God and for religion when "being against" would put one against humankind by siding with forces that tend, however inadvertently, to legitimate the wasting of human life. Elie Wiesel is fiercely humanistic. His humanism, however, remains tied to God and to religion, specifically to the Jewish traditions that inform his understanding and his refusal to understand both. The lesson here is that, without discussing, enlivening, and testing those ties in public, and in particular their ways of being for and against humankind, a critical resource for saving life and mending the world will be lost.

"By allowing me to enter his life, he gave meaning to mine." [33] Elie Wiesel's 1973 novel, *Le Serment de Kolvillàg* (*The Oath*), tells of a community that disappeared except for one surviving witness. It is a tale about that person's battle with a vow of silence. Azriel is his name, and Kolvillàg, his home in Eastern Europe, was destroyed in a twentieth-century pogrom prompted by the disappearance of a Christian boy. Ancient animosity renewed prejudice; prejudice produced rumor; rumor inflamed hate. Indicted falsely by the ancient, hateful accusation of ritual murder, Azriel and his fellow Jews were soon under threat.

Moshe, a strange, mystical member of the community, surrenders himself as the guilty party though no crime has been committed. But he does not satisfy the authorities and "Christians" of the town. Madness intensifies. The Jews begin to see that history will repeat, and they prepare for the worst. Some arm for violence; most gather strength quietly to wait and endure.

Permitted to speak to the Jews assembled in their ancient synagogue, Moshe envisions Kolvillàg's destruction. He knows the record of Jewish endurance, its long testimony against violence, but this seems to have done little to restrain men and women and even God from further vengeance. So Moshe persuades his people to try something different: "By ceasing to refer to the events of the present, we would forestall ordeals in the future."[34] The Jews of Kolvillàg become Jews of silence by taking his oath: "Those among us who will survive this present ordeal shall never reveal either in writing or by the word what we shall see, hear and endure before and during our torment!"[35]

Next comes bloodshed. Jewish spirits strain upward in smoke and fire. Only the young Azriel survives. He bears the chronicles of Kolvillàg—one created with his eyes, the other in a book entrusted to him for safekeeping by his father, the community's historian. Azriel bears the oath of Kolvillàg as well. Torn between speech and silence, he remains true to his promise.

Many years later, Azriel meets a young man who is about to kill himself in a desperate attempt to give his life significance by refusing to live it. Azriel decides to intervene, to find a way to make the waste of suicide impossible for his new friend. The way Azriel chooses entails breaking the oath. He shares the story of Kolvillàg in the hope that it will instill rebellion against despair, concern in the place of lethargy and indifference, life to counter death.

The oath of silence was intended to forestall ordeals in the future. Such forestalling, Wiesel testifies, must give silence its due; it must also break silence in favor of speech and action that recognize the interdependence of all human actions. "By allowing me to enter his life, he gave meaning to mine." Azriel's young friend echoes the insights that Elie Wiesel has shared with those who hear what he has to say. He also sums up the most valuable gain that could occur if we learned to talk well about religion in public: "By allowing me to enter his life, he gave meaning to mine." In its most basic meaning, this relationship is what public religious discourse in America is all about: revising, expanding, deepening the meanings of our American experience by entering each other's lives long enough to discover that our stories—very different though they may be—also convert our private needs into social relationships that give us yearnings, hopes, and dreams in common.

Giving Meaning to Our Lives

In October 1966, Wiesel began a series of public lectures at New York's Ninety-second Street Y, a prestigious Jewish cultural center. Each autumn since then, he has returned to that place where, among other things, he talks about religion in public. As he explores the many questions that his talks always raise, Wiesel's words are governed by themes that include the ten I have identified.

When Wiesel speaks at the Ninety-second Street Y, he focuses especially on biblical men and women, Talmudic interpreters and interpretations of biblical stories, and the masterful teachers of the Hasidic tradition that informs so decisively the Jewish perspective where he "sees it from." Finding them "close to us everywhere and always," he picks these subjects because they are "intriguing and demanding of investigation." [36] They have that quality because their stories are also ours. Just as the flaws and weaknesses of their characters can be seen in us today, so their hard-won wisdom and hard-earned dreams can produce insight for us now.

In 1991, Wiesel published a book called *Sages and Dreamers: Biblical, Talmudic, and Hasidic Portraits and Legends.* It presents twenty-five portraits, one from each of the annual series of lectures that Wiesel had given at the Ninety-second Street Y since 1966. The last chapter in the book is about "The Ostrowtzer Rabbi." It talks about a Hasidic dynasty that lasted for only two generations.

The dynasty's founder, Yehiel-Meir Halevy Helstock was born in Poland sometime in the early 1850s—the exact date is uncertain. His learning and powers of memory were awesome, his humility and compassion legendary, his desire to eliminate injustice and suffering impassioned. Rabbi Yehiel-Meir, says Wiesel, "ascribed all evil to come to the cardinal sin of gratuitous hatred." [37]

Again and again, Rabbi Yehiel-Meir returned to the biblical story of Joseph, who was victimized by his brothers' hate. In every way he knew, the Ostrowtzer rabbi encouraged people to stop hating each other. "Let us stop claiming that we alone are right, and all others are wrong," he implored. "Only then will redemption come." [38] Weakened by long years of fasting as well as by illness, Rabbi Yehiel-Meir died a few days after Purim, a joyous Jewish festival that celebrates redemption. But especially toward the end of his life, he had been increasingly tormented by nightmares.

The first Ostrowtzer rabbi had rejoiced when his people were happy.

"When they were sad," Wiesel adds, "he brought them consolation. He gave meaning to their lives."[39] The same might have been said of Rabbi Yehezkel, the son who succeeded him. He was known for his weeping. "When he prayed, when he delivered sermons, when he studied, people would see tears streaming down his face," Wiesel says of him. "He too saw the dark clouds covering Europe and he spoke about them."[40]

In the summer of 1942, the Germans liquidated most of the ghetto they had established in Ostrowtze. Along with a few hundred others, Rabbi Yehezkel and his immediate family remained alive for a time. By the end of year, however, the Germans had murdered them, too. The Ostrowtzer dynasty had come to an end.

The Ostrowtzer rabbis' yearning for things to change, for things to improve, was as intense as their dynasty was brief. Redemption eluded them, but their spiritual authority and Elie Wiesel's remains. Although the shadow of Birkenau cannot be removed from the earth, including American ground, its darkness may be lightened by talking about religion in public in ways that "stop claiming that we alone are right, and all others are wrong," by religious life that encourages us to "stop hating one another," and by public expressions of religion that drive home this truth: "To be free is important. To help others to be free is even more important."

NOTES

1. The quotations are from Randall Balmer, *Mine Eyes Have Seen the Glory: A Journey into the Evangelical Subculture in America,* expanded ed. (New York: Oxford University Press, 1993), 280. Balmer credits Harry Stout for the phrase "a nation of talkers."

2. For more about Elie Wiesel's life, see his autobiography, *All Rivers Run to the Sea: Memoirs* (New York: Alfred A. Knopf, 1995).

3. For the complete results of this poll, see Jennifer Golub and Renae Cohen, *What Do Americans Know about the Holocaust?* (New York: American Jewish Committee, 1993). The AJC commissioned the poll in late 1992. The findings were released in April 1993 to coincide with the fiftieth anniversary of the Warsaw ghetto uprising and the opening of the U.S. Holocaust Memorial Museum in Washington, D.C.

4. For information on these follow-up surveys, I am indebted to Lawrence Baron, "Holocaust Awareness and Denial in the United States: The Hype and the Hope," in *Lessons and Legacies III,* ed. Peter Hayes (Evanston: Northwestern University Press, 1997).

5. See Michael Ross, "Curtain Rises on a Museum of Bitter Lessons," *Los Angeles Times*, 23 Apr. 1993, A1, A17.

6. Elie Wiesel, "Let Him Remember," in *Against Silence: The Voice and Vision of Elie Wiesel*, 3 vols., ed. Irving Abrahamson (New York: Holocaust Library, 1985), 1:368.

7. The passage is from Isaiah 43:10.

8. Elie Wiesel, *The Accident*, trans. Anne Borchardt (New York: Avon Books, 1970), 96. This novel was published originally as *Le Jour* (Day) in 1961. The English translation appeared in 1962.

9. Five years later, in the spring of 1977, my acquaintance with Elie Wiesel deepened as I wrote *A Consuming Fire: Encounters with Elie Wiesel and the Holocaust* (Atlanta: John Knox, 1979). Although my friendship with this remarkable man means more to me than I can say, I have tried to respond to all of his books with published writing of my own. His prolific authorship makes that effort as daunting as it is rewarding.

10. John K. Roth, "Tears and Elie Wiesel," *Princeton Seminary Bulletin* 65 (Dec. 1972): 42.

11. Elie Wiesel, "Talking and Writing and Keeping Silent," in *Holocaust: Religious and Philosophical Implications*, ed. John K. Roth and Michael Berenbaum (New York: Paragon House, 1989), 362. This essay appeared originally in *The German Church Struggle and the Holocaust*, ed. Franklin H. Littell and Hubert G. Locke (Detroit: Wayne State University Press, 1974).

12. Elie Wiesel, *Night*, trans. Stella Rodway (New York: Bantam Books, 1986), 1, 109. This work was published originally as *La Nuit* in 1958. The English translation appeared in 1960. Earlier Wiesel published a Yiddish version of *Night*. Wiesel reduced its size for the French edition, which is about a hundred pages in print.

13. Wiesel, *Accident*, 123, 127.

14. Ibid., 97.

15. Elie Wiesel, "A Small Measure of Victory," in *Against Silence*, 3:224.

16. The U.S. Holocaust Memorial Museum carefully explores the multiple dimensions of interdependence between American policy and the destruction of the European Jews. Excellent books that address these issues include the following: Michael Berenbaum, *The World Must Know: The History of the Holocaust as Told in the United States Holocaust Memorial Museum*, with photographs edited by Arnold Kramer (Boston: Little, Brown, 1993); Deborah E. Lipstadt, *Beyond Belief: The American Press and the Coming of the Holocaust 1933-1945* (New York: Free Press, 1986); and David S. Wyman, *The Abandonment of the Jews: America and the Holocaust, 1941-1945* (New York: Pantheon Books, 1984).

17. Roth, "Tears and Elie Wiesel," 48.

18. Elie Wiesel, *A Jew Today*, trans. Marion Wiesel (New York: Random House, 1978), 164. This book was published originally as *Un juif aujourd'hui* in 1977.

19. This statement is from Elie Wiesel's foreword to Harry James Cargas, *Shadows of Auschwitz: A Christian Response to the Holocaust* (New York: Crossroad Publishing Company, 1990), ix. The emphasis is mine.

20. Elie Wiesel, "Telling the Tale," in *Against Silence*, 1:234. The emphasis is mine.

21. Elie Wiesel, "Exile and the Human Condition," in *Against Silence*, 1:183. The emphasis is mine.

22. Ibid., 1:182. The emphasis is mine.

23. Elie Wiesel, "The Use of Words and the Weight of Silence," in *Against Silence*, 2:79. The emphasis is mine.

24. Elie Wiesel, "Freedom of Conscience—A Jewish Commentary," in *Against Silence*, 1:210. The emphasis is mine.

25. Elie Wiesel, *Messengers of God: Biblical Portraits and Legends*, trans. Marion Wiesel (New York: Random House, 1976), 235. The emphasis is mine. This book was published originally as *Célébration biblique: Portraits et légendes* in 1975.

26. Elie Wiesel, *One Generation After*, trans. Lily Edelman and Elie Wiesel (New York: Avon Books, 1972), 95. The emphasis is mine. This book was published originally as *Entre deux soleils* in 1970. The English translation first appeared in that same year. See also Elie Wiesel, *The Testament*, trans. Marion Wiesel (New York: Summit Books, 1981), 9. This book was published originally as *Le Testament d'un poète juif assassiné* in 1980.

27. Elie Wiesel, "The Trial of Man," in *Against Silence*, 1:176. The emphasis is mine.

28. See, for example, *Souls on Fire: Portraits and Legends of Hasidic Masters*, trans. Marion Wiesel (New York: Random House, 1972), published originally as *Célébration hassidique: Portraits et légendes*, 1972; *Four Hasidic Masters and Their Struggle Against Melancholy* (Notre Dame, Ind.: University of Notre Dame Press, 1978); *Somewhere a Master: Further Hasidic Portraits and Legends*, trans. Marion Wiesel (New York: Summit Books, 1982), published originally as *Contre la mélancolie: Célébration hassidique II*, 1981; and *Sages and Dreamers: Biblical, Talmudic, and Hasidic Portraits and Legends*, trans. Marion Wiesel (New York: Summit Books, 1991).

29. Wiesel, *Souls on Fire*, 133.

30. Ibid., 198.

31. Ibid., 245.

32. Ibid., 254.

33. Elie Wiesel, *The Oath*, trans. Marion Wiesel (New York: Random House, 1973), 16. The emphasis is mine. This novel was published originally as *Le Serment de Kolvillàg* in 1973.

34. Ibid., 239.

35. Ibid., 241.

36. Wiesel, *Sages and Dreamers*, 13.
37. Ibid., 434.
38. Ibid., 434.
39. Ibid., 431.
40. Ibid., 438.

Deepening Talk about Religion

The River sang and sings on.
        —MAYA ANGELOU, *"On the Pulse of Morning"*

American life contains so much that can tempt, entangle, trap, corrupt, and ruin us. The key problem that Americans face as the twenty-first century approaches is how to live together in ways that help one another to be free. This book has argued that such concerns are either central to or at least never far removed from religious themes and contents. Thus, good talk about religion is an essential ingredient to meeting the most important challenge that American life poses.

As we Americans pass each other on the street, in our places of work and business, even in our homes, we do not know enough about what is most deeply on our minds and in our hearts. If we shared those thoughts and feelings more openly and honestly, we would be surprised, or at least instructed, because of the common ground we would discover. To find this common ground, we Americans would have to be as honest about our fears and prejudices as about our hopes and dreams. In doing so, however, we would rediscover that we live in the same country and that our destinies are related and interdependent. We would rediscover that we all need new beginnings in our lives from time to time, that we want our lives to matter, to make sense, and even to be created, as some traditions say, in the image of God. Drawing this book to a conclusion, its epilogue offers some recapitulating illustrations—stories new and old—to deepen talk about religion, which is work that we Americans need to do to keep our country alive and well.

Bible Stories

If the American Dream is about freedom and about freedom of choice in particular, then the Bible fits right in. At least it does when you consider that in English alone there are some four hundred and fifty versions from which Americans can choose in the late 1990s. Among the several publishing houses that compete for a share in the lucrative biblical marketplace, Thomas Nelson of Nashville, Tennessee, is the world's largest producer of Bibles. Combining translations, bindings, papers, print sizes, and "study helps" in multiple and imaginative ways, Nelson has printed more than a thousand editions of the Bible, a book that can be found in nine out of ten homes in the United States.

According to Gayle White, who writes occasional business reports for the Cox News Service, industry figures peg the average number of Bibles per American household at four.[1] In addition to the old King James version, which is still quite popular, the Bibles bought by Americans reflect consumer interests as well as market niches nurtured and filled by publishers. "Study Bibles," as they are called, are increasingly preferred. They often contain maps, charts, and explanations that interpret the biblical texts. Nelson's recent *Word in Life Study Bible*—"fresh as your morning newspaper," said the advertising that promotes it—features page designs that mimic *USA Today*.

Women buy most of the Bibles sold in the United States. So there are editions designed especially for working women, or for mothers who stay at home, or for those who are pregnant. A special Bible for men matched the *Women's Devotional Bible* that has been marketed successfully since its appearance early in the 1990s, but even promotions for the *Men's Devotional Bible* have been pitched to women, the assumption being that they will buy it for their men.

Gimmicks do not always generate steady biblical sales. So it is unclear whether the rhyming New Testament will be around for long. Much more important and deserving of attention is the American Bible Society's 1995 Contemporary English Version of the Bible. Ten years in the making, the CEV features a New Testament translation—which first appeared in 1991—that remains faithful to the original texts and eliminates anti-Jewish phrasing that has intensified antisemitism for centuries. Its first press run was one million copies.

Do not look for biblical variety or sales to dwindle anytime soon. As much as the market will bear, there is likely to be a special version of the Bible for most of our private needs and public selves. Americans from different ethnic groups and those who speak languages other than English —along with athletes, environmentalists, overworked executives, and recovering addicts of one kind or another—to say nothing of people with particular denominational affiliations, are just a few of the many distinctive audiences that publishers and retailers hope their Bibles will attract. More Bibles are being purchased in the United States than ever before. With sales topping $400 million per year, this big and serious business is an immense public expression of religion.

If the publishing and selling of Bibles in the United States is big and serious business, how about reading of the Bible, hearing and heeding what it has to say? A book bought is not the same as a book read, a rule that makes no exception for scripture. When Elie Wiesel lectures about Ruth and Solomon, Daniel and Esther, at the Ninety-second Street Y in New York City, perhaps he can assume that his audience knows the outlines, if not the details, of the biblical narratives about those fascinating characters. But he probably does not assume too much in that regard, for if his teaching experiences are like mine, one cannot take for granted that biblical stories are nearly as well known as our American buying and selling of Bibles suggests. That is why Wiesel tells and retells his biblical stories in public. Shared in that way, those narratives can inform our discourse in ways that enlighten our lives.

With that possibility in mind, consider that the Bible is haunted by waters. For example, the story in Genesis tells us that creation began with God's spirit moving over the face of the waters. Day and night, sky and earth, rocks and trees, men and women—all that we see, and every place we "see it from," has sources in the deep. When God planted a garden in Eden, a river was provided to water it.[2] For biblical narrators, who lived in parched places and dry times, that detail could not be overlooked.

Later, when Moses led his people out of their Egyptian bondage, the sea almost thwarted the Exodus. But the waters parted and the Israelites got through.[3] Soon enough, however, Moses found his followers turning against him because they were nearly dying of thirst in the Sinai's desert. Strike the rock at Horeb, God told him, and water will come out of it, so that the people may drink.[4] Later still, and perhaps with Horeb's spring in mind, the prophet Amos—a shepherd, he knew the value of water—provided a well-remembered image when he urged his people to "let justice roll down like waters, and righteousness like an ever flowing stream." [5] And when Isaiah spoke of the word of God, contending that it does not return to God empty, the prophet compared that word to the rain and snow that "come down from heaven, and do not return there until they have watered the earth, making it bring forth and sprout, giving seed to the sower and bread to the eater." [6]

All four of the New Testament's gospels about the life of Jesus emphasize that he was baptized in the River Jordan, an act whose symbolic repetition even now uses water to identify a person as one of his followers. Wells were often the meeting places where Jesus talked to people. When he wanted to illustrate how people should treat one another, he frequently emphasized the importance of simple but vital acts—like quenching someone's thirst with a cup of water. Many New Testament stories locate Jesus around the Sea of Galilee. Its shores and currents provided some of the key places where he "saw it from." The New Testament's stories indicate that Jesus taught people by the sea, encouraged them, and fed them when a boy brought him fish and bread. The sharing made the feeding possible. In the same vicinity, he strengthened and cared for his disciples, among them James and John, Peter and Andrew—fishermen who made their living from the sea. At his last supper with them, not long before Roman power crucified him in Jerusalem, Jesus poured water into a basin and washed their feet.

Seeing those waters from the perspectives of Easter, the closing chapters of Revelation, the New Testament's final book, map a mural. From the throne of God, who is "the Alpha and the Omega, the first and the last, the beginning and the end," there flows "the river of the water of life." On both sides of that river stands the tree of life, its leaves for "the healing of the nations." God, who is "making all things new," promises to give water to the thirsty as "a gift from the spring of the water of life." As that happens, "death will be no more; mourning and crying and pain will be no more, for the first things have passed away." [7]

Things have been passing away for a long time. Water has been one reason why. Although life cannot exist without it, water also has destructive power. According to biblical narratives, for example, well before the introduction of Moses, Amos, or Jesus, let alone American life in the late twentieth century, human history nearly ended when the whole earth was engulfed by a flood. The story in Genesis is awesome and somber, if not a cause for protest and resistance. Creation, even with all its beauty and grandeur, was to be wiped out. But why?

Genesis says that "the earth was corrupt in God's sight, and the earth was filled with violence." As Elie Wiesel suggests, when the biblical text speaks of corruption, the word refers to more than a scandal here or a cover-up there.[8] Thoroughgoing disdain for the well-being of creation, and especially disrespect that breeds hatred among people, is where the emphasis falls. In ten generations things had passed from order to chaos. From God's perspective, humankind had betrayed God's trust and shown itself unworthy of God's kindness. Indeed, God found the wickedness of humankind so deep that creation—at least the part involving humankind—seemed a tragic mistake. Having seen too much, God thought humankind was beyond redemption. So, one disaster called for another. The world would drown in a "flood of waters."[9]

Was there nothing to reverse God's decision? Sometimes the Bible suggests that God's judgments are subject to change and self-correction. Genesis even indicates that on this occasion God's judgment was self-corrective more than once. Having decided to wipe out humankind because the original decision to create humanity had been a mistake, God could not do it, at least not completely, because "Noah found favor in the sight of the Lord."

Who was Noah? Even if nine out of ten of our American homes possess a Bible, even if the average number of Bibles per American household is four, most of us would have difficulty answering that question in detail. Still, the story of Noah and the ark is part of a memory widely, if dimly, shared in American experience. The reason? Noah was haunted by waters as no one else has been before or since.

Significantly, when Elie Wiesel published a selection of his lectures from the annual series at the Ninety-second Street Y, that public expression of religion began with Noah. As Wiesel pointed out, Genesis says simply that Noah was "a righteous man, blameless in his generation." He "walked with God," the biblical account continues, and the result was that he was entrusted with unprecedented work.

The Bible states that Noah "did all that God commanded him." God's command directed Noah to build an ark to withstand the coming flood. The design had to be precise, the measurements exact, the materials flawless, the construction perfect, the project completed on time. Building the ark, however, was only the beginning. Noah's task—apparently he alone was found trustworthy to do it—entailed ensuring that the ark would contain at least two of every living thing. Those creatures would join Noah and his immediate family to provide a new beginning. After forty days and nights of rain, after a deluge that would purge the earth, that new beginning might yet make good God's creative dreams.

Noah pleased God. We are in his debt as well as in God's, for without Noah, everything in creation might have been lost. But what about God? Did God please Noah? How well did God's plan turn out?

Water covered the earth. But as God had promised, the waters eventually subsided. Noah survived, and, after the ark was emptied, he built an altar and made an offering. Strangely, however, the Bible does not say how Noah felt. Indeed, the storytellers put hardly any words into his mouth. God is constantly telling Noah what to do, but there is no dialogue. A man of few words and very few questions, Noah simply does what God commands.

Could Noah have been happy after the flood was over? Perhaps he was relieved, afraid of what might happen next, thankful, all of those emotions and more. But in spite or even because of his silence, it is hard to see Noah as fully human without his wondering uneasily about the catastrophe—about the God as well as the corruption—that had left him, in his own way, a victim along with everyone else who had been swept away.

Was it so obvious that Noah was the one who should have been spared? Was it so obvious that everyone else should have been doomed? Was it so obvious that God had done the right thing? Questions were not Noah's strongest suit. He was more practical than philosophical. His feelings—whatever they were—turned him to work. Far from being interested in any more sailing, to say nothing of a maritime career, he became, the biblical story says, "a man of the soil."

A vineyard was the first thing Noah planted. When the first wine was made, maybe those unanswered, and even unanswerable, questions were raised by Noah after all. In any case, Noah wasted no time: he got drunk. Meanwhile, God vowed "never again." No more would God visit such devastation on the earth. From time to time, rainbows in the sky are intended to be reminders of that promise.

The new beginning did not last. Having started so tragically, so violently, how could it? Perhaps even God was not surprised. One strand of the Genesis story—it is barely alluded to, perhaps because it is so ominous—contains a disturbing subtext. It hints that God vowed never again to "destroy every living creature as I have done" in spite or even because of awareness that humankind, having been created by God and in God's own image, possessed a heart whose inclinations would never be entirely free of evil. The prospect with which the biblical story of Noah leaves us, then, is not for perpetual peace and prosperity, let alone perfection and utopia. As long as men and women inhabit the earth, creation will be in need of mending—so much so that even Noah scarcely could have guessed how much humankind would need consolation and promise, which are the meanings of his name.

American Stories

If the Bible is haunted by waters, from time to time American life has been, too. Most of us do not need to count back even ten generations before there are ocean-spanning or river-crossing journeys in our histories. Sometimes voluntary, often not, those passages severed human ties for the sake of new beginnings, some of them religiously inspired. For a time, the oceans isolated the country and gave it protection. But we are a seafaring people, too, and increasingly our economic future hinges on interdependence that navigation of the world's oceans makes both possible and necessary.

We have moved beyond the days when exploration and settlement of the country's interior required transportation that depended on rivers, lakes, and canals. Yet the nation's commerce, especially the well-being of many of our major cities—Chicago and Detroit, Pittsburgh and Cincinnati, Minneapolis and St. Paul, St. Louis and New Orleans, to name a few—still relies on those waterways. Elsewhere, particularly in the vast expanses of the American West where the land is dry, the rainfall scant, and, as Wallace Stegner says, "green [ceases] to be the prevailing color of the earth," we are haunted by waters because of the threats posed by their absence.[10] Thus, in the winter of 1992–93, Americans who lived there welcomed long-awaited rain that made the desert a blooming spectacle and colored the mountains so deeply white with an abundant snowfall that serious droughts in states such as California could be announced officially at an end, if only for a time. Not a few Americans gave thanks religiously for that abundance, for neither our private needs nor our public selves control season and climate, and from time to time those same needs and selves break through the charade of our self-sufficiency to reveal how utterly dependent we are on natural conditions that are not accountable to our wishes.

Four winters later, floods deluged much of northern California and the Pacific Northwest, a condition that also devastated the nation's midwestern heartland in both 1993 and 1997. Although the Great Flood of '93, as it came to be called, fell short of the epic one that Noah survived, it still took a huge toll: It claimed more than forty lives, left 30,000 to 40,000 people homeless in eight midwestern states, and disrupted the lives of hun-

dreds of thousands more. Conservative estimates placed the damage costs
at $10 billion, a severe blow to the American economy at the time, which
was struggling to recover from deficits and debts and the ravages of a recession in which it had been mired. But there were no numbers, however
large, to sum up the suffering of individuals and the anxious uncertainty
of communities whose hopes and dreams were swamped by waters that
rose, broke through levees and lines of sandbags, and then stayed high, on
and on.

At the time, residents of Des Moines, Iowa, or St. Joseph, Missouri,
could have identified with the lyric's irony if their country-western disc
jockeys had played the song that laments how sometimes "parched we
stand knee-deep in a river dying of thirst." But the reasons they could do
so had nothing whatsoever to do with drought. They involved conditions
all too reminiscent of Noah's story. For the water treatment plants in those
towns were shut down for days by the most destructive flood in recorded
memory to sweep beyond the banks of the Missouri and Mississippi rivers
and their tributaries.

If some of the flood reports were infused with irony, others took
on nearly apocalyptic dimensions. Just before 10:00 A.M. on Thursday,
July 22, the bell in a 300-year-old Catholic church warned that the end was
at hand for the historic community of Kaskaskia Island.[11] The island had
been formed in 1881, when the Mississippi's course suddenly switched to
the east during another flood. Earlier in the nineteenth century, Kaskaskia
had been the territorial capital of Illinois, and the original settlement of the
place dated back to time before the American Revolution. French exploration of the Mississippi had led to the establishment of a fort at Kaskaskia.
In 1741 the king of France recognized the residents' bravery by giving the
community a 650-pound bronze bell. Not long thereafter, its ringing would
celebrate American independence and nationhood.

Two centuries later, the courage of Kaskaskia's residents was never in
doubt, but even their valiant efforts were not enough to shore up the fifty-
foot-high levee that had kept the Great Flood of '93 at bay for days. The
mighty Mississippi was not to be denied. When a sixty-foot section of the
Kaskaskia Island levee burst at midmorning on that Thursday in July, those
who remained among the community's 150 residents had to flee for their
lives as the flood waters submerged not only their homes and the last rem-
nants of the old French fort but the island's entire 15,000 acres as well. In
a scene reminiscent of Noah's story, Kaskaskia's refugees, along with the

animals they had saved, waited for rescue on the little dry land that remained atop the levee that had failed to hold.

When a breach in the fifty-two-mile-long levee near Hull, Illinois, inundated 45,000 acres of prime farmland in that region, levee workers climbed trees to save their lives only to find that snakes had gotten there first. It took helicopters to rescue those men from double jeopardy. "It will stop raining," the Rev. Jesse Jackson was quoted as saying at a small Baptist church in St. Louis on Sunday, July 25. "It's time for the rainbow." [12] True enough on both counts, and yet the next day's radio news reports announced that more rain was forecast for midwestern cities, towns, and farms that had already been declared disaster areas weeks before.

Meanwhile there were those who believed that the flood happened, as one homemaker fathomed it, "because God wanted it." [13] Some of the "flood theology" was even more explicit. According to one person who spoke on KMOX's popular afternoon call-in show in St. Louis, the deluge was God's judgment against the river boat gambling that many riverfront towns have banked on to bolster their sagging economies. [14]

Those reports, however, seemed to be exceptions that proved a rule of a different kind, for although some Americans may have seen human shortsightedness or even folly—through bad land management, for example, or insufficient flood control strategies—as contributing to the flood, relatively few turned to divine intention, to say nothing of God's wrath, for an "explanation" of the flood's fury. Still, as revealed in stories that deserve to be more widely known than they will ever be, the human responses to the Great Flood of '93 were, among other things, a vast public expression of religion.

One evening that July, for example, the television news focused on a midwestern community's sand-bagging effort to save its church. Later in the month, an Associated Press photographer found Randolph, Illinois, county sheriff Ben Picou and another helper waist-deep in water that had filled the old Catholic church on Kaskaskia Island. They were pictured risking their lives to save the sacred symbols of a community: a priest's robes and a crucifix. [15]

No one will ever be able to count how many prayers were said, how many religious services were held (many, no doubt, with Noah in mind), in the teeth of the flood. No one will ever be able to count the questions—often provoked by religious yearning or protest—that the flood raised, either. But perhaps even more incalculable are the acts of relief, help, and healing that poured out from ordinary American people who did the right things, the good things, during the disaster. They were epitomized by people in Des Moines. Having been helped when the surging Raccoon River left them without running water, they made a point of sending water supplies to St. Joseph, Missouri, as that city suffered the same fate when the Missouri River crested there.

Even while Congressional gridlock delayed flood relief that the government needed to deliver swiftly, individuals and groups from all around the country, but especially in the Midwest, rallied to meet basic human needs. Hard to measure and quantify though they would be, surely many of those helping hands embodied, at least in part, expressions of religious conviction.

With the flood still raging, President Bill Clinton spoke to the ninety-six young men who had gathered in Washington, D.C., for the annual meeting of Boys Nation. At the same meeting thirty years before, Bill Clinton, a delegate from Hope, Arkansas, had met President John F. Kennedy. Their handshake made him think deeply about public service and even about the presidency. "Until the American people can overcome their cynicism," President Clinton told the next generation at Boys Nation, "it is going to be very difficult for us to solve the problems of this country." [16] The President's point was well taken, but it needed to be supplemented by the stories he had seen and heard only a few days before when he visited with victims of the Great Flood of '93.

In the Midwest, President Clinton—like Americans all around the country—had witnessed a vast outpouring of relief. It was governed not by selfishness but by awareness that life, especially its hopes and dreams, is shared. It was motivated primarily not by "what's in it for me," but by "how can I help them?" Cynicism did not seem to be much in evidence there. Grief—of course. Discouragement—obviously. Frustration—certainly. Opportunism—sometimes. But cynicism?—no. Haunted by waters, Americans rallied to deal with their problems in ways that displayed courage and conviction capable of overcoming cynicism and much, much more. Americans did so because "at the end of every hard earned day," as Bruce Springsteen sings in "Nebraska," his 1982 album, "people find some reason to believe."

Springsteen's "Reason to Believe" speaks about people gathered together for baptism in a river, for a wedding by the riverside. At the end of every hard earned day during the Great Flood of '93, the reasons to believe were not just me, myself, and I. Certainly they were not a matter of self-reliance alone, either. The flood was too big, too much, for that. Its haunting waters drove home the point that our reasons to believe must include you, them, and us, or those reasons will be too frail, too insignificant to withstand their being washed away.

Reasons to Believe

Lasting, durable reasons to believe are social. Although they are expressed through individual lives, their transcendent meanings are greater than the lives of individuals because social life inherently contains normative, moral expectations. Moreover, a society's moral order, as sociologist Émile Durkheim said, "abounds in the religious."[17] Especially in American life, the moral order cannot be divorced from religion's public presence.[18]

It was no coincidence that Noah built an altar at the end of the biblical flood. Likewise, in the wake of the Flood of '93, important public expressions of religion and significant talk about religion in public could be found. Thus, as we engage in what Durkheim called "remaking," which includes the slow cleanup after the waters of crisis recede and the adrenaline of cooperation is likely to flow less freely, we Americans should hope that our responses to the needs of American life will continue to include what Durkheim identified as religiously motivated "reunions, assemblies and meetings where the individuals, being closely united to one another, reaffirm in common their common sentiments."[19] Otherwise we will be needlessly bereft of hope we need to give one another.

One way to think further about such possibilities involves another occasion when, not literally but symbolically, the nation was haunted by waters: President Clinton's first inaugural, which took place on January 20, 1993. In Washington, D.C., the day was clear and bright. For many Americans, hopes were high. Midwestern farmers looked forward to a productive year, not suspecting that a summer flood would wash it away. Thirty years earlier, John F. Kennedy had invited a poet, Robert Frost, to favor his inaugural with verse. Bill Clinton revived the practice. What he said on that 1993 inauguration day has been forgotten by most of us, but the voice and words of the poet, Maya Angelou, are better remembered. "On the Pulse of Morning," she called the poem written for that civic-religious occasion when a newly elected president takes the constitutionally prescribed oath of office—with a hand on the Bible and a "so help me God"—to "preserve, protect, and defend the Constitution of the United States."

"A Rock, a River, a Tree," Angelou's poem began. Drawing on the rich religious tradition of the spiritual songs from which she took those images, her words had much for the nation to hear. As Angelou filled their voices, the Tree spoke, the Rock cried out, and "the River sang and sings on." [20] Their message saw things from perspectives that are awesome—realistic and yet hopeful, encouraging though somber, beautiful in spite of tragedy, painfully and therefore redemptively honest: "History, despite its wrenching pain, / Cannot be unlived, but if faced / With courage, need not be lived again."

In the poet's voice the breaking of hearts could be heard, but also the breaking of the day. No day's beginning could be perfectly new, but in the sense of trying again, sticking at it, refusing to give up, each morning does bring a chance to begin again. Through the poet's voice, the Rock, the Tree, and the River that are our country appealed to us to "Give birth again / To the dream." They urged us to mold it, and to let it mold us, into the shape of our most private needs. They encouraged us to sculpt it, and to let it sculpt us, into the image of our most public selves. If that can happen, Maya Angelou's poem—an expression of religion as public as it was profound—affirmed that we Americans could find the grace to look each other in the face "And say simply / Very simply / With hope— / Good morning."

What Do We Owe One Another?

There are signs that such grace will be much needed as American life moves into the twenty-first century. Many of those signs are economic, and we can locate them by noting that soon after his 1993 inauguration, President Clinton nominated his Rhodes Scholar friend, Robert B. Reich, to be secretary of labor. A political economist from Harvard, Reich is an insightful writer whose books include *The Work of Nations*. Although it says little explicitly about religion, few books cry out more forcefully about the importance of talking about religion in public in the 1990s. Here is why.

In *The Work of Nations,* Reich fears that Americans will be trapped by what he calls "vestigial thinking." One key facet of such thought is the belief that economies are national entities. Another is the adage that a rising tide raises all arks, as Noah might have paraphrased the maxim. According to Reich, those ways of thinking are dangerously out of touch with reality, because "national borders no longer define our economic fates. We are now in different boats, one sinking rapidly, one sinking more slowly, and the third rising steadily." [21]

In the early years after World War II, the American economy ruled the roost, and the American people tended—not perfectly, but generally—to prosper together as our corporations grew and the nation's wealth advanced apace. The rest of the world, however, was not standing idly by. Nor, by any means, were American economic interests governed entirely by perspectives that ignored opportunities overseas. Within a few decades, before most of us knew what it meant, the American economy was so interlocked and interdependent with global forces that the label "Made in the U.S.A." applied less and less literally to more and more firms, products, and the labor that designed, engineered, and manufactured them.

These developments affected the American workforce, and especially relationships among its various sectors. As we entered increasingly into the age of computerized high technology, Americans were also increasingly divided in Reich's different economic boats, even if they did not fully realize that fact and its consequences.

According to Reich, those boats are basically three in number (174). The first contains people who perform what Reich calls "routine production services." Akin to work on factory assembly lines, these jobs are destined to be as low-paying as they are repetitive, partly because they can usually be done anywhere in the world for the relatively low costs that a labor pool composed of surplus people can provide.

A second boat includes those who provide "in-person services." Their work does require being situated locally—the plumbing at my house, for example, can only be conveniently repaired in Claremont, California. Unlike the workers in routine production services, moreover, the need for personal services may be growing while the number of workers needed for routine production work is in decline. But that scenario does not leave an especially bright outlook for in-person service workers. As people flood into those careers—how many nail-care salons or tattoo parlors does the nation need?—the opportunities for financial gain are compromised.

Only for the third group, those who offer "symbolic-analytic services," does the economic future remain truly exciting. Yet here is one part of the rub as far as we Americans are concerned. These folks—adept at identifying and solving the problems of the modern, computerized economy because they are trained to think abstractly, to experiment, to collaborate, and to broker talent and expertise—can also be found all around the world. The United States may have had a temporary corner on this part of the market, but American hegemony in this area is by no means assured. Even if it were, the segregation of workers into three categories finds Americans moving in directions that will keep widening the gap between the richer and the poorer among us. More than that, we can no longer assume, as we were long able to do, that Americans have economic interests sufficiently in common to give us the grace to look into each other's eyes and, as Maya Angelou put it, say "Very simply / With hope— / Good morning."

Reich is troubled by the map of our country that results when he asks himself where he "sees it from" and sketches the mural that responds. Loyalties to places and traditions, persons and communities, were once meshed tightly with economic self-interest. But to assume that we still inhabit a world like that would be vestigial thinking with a vengeance. The Great Flood of '93 may have brought us together for a time, but what happens when the waters no longer haunt us quite so much? What happens when we return not to business "as usual" but to business whose international stress and strain will question, in Reich's words, "whether the habits of citizenship are sufficiently strong to withstand the centrifugal forces of the new global economy" (304).

"What do we owe one another," wonders Reich, "as members of the same society who no longer inhabit the same economy?" (303). That question is serious in a nation where, from January 1993 to December 1995, some 3.8 million workers lost a job they had held for three years or more, most of these losses occurring because of corporate restructuring and downsizing; where the buying power of middle-class American wages has been stagnant for a decade; where 20 percent of American children under the age of eighteen live below the poverty line.[22] A few more facts indicate why Reich's query is crucial: Nearly 40 percent of the nation's wealth belongs to 1 percent of the people. The pay ratio of chief executives to average workers in large American corporations has gone from 41-to-1 in the mid-1970s to 187-to-1 in the mid-1990s. The household incomes of those in the bottom 40 percent of the American economy have slipped over the past twenty years—when adjusted for inflation—while the nation's income growth has primarily benefited households in the top 20 percent. As the twenty-first century approaches, no political issue in the United States will be more central than the growing inequality between the haves, the have-nots, and those in the middle who feel they are on a treadmill that makes them run faster and faster just to stay in place.

Bill Posey, a member of the Florida House of Representatives, summed up his view of the American economic situation by trenchantly observing, "Unless people are independently wealthy, they're going to work, they're going on welfare, or they're going to steal."[23] Any society—and Americans are not exceptional in this regard—will be flooded by chaos unless, in

Durkheim's words, it finds ways of "upholding and reaffirming at regular intervals the collective sentiments and the collective ideas which make its unity and its personality."[24]

What do we Americans owe one another? Reich ponders whether we have the will to answer his question well. He makes the conventional appeals that we need better education, deeper devotion to citizenship, improved moral sensitivity, and greater awareness that our humanity is shared with others. Reich does not speak explicitly about religion, but at least indirectly he calls attention to its importance. "Without a real political community in which to learn, refine, and practice the ideals of justice and fairness," Reich contends, we "may find these ideals to be meaningless abstractions" (309). Americans are unlikely to have the kind of political community that Reich rightly thinks we need unless we learn to do a better job of talking about religion in public.

One obstacle in achieving that goal might be that we Americans just do not have time to think and talk about religion's public significance because we are flooded by work, a consideration that leads to *The Overworked American*. Authored by another Harvard economist, Juliet B. Schor, this study shows that leisure time is unexpectedly in decline for many Americans despite the fact that more than 40 percent of Americans affirm that the main purpose of work is to make leisure possible.[25] Computers, the Internet, the World Wide Web, cellular phones, fax and copy machines—far from creating more time, modern capitalism's latest technology has actually intensified the demands of the workplace. That technology creates an expectation as tempting as it is deceptive, namely, that one can and must work faster and thereby accomplish more. A common result, however, is too many commitments and too little time to fulfill them.

To understand this counterintuitive outcome, Schor explores economic history, current labor practices, and conflicting senses of expectation. Her book criticizes capitalism from within. It also concludes with modest notes of hope. Running breathlessly on a treadmill of work-and-spend, we Americans have imprisoned ourselves in what Schor calls a "squirrel cage." Nevertheless, she says, the treadmill can be slowed; an exit from the cage may be found.

Schor faced many problems in writing this book. Not the least of them was that its topic, and certainly its title, might seem out of place in the 1990s. A book about the underworked if not the unemployed American might have seemed more timely. When Schor's book appeared in the early 1990s, everyday news included mounting layoffs and stubborn unemployment statistics. Even if those statistics have improved later in the decade, Schor's contention is still apt when she argues that overwork for some and too little work or none at all for others remain key pieces in our economic puzzle.

The guiding principle of a capitalist system such as ours, argues Schor, is not primarily employment but profitability. Profitability may result in high employment rates; but when that relationship does hold, we have a happy coincidence more than a necessary condition. Particularly during the last twenty-five years, mergers and takeovers, market uncertainties, and increasing pressures from foreign competitors have intensified cost-cutting measures. Instead of adding to the wage and benefit bill that the hiring of new personnel entails, American enterprise has restructured, frequently "downsized," and then expected more and more from its existing workforce. In this same period, especially now that politicians of all stripes echo Bill Clinton's mantra, "the era of big government is over," government has been unwilling or unable to provide work for the unemployed. Meanwhile the pace and length of the work week increases for those who are employed, a condition aggravated in times when high levels of unemployment or underemployment weaken the bargaining power of unions. Thus, gaps widen and inequities deepen between the overworked and those at the other end of the spectrum. The existence of large numbers of overworked and unemployed Americans is not at all the paradox it appears to be at first glance. As Schor sees the situation, the two conditions feed on each other.

While unemployment rose in the 1970s, Schor notes, there were reformers who urged shorter, not longer, weekly hours for the existing workforce. Such reductions, the reformers argued, would spread jobs around and put millions of people back to work. For the most part, those proposals fell on deaf ears, even as unemployment worsened in the 1980s. Striving to figure out why a philosophy of work sharing has been so largely ignored, Schor's inquiry probes capitalism's logic, its history, and late twentieth-century practice.

Schor's data analysis yields telling results. For example, after taking care of business, job, and household obligations, contemporary Americans average only sixteen and a half hours of leisure per week. For many Americans, working hours are longer than they were forty years ago, and those hours have risen steadily during the last twenty years. If current rates continue, that labor force will be working hours comparable to those that were common in the 1920s. This change was unexpected and therefore it long went unnoticed. After all, the conventional economic wisdom promised that the progress of capitalism and technology would provide more leisure, not less.

If such trends caught the nation unawares, by no means does Schor consider them inevitable. In similar economic circumstances—for example, those of France or Germany—she discovered that typical manufacturing employees worked 320 hours less per year than their American counterparts. Nor was a lack of American productivity the culprit that some critics made it out to be. Schor discerned steady increases in productivity. In less than fifty years, the 1948 productivity level of American workers more than doubled, but the decisions taken and choices made did not use that dividend to reduce working hours.

Instead of working less, Americans followed the urge to "shop 'til you drop." Spreading the affliction of work-and-spend, the "malling" of America has been both a cause and an effect of still other facts that Schor documents in cross-country comparisons: In a country where shopping is both a national passion and a problematic kind of leisure activity, Americans shop three to four times as many hours as their Western European counterparts. Living in history's most consumer-oriented society, we also spend a higher percentage of our incomes. Citing U.S. government statistics, Schor illustrates what that economic power buys: "In the five years between 1983 to 1987, Americans purchased 51 million microwaves, 44 million washers and dryers, 85 million color televisions, 36 million refrigerators and freezers, 48 million VCRs, and 23 million cordless telephones— all for an adult population of only 180 million." [26]

Most Americans share a standard of material comfort that humankind has never seen before, but the leisure to enjoy the time of our lives is itself consumed by the necessity to work more and more. Otherwise there is no hope to maintain and pay for, let alone expand, the material standard of living we Americans expect. Schor underscores that this pattern of work-and-spend is by no means entirely the result of a self-consciously chosen American addiction to consumption. Other forces are at work as well. Profitability, for instance, entails that more and more must be bought and sold. That spiral discourages shorter hours or sabbaticals for the existing workforce. Its time is too valuable; overtime is better than time off, especially when it can be extracted from salaried employees whose work week sometimes seems endless.

Again, Schor points out that apparently inevitable trends are not that way in fact. In the nineteenth and early twentieth centuries, reducing work time was a central concern in the United States. Those battles were not easy, but the hours of the work week did decline significantly during that period. As recently as the 1950s, there were even predictions that the American work week might become so short that leisure would be a prob-

lem: How would we fill all the spare time so that stifling boredom did not
intrude? Nearly half a century later, Schor concludes that times have indeed changed. Part of the change was signaled by the growing presence of
women in the workforce. With that development came concern about "the
second shift" as women tried to deal with the overload of managing jobs
and households. Men felt new pressures, too. In the 1990s, far from being
concerned about a surfeit of leisure time, there is national concern that
children are too often "home alone," work-related stress is on the rise, and
basics such as proper food and rest are slighted as Americans work longer
and harder to sustain the dubious hope that more consumption will add
meaning to their lives.

Schor thinks Americans lack a proper sense of proportion. She would
like us to work shorter hours and consume less. Doing so would enrich life
by increasing our "quality time." We are a harried people. Surveys often
show that Americans are prepared, at least in principle, to receive less pay
in exchange for more free time. Yet in practice even vacation time goes un-
used because people feel pressures not to leave their work behind. As Schor
understands, however, neither agreement with her scenario nor even recognition of ourselves as overworked Americans will be enough to induce the
changes that her recommendations require. That task will be much more
difficult because it goes beyond changing our habits of work and consumption. It requires tangling with the logic of American capitalism as well.

Putting her argument in "its starkest terms," Schor contends that "leisure
exists *in spite of* rather than as a result of capitalism" (7). Not only does
the capitalist market system create work, but also "key incentive structures of capitalist economies contain biases toward long working hours"
(7). Those structures are supported by a construct called *homo economi-
cus*. Contrary to the assertions of capitalist economic theory and practice,
"economic man" is *not* a creature given birth by nature. Rather, its origins
are twin teachings that are as plausible, potent, and profitable as they are
paradoxical: (1) human desires are infinite; and (2) every rational human
being will keep trying to maximize the fulfillment of those desires. Having
learned those capitalist teachings well, perhaps too well for our own good,
Americans run hard on the work-and-spend treadmill and trap each other
in Schor's "squirrel cage."

Schor offers a multidimensional remedy. It includes altering employers'
incentives, achieving gender equity, and demystifying the attraction of ever-
greater consumption. At the foundation of all her recommendations is reevaluation of time itself. Benjamin Franklin taught Americans that time is
money, but his students took the lesson more literally than he may have

intended. Franklin's concern was for people to use time productively and not to waste it. Capitalism's later American generations went further. For them, in Schor's words, "Franklin's aphorism took on new meaning, not only as prescription, but as actual description. Money buys time, and time buys money. *Time itself had become a commodity*" (139).[27]

Schor's reevaluation reverses that trend. It would restore free time—not just the sort of "rest and relaxation" that we use to combat fatigue but the kind that is needed to care for others, to educate oneself, to get involved in civic projects. Leisure of the latter kind would make our communities healthier. Schor suspects that another benefit would be improved performance on the job when we are working to earn our pay. She acknowledges that many barriers block the way toward acceptance of her views, perhaps first and foremost American corporations. Even in those quarters, however, she sees signs of change. Along with public opinion that may be growing in her favor, Schor looks especially toward environmental and women's groups, the children's lobby, a revitalized trade-union movement, and government policies as major forces that could aid the cause of *The Overworked American*.

Is there a place for religion in this work? Schor does not say explicitly, but at every turn her analysis raises issues that have religious dimensions because they all involve fundamental considerations about what is good, right, and most worthy of our loyalty. Her concerns are about the priorities that can help us to locate what deserves to be called sacred and to possess a sense of the whole in which we have meaningful places.

Reich and Schor scarcely mention religion overtly. They do not write about rivers, and they do not seem to be haunted by waters, either. And yet in a way they do and are. They worry that the tides, failing to raise all boats, may be against us. Their reflections flood us Americans with questions about ourselves. Those questions ask who we are, what we value most, what we must save as our streams of consciousness rush on. At least implicitly they are writing about the place of religion in public life, and their economic language is not as far removed from religious discourse as it may appear to be at first. We Americans overlook important resources for addressing the issues they raise unless public religious discourse infuses our most pressing public policy considerations.

The Right Questions

Contemporary public policy considerations involve questions about the help that we Americans need to give each other so that we can do a better job of living together in ways that keep us free. As they invite public religious discourse, those questions take us Americans to many places. For example, they can lead far to the west of Harvard Yard and Washington, D.C. They can lead us well beyond the floodplains of the Missouri and the Mississippi, to the western side of the Continental Divide where the Big Blackfoot River gushes through the mountains of Montana on toward the Columbia, its waters headed not for the Atlantic or the Gulf of Mexico but for the Pacific Ocean.

Norman Maclean knew the Big Blackfoot well, because along with his father, a Presbyterian minister, and his brother, Paul, Maclean was a fly fisherman. Norman Maclean was also a gifted writer, and thanks to his story, *A River Runs Through It,* and the beautiful film adaptation of it produced by Robert Redford and Patrick Markey in 1992, millions of Americans came to love that river, too.

In his family, says Maclean, telling the story from the perspective of an aging man who looks back on his youth, "there was no clear line between religion and fly fishing."[28] They were joined in the human ties of the Maclean family because even though Norman's father believed, "as a Scot and a Presbyterian . . . that man by nature was a mess and had fallen from an original state of grace," he also taught that good gifts could be ours and that the point was to use them together, as the *Westminster Shorter Catechism* put it, "to glorify God, and to enjoy Him forever" (2).

In the Maclean household, fly fishing proved the part about good gifts. The river was there. The trout were, too. They were gifts that nothing human could account for. Catching a trout, especially in a river like the Big Blackfoot, was also a matter of grace, a conviction that led Maclean's father to teach his boys that "grace comes by art and art does not come easy" (5).

Paul and Norman grew up. Their parents aged. Yet the lessons and joys, the ethics and sacred rites of fly fishing endured. They put one in a tradition. To belong in that tradition meant training and discipline, respect and awe, care and commitment, courage and force of will, memory and hope. Without those qualities, the art would be lost, the grace forgotten, the good gifts abused, even the trout disdained and the river disrespected.

It turned out that Paul was the best fisherman in the Maclean family. But fly fishing, though it can be a symbolic expression of living well, is only a part of living after all, and it did not prevent Paul's life from being troubled and troubling. Paul was a gambler. As a journalist, he exposed corrupt people who wanted to remain covered up. As a lover, he broke racial taboos. His debts as a card player only got him into more difficulty.

His life was taken from him in an untimely way—the Macleans were never quite sure why. They did not talk very much about Paul's death or their grief, though he was never far from the family's mind. Just a few words— "he was beautiful"—summed up how they felt about him.

Norman and his father both wondered, sometimes out loud to each other, if they could have helped Paul more or better. Honestly, they were not quite sure, haunted as they remained by the fact that, as Norman's father once said, "it is those we live with and love and should know who elude us" (113).

Considering such things, Maclean asked himself and us, "how can a question be answered that asks a lifetime of questions?" (112). Considering such things some more, he also recalled his father's reflections about help. "Help," the senior Maclean had said, "is giving part of yourself to somebody who comes to accept it willingly and needs it badly" (89). Help, real help, is not something anyone can give or get alone. That is what makes help, real help, harder and less frequent than it seems it ought to be. "Either we don't know what part to give or maybe we don't like to give any part of ourselves," Norman's father had gone on to say. "Then, more often than not," he continued, "the part that is needed is not wanted. And even more often, we do not have the part that is needed" (89). Ready and willing to help as we may be, Norman's father concluded, we have to keep asking what is needed, after all.

As the musings of economists such as Reich and Schor make clear, as presidential inaugurations and the poetry that graces them bear witness, as the Great Flood of '93 and the Bible's timeless stories, Noah's among them, testify, the issue—what is needed, after all—is one that we have to talk about in public, and surely it involves religion in fundamental ways. Thus, it is instructive to observe one thing more before leaving Norman Maclean's meditative story about faith and fishing, broken hearts and fragile lives, and the help and healing—the grace—that people need.

The story ends with Norman Maclean alone in "the Arctic half-light of the canyon" where the Big Blackfoot flows. There, as "all existence fades to a being with my soul," he casts a line into the water with "the hope that a fish will rise." As he waits, expectantly, for that grace, his vision embraces the river. "The river," he muses, "was cut by the world's great flood and runs over rocks from the basement of time. On some of the rocks are timeless raindrops. Under the rocks are the words, and some of the words are theirs" (113).

What are those words? What do they say? What do they mean? What sense of the whole, what understanding of the sacred, do they invite? Norman Maclean does not tell us explicitly. But as the river sang and sings on, the messages in those words are there to be discovered in the deepest yearnings of our hearts, and they are there to be shared as best we can in the stories of our lives. As those private needs and public selves mix and mingle together, I find them saying these things in conclusion:

There is much in American life that separates us. The chapters that have gone before testify to that. Religion and talk about it have been large factors in those divisions, but public expressions of religion can and should have a different part to play. Successful talk about religion in America helps people to live together in ways that keep us free. It does so particularly by helping us Americans to focus critically on the right questions: What is good? What may be better? What is the best that we can do? What is just? What most deserves one's loyalty? What is most important? What is worth dying and living for?

Such questions cannot be discussed, at least not completely, without putting religion on the table. Only as religion is expressed openly and examined publicly will the deepest insights contained in those questions be obtained.

Focusing on the right questions will not guarantee anything like unanimity about their answers, and we pluralistic Americans should be grateful for that, for unanimity is not what matters most in American life. But if public discourse about religion can help us to consider the right questions together, an essential step in living together well will have been taken.

The goal of pursuing the right questions together is to learn, change, and grow, and then to act in accordance with the understanding that our sharing builds. Such work requires sincerity, respect, give-and-take among people who see each other as equals. It enjoins openness to explore basic assumptions and points of disagreement, willingness to try to see other people's points of view "from within," and the mutual understanding and criticism on which deepening trust depends. The right kind of talk about religion in America will help us to express our private needs and public selves in ways that save our country and make it better.

NOTES

1. Gayle Cox, "Good Book to Print," *Star Tribune* (Minneapolis edition), 19 July 1993, 1D. I am indebted to Cox's article for information about the Bible publishing industry in the United States.

2. Genesis 1 and 2.

3. Exodus 14:21–31.

4. Exodus 17:1–7.

5. Amos 5:24.

6. Isaiah 55:10.

7. Revelation 21 and 22.

8. See Elie Wiesel, *Sages and Dreamers: Biblical, Talmudic, and Hasidic Portraits and Legends* (New York: Summit Books, 1991), 24. My discussion is indebted to Wiesel's reflections on Noah in *Sages and Dreamers,* 19–34.

9. Genesis 6–9 contains the narratives about Noah from which my discussion and its quotations are drawn.

10. Wallace Stegner, *Where the Bluebird Sings to the Lemonade Springs* (New York: Penguin, 1992), 68.

11. For more details on Kaskaskia Island, see Dean E. Murphy and Louis Saha-gun, "Levee Break Wipes Out Historic Illinois Island," *Los Angeles Times,* 23 July 1993, A1, A20.

12. The quotation is from Roger Petterson's Associated Press report as it appeared in the *Inland Valley Daily Bulletin,* 26 July 1993, A5.

13. See the *Star Tribune* (Minneapolis edition), 15 July 1993, 14A.

14. See, for example, *Newsweek,* 26 July 1993, 25.

15. I found this photograph on the front page of the *Inland Valley Daily Bulletin,* 23 July 1993. A public expression of religion in its own right, the picture appeared in many Associated Press-affiliated newspapers around the country.

16. The quotation is taken from Christopher Connell's Associated Press report in the *Inland Valley Daily Report,* 25 July 1993, A5.

17. Émile Durkheim, *Sociology and Philosophy,* trans. D. F. Pocock (New York: Free Press, 1974), 48. The quotation is from Durkheim's essay "The Determination of Moral Facts," which appeared in 1906.

18. For more on this point, see Guenter Lewy, *Why America Needs Religion: Secular Modernity and Its Discontents* (Grand Rapids, Mich.: Eerdmans, 1996). An agnostic, Lewy nevertheless believes that decline is at hand when a society's morality is severed from religious roots.

19. Émile Durkheim, *The Elementary Forms of the Religious Life,* trans. Joseph Ward Swain (New York: The Free Press, 1965), 475.

20. Maya Angelou, *On the Pulse of Morning* (New York: Random House, 1993).

21. Robert B. Reich, *The Work of Nations: Preparing Ourselves for 21st-Century Capitalism* (New York: Vintage Books, 1992), 208. Subsequent page references are to this edition and are given parenthetically in the text. The book appeared originally in 1991.

22. The loss of jobs due to corporate restructuring took place at a slower rate in mid-decade than it did earlier in the 1990s. In the 1990s, there has also been a net gain in jobs in the United States, but many of these jobs do not pay as well as

the ones that were lost, and older workers have often had considerable difficulty in finding comparable positions. See "Rate of Job Loss Through Firm Restructurings Slows," *Los Angeles Times,* 23 Aug. 1996, D12.

23. Posey is quoted by Richard Reeves in "What Happens If There Isn't Work," *International Herald Tribune,* 29 Nov. 1995, 10.

24. Durkheim, *Elementary Forms of the Religious Life,* 474–75.

25. John Robinson, director of the Americans' Use of Time Project at the University of Maryland, would disagree. If we feel pressed for time, the problem, he believes, has less to do with longer working hours—by his reckoning the average work week has declined for men and women since 1965—than with the way we perceive our uses of time. See Lianne Hart, "Rat Race: It May Be Less Swift," *Los Angeles Times,* 11 Dec. 1996, A5.

26. Juliet B. Schor, *The Overworked American: The Unexpected Decline of Leisure* (New York: Basic Books, 1991), 108–9. Subsequent page references are given parenthetically in the text.

27. The italics are Schor's. Using reflections on the American Dream and Benjamin Franklin as points of departure, Robert Wuthnow's *Poor Richard's Principle: Recovering the American Dream Through the Moral Dimension of Work, Business, and Money* (Princeton, N.J.: Princeton University Press, 1996) investigates why "the relationship between economic life and the quest for deeper human values . . . is becoming increasingly problematic" (6). Wuthnow sees Americans grappling with questions: "How should we live? How much should we work? How much money do we really need? What goals are we trying to accomplish anyway?" (7). Wuthnow argues that "Americans must recover a moral language in which to bring their deeper human values directly to bear on their economic decisions" (9). One problem, however, is that we do not know very well how to carry on public discourse about such matters. A step toward recovery of such discourse, which has a long tradition in American life even though it has been largely forgotten in the late twentieth century, involves "listening to the ways in which people make sense of their lives" (13). Wuthnow's approach complements the one I advocate concerning talk about religion in public.

28. Norman Maclean, *A River Runs Through It and Other Stories* (New York: Pocket Books, 1992), 1. Subsequent page references are to this edition and are given parenthetically in the text. Maclean's story was published originally in 1976.

Abrahamson, Irving, ed. *Against Silence: The Voice and Vision of Elie Wiesel*. 3 vols. New York: Holocaust Library, 1985.

Adams, James Truslow. *The Epic of America*. [1931]; Boston: Little, Brown, 1934.

Albanese, Catherine L. *America: Religions and Religion*. 2d ed. Belmont, Calif.: Wadsworth, 1992.

Améry, Jean. *At the Mind's Limits: Contemplations by a Survivor on Auschwitz and Its Realities*. Trans. Sidney Rosenfeld and Stella P. Rosenfeld. New York: Schocken Books, 1986.

Angelou, Maya. *On the Pulse of Morning*. New York: Random House, 1993.

Audi, Robert, and Nicholas Wolterstorff. *Religion in the Public Square: The Place of Religious Convictions in Political Debate*. Lanham, Md.: Rowman and Littlefield, 1996.

Balmer, Randall. *Grant Us Courage: Travels along the Mainline of American Protestantism*. New York: Oxford University Press, 1996.

———. *Mine Eyes Have Seen the Glory: A Journey into the Evangelical Subculture in America*. New York: Oxford University Press, 1993.

Bell, Derrick. *Faces at the Bottom of the Well: The Permanence of Racism*. New York: Basic Books, 1992.

———. *Gospel Choir: Psalms of Survival for an Alien Land Called Home*. New York: Basic Books, 1996.

Bellah, Robert N. *The Broken Covenant: American Civil Religion in Time of Trial*. 2d ed. Chicago: University of Chicago Press, 1992.

Bellah, Robert N., Richard Madsen, William M. Sullivan, Ann Swidler, and Steven M. Tipton. *The Good Society*. New York: Alfred A. Knopf, 1991.

———. *Habits of the Heart: Individualism and Commitment in American Life*. New York: Harper & Row, 1985.

Bennett, William J. *The Index of Leading Cultural Indicators: Facts and Figures on the State of American Society*. New York: Simon & Schuster, 1994.

———, ed. *The Book of Virtues: A Treasury of Great Moral Stories*. New York: Simon & Schuster, 1993.

———, ed. *The Children's Book of Virtues.* New York: Simon & Schuster, 1995.

———, ed. *The Moral Compass: Stories for Life's Journey.* New York: Simon & Schuster, 1995.

Berenbaum, Michael. *The World Must Know: The History of the Holocaust as Told in the United States Holocaust Memorial Museum.* Boston: Little, Brown, 1993.

Berger, Peter L. *A Far Glory: The Quest for Faith in an Age of Credulity.* New York: Free Press, 1992.

———. *The Sacred Canopy: Elements of a Sociological Theory of Religion.* Garden City, N.Y.: Doubleday Anchor Books, 1967.

Berman, Phillip L. *The Search for Meaning: Americans Talk about What They Believe and Why.* New York: Ballantine Books, 1990.

Berneking, Nancy, and Pamela Carter Joern, eds. *Re-Membering and Re-Imagining.* Cleveland: Pilgrim Press, 1995.

Bernstein, Richard J. *Beyond Objectivism and Relativism: Science, Hermeneutics, and Praxis.* Philadelphia: University of Pennsylvania Press, 1983.

Berry, Wendell. *The Unsettling of America.* New York: Avon, 1977.

Bloom, Harold. *The American Religion: The Emergence of the Post-Christian Nation.* New York: Simon & Schuster, 1992.

Cady, Linell E. *Religion, Theology, and American Public Life.* Albany: State University of New York Press, 1993.

Cargas, Harry James. *Shadows of Auschwitz: A Christian Response to the Holocaust.* New York: Crossroad, 1990.

Carter, Stephen L. *The Culture of Disbelief: How American Law and Politics Trivialize Religious Devotion.* New York: Basic Books, 1993.

Castuera, Ignacio, ed. *Dreams on Fire/Embers of Hope: From the Pulpits of Los Angeles after the Riots.* St. Louis: Chalice Press, 1992.

Chopp, Rebecca S. *The Power to Speak: Feminism, Language, God.* New York: Crossroad, 1991.

Cohen, Michael Lee. *The Twentysomething American Dream: A Cross-country Quest for a Generation.* New York: Dutton, 1993.

Current, Richard N., ed. *The Political Thought of Abraham Lincoln.* Indianapolis: Bobbs-Merrill, 1967.

Dawson, John. *Healing America's Wounds.* Ventura, Calif.: Regal Books, 1994.

Delbanco, Andrew. *The Death of Satan.* New York: Farrar, Straus and Giroux, 1995.

Dewey, John. *A Common Faith.* New Haven: Yale University Press, 1952.

Dillard, Annie. *The Writing Life.* New York: HarperCollins, 1989.

Durkheim, Émile. *The Elementary Forms of Religious Life.* Trans. Joseph Ward Swain. New York: Free Press, 1965.

———. *Sociology and Philosophy.* Trans. D. F. Pocock. New York: Free Press, 1974.

Ellison, Ralph. *Invisible Man.* New York: Vintage Books, 1982.

Evans, Sara M., and Harry C. Boyte. *Free Spaces: The Sources of Democratic Change in America.* New York: Harper & Row, 1986.

Fay, Martha. *Do Children Need Religion? How Parents Today Are Thinking about the Big Questions.* New York: Pantheon Books, 1993.

Finke, Roger, and Rodney Stark. *The Churching of America, 1776-1990: Winners and Losers in Our Religious Economy.* New Brunswick, N.J.: Rutgers University Press, 1992.

Fossum, Robert H., and John K. Roth. *The American Dream.* Durham: British Association for American Studies, 1981.

———, eds. *American Ground: Vistas, Visions, and Revisions.* New York: Paragon House, 1988.

Fukuyama, Francis. *Trust: The Social Virtues and the Creation of Prosperity.* New York: Free Press, 1995.

Gallup, George H., Jr., and Timothy Jones. *The Saints among Us.* Harrisburg, Pa.: Morehouse, 1992.

Garreau, Joel. *The Nine Nations of America.* Boston: Houghton Mifflin, 1981.

Golay, Michael, and Carl Rollyson. *Where America Stands, 1996.* New York: John Wiley, 1996.

Goldhagen, Daniel Jonah. *Hitler's Willing Executioners: Ordinary Germans and the Holocaust.* New York: Alfred A. Knopf, 1996.

Hamilton, William. *A Quest for the Post-historical Jesus.* New York: Continuum, 1993.

Hatch, Nathan. *The Democratization of American Christianity.* New Haven: Yale University Press, 1989.

Herrnstein, Richard J., and Charles Murray. *The Bell Curve: Intelligence and Class Structure in American Life.* New York: Free Press, 1994.

Hewitt, Hugh. *Searching for God in America.* Dallas: Word Publishing, 1996.

James, William. *The Varieties of Religious Experience: A Study in Human Nature.* New York: Doubleday Image Books, 1978.

Johnson, Douglas, and Cynthia Sampson, eds. *Religion, The Missing Dimension of Statecraft.* New York: Oxford University Press, 1994.

Johnson, Elizabeth A. *She Who Is: The Mystery of God in Feminist Theological Discourse.* New York: Crossroad, 1992.

Kellner, Mark A. *God on the Internet.* Foster City, Calif.: IDG Books Worldwide, 1996.

Kemmis, Daniel. *Community and the Politics of Place.* Norman: University of Oklahoma Press, 1990.

Kosmin, Barry A., and Seymour P. Lachman. *One Nation Under God: Religion in Contemporary American Society.* New York: Harmony Books, 1993.

Kreeft, Peter. *Everything You Ever Wanted to Know about Heaven . . . But Never Dreamed of Asking.* San Francisco: Ignatius, 1990.

Kühl, Stefan. *The Nazi Connection.* New York: Oxford University Press, 1995.

Lamb, David. *A Sense of Place: Listening to Americans.* New York: Times Books, 1993.

Laumann, Edward O. *Social Organization of Sexuality: Sexual Practices in the United States.* Chicago: University of Chicago Press, 1994.

Lerner, Michael. *The Politics of Meaning: Restoring Hope and Possibility in an Age of Cynicism.* Reading, Mass.: Addison-Wesley, 1996.

Lerner, Michael, and Cornel West. *Jews and Blacks: Let the Healing Begin.* New York: G. P. Putnam's Sons, 1995.

Linenthal, Edward Tabor. *Preserving Memory: The Struggle to Create America's Holocaust Museum.* New York: Viking Penguin Books, 1995.

———. *Sacred Ground: Americans and Their Battlefields.* 2d ed. Urbana: University of Illinois Press, 1993.

Lipstadt, Deborah E. *Beyond Belief: The American Press and the Coming of the Holocaust, 1933–1945.* New York: Free Press, 1986.

Littell, Franklin H., and Hubert G. Locke, eds. *The German Church Struggle and the Holocaust.* Detroit: Wayne State University Press, 1974.

Maclean, Norman. *A River Runs Through It and Other Stories.* New York: Pocket Books, 1992.

Masumoto, David Mas. *Epitaph for a Peach: Four Seasons on my Family Farm.* San Francisco: HarperSanFrancisco, 1995.

McDannell, Colleen, and Bernhard Lang. *Heaven: A History.* New Haven: Yale University Press, 1988.

McFague, Sallie. *Models of God: Theology for an Ecological, Nuclear Age.* Philadelphia: Fortress Press, 1987.

Mead, Sidney. *The Lively Experiment.* New York: Harper & Row, 1963.

Miles, Jack. *God: A Biography.* New York: Alfred A. Knopf, 1995.

Miles, Margaret R. *Seeing and Believing: Religion and Values in the Movies.* Boston: Beacon Press, 1996.

Moore, R. Laurence. *Selling God: American Religion and the Marketplace of Culture.* New York: Oxford University Press, 1994.

Moore, Thomas. *Care of the Soul: A Guide for Cultivating Depth and Sacredness in Everyday Life.* New York: HarperCollins, 1992.

———. *The Reenchantment of Everyday Life.* New York: HarperCollins, 1996.

———. *Soul Mates: Honoring the Mysteries of Love and Relationship.* New York: HarperCollins, 1994.

Neuhaus, Richard John. *America Against Itself: Moral Vision and the Public Order.* Notre Dame, Ind.: University of Notre Dame Press, 1992.

Niebuhr, Reinhold. *The Irony of American History.* New York: Charles Scribner's Sons, 1952.

Nord, Warren A. *Religion and American Education: Rethinking a National Dilemma.* Chapel Hill: University of North Carolina Press, 1995.

Norris, Kathleen. *Dakota: A Spiritual Geography.* Boston: Houghton Mifflin, 1993.

Nuland, Sherwin B. *How We Die: Reflections on Life's Final Chapter.* New York: Random House, 1993.

Patterson, James, and Peter Kim. *The Day America Told the Truth: What People Really Believe about Everything That Matters.* New York: Prentice-Hall, 1991.

———. *The Second American Revolution.* New York: William Morrow, 1994.

Ravitch, Diane, ed. *The American Reader: Words That Moved a Nation.* New York: HarperCollins, 1991.

Reeves, Thomas C. *The Empty Church: The Suicide of Liberal Christianity.* New York: Free Press, 1996.

Reich, Robert B. *The Work of Nations: Preparing Ourselves for 21st-Century Capitalism.* New York: Vintage Books, 1992.

Rich, Adrienne. *An Atlas of the Difficult World: Poems, 1988-1991.* New York: W. W. Norton, 1991.

Rittner, Carol, and John K. Roth, eds. *Different Voices: Women and the Holocaust.* New York: Paragon House, 1993.

Roberts, Sam. *Who We Are: A Portrait of America Based on the Latest U.S. Census.* New York: Times Books, 1993.

Roof, Wade Clark, ed. *Religion in the Nineties,* The Annals of the American Academy of Political and Social Sciences, vol. 527 (May 1993). Newbury Park, Calif.: Sage Periodicals Press, 1993.

Roof, Wade Clark, with the assistance of Bruce Greer, Mary Johnson, Andrea Leibson, Karen Loeb, and Elizabeth Souza. *A Generation of Seekers: The Spiritual Journeys of the Baby Boom Generation.* New York: HarperCollins, 1993.

Roth, John K. *A Consuming Fire: Encounters with Elie Wiesel and the Holocaust.* Atlanta: John Knox, 1979.

Roth, John K., and Michael Berenbaum, eds. *Holocaust: Religious and Philosophical Implications.* New York: Paragon House, 1988.

Rouner, Leroy S. *To Be at Home: Christianity, Civil Religion, and World Community.* Boston: Beacon Press, 1991.

Royce, Josiah. *The Philosophy of Loyalty.* [1908]; Nashville: Vanderbilt University Press, 1995.

Rubenstein, Richard L. *After Auschwitz: History, Theology, and Contemporary Judaism.* 2d ed. Baltimore: Johns Hopkins University Press, 1992.

———. *The Age of Triage: Fear and Hope in an Overcrowded World.* Boston: Beacon Press, 1983.

———. *The Cunning of History: The Holocaust and the American Future.* New York: Harper Torchbooks, 1987.

Rubenstein, Richard L., and John K. Roth. *Approaches to Auschwitz: The Holocaust and Its Legacy.* Louisville: Westminster/John Knox, 1987.

Russell, Jeffrey Burton. *A History of Heaven.* Princeton: Princeton University Press, 1997.

Ryan, Alan A., Jr. *Quiet Neighbors: Prosecuting Nazi War Criminals in America.* San Diego: Harcourt Brace Jovanovich, 1984.

Samuelson, Robert J. *The Good Life and Its Discontents: The American Dream in the Age of Entitlement, 1945–1995.* New York: Times Books, 1995.

Sandel, Michael J. *Democracy's Discontent: America in Search of a Public Philosophy.* Cambridge, Mass.: Harvard University Press, 1996.

Sanders, Scott Russell. *Staying Put: Making a Home in a Restless World.* Boston: Beacon Press, 1993.

Schor, Juliet B. *The Overworked American: The Unexpected Decline of Leisure.* New York: Basic Books, 1991.

Sereny, Gitta. *Albert Speer: His Battle with Truth.* New York: Alfred A. Knopf, 1995.

——. *Into That Darkness: An Examination of Conscience.* New York: Vintage Books, 1983.

Smith, Anna Deavere. *Twilight: Los Angeles, 1992 — On the Road: A Search for American Character.* New York: Anchor Books, 1994.

Staff, *Los Angeles Times. 4:31: Images of the 1994 Los Angeles Earthquake.* Los Angeles: Los Angeles Times Syndicate, 1994.

——. *Understanding the Riots: Los Angeles before and after the Rodney King Case.* Los Angeles: Los Angeles Times, 1992.

Stegner, Wallace. *Where the Bluebird Sings to the Lemonade Springs.* New York: Penguin, 1992.

Styron, William. *Sophie's Choice.* New York: Random House, 1979.

Thomas, Laurence Mordekhai. *Vessels of Evil: American Slavery and the Holocaust.* Philadelphia: Temple University Press, 1993.

Thompson, Hunter S. *Fear and Loathing in Las Vegas: A Savage Journey to the Heart of the American Dream.* New York: Warner Books, 1982.

Tinder, Glenn. *The Political Meaning of Christianity: The Prophetic Stance.* New York: HarperCollins, 1991.

Tocqueville, Alexis de. *Democracy in America.* 2 vols. Ed. J. P. Mayer, trans. George Lawrence. Garden City, N.Y.: Anchor Books, 1969.

——. *Journey to America.* Ed. J. P. Mayer, trans. George Lawrence. Garden City, N.Y.: Anchor Books, 1971.

Updike, John. *Rabbit at Rest.* New York: Alfred A. Knopf, 1990.

——. *Rabbit Is Rich.* Greenwich, Conn.: Fawcett, 1982.

——. *Rabbit Redux.* Greenwich, Conn.: Fawcett, 1972.

——. *Rabbit Run.* Greenwich, Conn.: Fawcett, 1965.

Wallimann, Isidor, and Michael N. Dobkowski, eds. *Genocide and the Modern Age: Etiology and Case Studies of Mass Death.* Westport, Conn.: Greenwood Press, 1987.

Wattenberg, Ben J. *Values Matter Most: How Republicans or Democrats or a Third Party Can Win and Renew the American Way of Life.* New York: Free Press, 1995.

Weiss, John. *Ideology of Death: Why the Holocaust Happened in Germany.* Chicago: Ivan R. Dee, 1996.

West, Cornel. *Race Matters.* Boston: Beacon Press, 1993.

West, Nathanael. *The Day of the Locust.* New York: New American Library, 1983.

Wiesel, Elie. *The Accident*. Trans. Anne Borchardt. New York: Avon Books, 1970.

———. *All Rivers Run to the Sea: Memoirs*. New York: Alfred A. Knopf, 1995.

———. *Four Hasidic Masters and Their Struggle Against Melancholy*. Notre Dame, Ind.: University of Notre Dame Press, 1978.

———. *A Jew Today*. Trans. Marion Wiesel. New York: Random House, 1978.

———. *Messengers of God: Biblical Portraits and Legends*. Trans. Marion Wiesel. New York: Random House, 1976.

———. *Night*. Trans. Stella Rodway. New York: Bantam Books, 1986.

———. *The Oath*. Trans. Marion Wiesel. New York: Random House, 1973.

———. *One Generation After*. Trans. Lily Edelman and Elie Wiesel. New York: Avon Books, 1972.

———. *Sages and Dreamers: Biblical, Talmudic, and Hasidic Portraits and Legends*. Trans. Marion Wiesel. New York: Summit Books, 1991.

———. *Somewhere a Master: Further Hasidic Portraits and Legends*. Trans. Marion Wiesel. New York: Summit Books, 1982.

———. *Souls on Fire: Portraits and Legends of Hasidic Masters*. Trans. Marion Wiesel. New York: Random House, 1972.

———. *The Testament*. Trans. Marion Wiesel. New York: Summit Books, 1981.

Wills, Gary. *Under God: Religion and American Politics*. New York: Simon & Schuster, 1990.

Wuthnow, Robert. *Acts of Compassion*. Princeton, N.J.: Princeton University Press, 1991.

———. *God and Mammon in America*. New York: Free Press, 1994.

———. *Poor Richard's Principle: Recovering the American Dream Through the Moral Dimension of Work, Business, and Money*. Princeton, N.J.: Princeton University Press, 1996.

———. *Producing the Sacred: An Essay on Public Religion*. Urbana: University of Illinois Press, 1994.

———. *Sharing the Journey: Support Groups and America's New Quest for Community*. New York: Free Press, 1994.

———. *The Restructuring of American Religion: Society and Faith Since World War II*. Princeton, N.J.: Princeton University Press, 1988.

———, ed. *"I Come Away Stronger": How Small Groups Are Shaping American Religion*. Grand Rapids, Mich.: Eerdmans, 1994.

Wuthnow, Robert, and Virginia Hodgkinson & Associates. *Faith and Philanthropy in America*. San Francisco: Jossey-Bass, 1990.

Wyman, David S. *The Abandonment of the Jews: America and the Holocaust, 1941–1945*. New York: Pantheon, 1984.

———. *Paper Walls: America and the Refugee Crisis, 1938–1941*. Amherst: University of Massachusetts Press, 1968.

Young, James E. *The Texture of Memory: Holocaust Memorials and Meaning*. New Haven: Yale University Press, 1993.

Zinsser, William. *American Places*. New York: HarperCollins, 1992.

Abortion, 47, 132
Abraham, 209
Accident, The (Wiesel), 202–5
Acting/doing, 208–13
Adams, James Truslow, 41n; *The Epic of America*, 28
Adams, Sharon, 149
After Auschwitz (Rubenstein), 169–75, 184, 190–91, 191–92nn
Age of Triage, The (Rubenstein) 184–90; God in, 186
AIDS epidemic, 47, 82, 100, 185
Allen, Henry, 201
Altizer, Thomas, 169, 192n
"Amazing Grace," 75, 87n, 145
American citizens, 33
American culture, 14, 26, 113, 136, 196; religion and, 10, 127
American Dream, 26, 41–42n, 77–85, 103, 117n, 149, 178, 180, 207, 242n; and the common good, 69–77; CNBC television program ("Achieving the American Dream"), 79–82; failure of, 84; freedom and, 220; and the Holocaust, 200–202; perspectives on, 28–40; place of religion in, 83; religious underpinnings of, 180; and "twenty-somethings," 55–56; wealth and, 98; women and, 82
American flag, 70, 129; burning of, 86n
American government, 69, 72, 136, 234
American Jewish Committee (AJC), 198, 215n
American mobility, 40–41n
American music, 74–75, 87–88nn, 165n,

226, 228, 230; religious themes in, 57–58
American people, 6, 9, 73, 75, 196, 228, 231; help given by, 227–28
American places, 19, 58, 67n, 73, 76–77; literature of, 88n
American religious thought, 17n
American Revolution, 91, 226
"American's Creed, The," 87n
American society, 12, 75
American workforce, 231–32; downsizing, 234; employment of, 233–34; job loss in, 241–42n
"America the Beautiful," 75, 88n, 162
Améry, Jean: *At the Mind's Limits*, 179–80. *See also* Maier, Hans
Amos, 222
Andresen, Martha, 126
Angelou, Maya, 197; "On the Pulse of Morning," 219, 229–30
Angels, 65n
Anti-Judaism. *See* Antisemitism
Antisemitism, 34, 43n, 176, 184
Applewhite, Marshall, 45
Arguments, 12–13, 15, 21
Armstrong, Louis, 36
Atlas of the Difficult World, An (Rich), 20–22
At the Mind's Limits (Améry), 179–80
Auschwitz, 26, 40, 167, 169, 179, 195; and the American Dream, 32–33, 36–37, 200–201; Birkenau, 195, 205–6, 215; and Rubenstein's theology, 172–74; and Wiesel, 199–200, 204–8
Awareness, 2, 233

Baby boomers, 54–55, 93
Bad Religion, 75
Bailey, F. Lee, 145
Balmer, Randall, 196; *Mine Eyes Have Seen the Glory*, 57
Baltimore, Md., 129–32
Baseball, 7–10, 16–17, 18n, 38, 137
Baseball (Burns film), 18n
Bates, Katherine Lee, 75, 88n
Belief(s), 1, 3, 17, 17n, 39, 44, 61–64n; American, 90–120, 209, 228–39; in angels, 118n; in God, 105, 110; in God of history, 169, 190; in heaven, 118n; imposition of religious, 136; in life after death, 105; in religion, 190–91; religious, 105–9, 133; and "twentysomethings," 55–56; "Yuppie," 54–55
Bell, Derrick: *Faces at the Bottom of the Well*, 165n
Bellamy, Francis, 71
Bell Curve, The (Herrnstein and Murray), 186, 194n
Bennett, William J., 86–87nn, 119n, 138n; *The Book of Virtues*, 73–74; *The Index of Leading Cultural Indicators*, 74–75
Berenbaum, Michael, 176–77
Bergen-Belsen, 179
Berman, Phillip, 44; *The Search for Meaning*, 50–52
Berry, Wendell, 88n; *The Unsettling of America*, 77
Bey, Twilight, 159
Bhabha, Homi, 158–59
Bible, 62n, 64n, 95, 143–44, 207, 209–10, 229; elimination of anti-Jewish themes in New Testament, 220–21; New Testament, 176, 220, 222; number in American homes, 220; sales of, 221; stories, 220–25; versions of, 220–21; women as buyers of, 220
Biblical scholarship, 62n
Big Blackfoot River, 238–40
Bill of Rights, 46
Black, Don, 123
Black, Hugo, 42n
Boesche, Roger, 194n
Book of Virtues, The (Bennett), 73–74
Bosnia, 168
Bow, Clara, 124

Bradshaw Seminar for Young Professionals and the Humanities, 126–27, 130, 139n
Branch Davidians, 46
Breaking the Waves (film), 57
Brennan, William, 192n
Briseno, Theodore J., 152, 154
Brown, Jim, 79
Buchenwald, 200
Buddha, 188
Buddhists, 56, 93
Bull Durham (film), 10
Burns, Ken: *Baseball*, 18n
Bush, George, 38, 154
Butler, Brett, 8

California, 23–24, 92, 143, 225; demography of, 23; economy of, 24, 149; Proposition 187, 183; Southern, 148–52
California Council for the Humanities, 40n, 88n, 126–27
California Dream, 24
Campbell, Jim, 60n
Canada, 23
Capitalism, 233–37; logic of, 236; profitability, 233
Capital punishment, 132
Care of the Soul (Moore), 52
Carnegie, Andrew, 194n
Carroll, James, 131
Carter, Jimmy, 45
Carter, Stephen L.: *The Culture of Disbelief*, 132–37
Case studies, 12–14, 90, 166
Castuera, Ignacio: *Dreams on Fire/Embers of Hope*, 160–63
Catechism of the Catholic Church, 50
Celestine Prophecy, The (Redfield), 50
Censorship, 115n
Center for a New American Dream, 41–42n
Chancellor, John, 18n
Chaves, Mark, 119n
Chavis, Ben, 79, 88n
Chicago, Ill., 78–82, 85, 175
Childhood, 99
Choiceless choice, 36
Chopp, Rebecca, 53
Christian Coalition, 45, 93

Christianity, 17, 111, 187; American, 34; contempt for Jews in, 176; as necessary condition for the Holocaust, 204
Christian-Jewish relations, 130-31
Christians, 56, 111, 172, 174, 212-13; American, 93
Church burnings, 46, 60n
Churches: decline of mainline, 120n
Cisneros, Henry, 79
Citizenship, 67n
Civil Liberties Act (1988), 34
Claremont, Calif., 24-26, 40, 126
Claremont Graduate School, 126, 131
Claremont McKenna College, 25-26, 154
Claremont Presbyterian Church, 25-26
Clark, Marcia, 145
Clergy, 102, 116n
Clinton, Bill, 28, 46, 138n, 141n, 146-47, 200, 228-229, 234
Cloning, 47
Close, Glenn, 126
Cochrane, Johnnie, 145
Cohen, Michael Lee, 55-56, 66n
Cold War, 78
Columbus, Christopher, 71
Commitment, 90; Christian, 107; religious, 106
Common good, 5, 15, 31, 52, 83, 96, 105, 112, 115n, 127, 181; language and, 155-56; qualities of, 75-77
Common ground, 14-17, 52-53, 77, 121, 130, 142, 155, 206, 219
Common values, 139n
Commonwealth, 75
Communication, 4-5
Communism, 78
Community, 3-4, 12, 15, 26, 75, 102, 110, 156, 162; desire for, 140n, 232-33; sacred symbols of, 227
Compassion, 112, 209-10
Concentration camps, 33, 167, 203. *See also individual names*
Confidence: in American institutions, leaders, professions, 101-2, 115-16n; in church, 115n; in Congress, 115n; in criminal justice system, 115n; in government, 101, 116n; in military, 101, 115-16n; in organized religion, 116n; in police, 115-16n
Confucius, 188

Conversion, 51
Council of Trent, 50
Covenant, 173; and doctrine of election, 187-88
Cox, Harvey, 163-64n
Creationism, 47
Crime, 57, 96
Croatia, 168
Crossing the Threshold of Hope (John Paul II), 50
Cults, 66n
Culture of Disbelief, The (Carter), 132-37
Cunning of History, The (Rubenstein), 175, 178, 184
Cynicism, 228

Daly, Mary, 53
Darden, Christopher, 145
Darwin, Charles, 194n
Davidson, Gordon, 155
Day Americans Told the Truth, The (Patterson and Kim), 90, 94-113, 113-19nn
Day of the Locust, The (West), 142-44, 162
Dayton Accords, 168
Dead Man Walking (film), 57
Dean, William, 1, 17n, 128; *The Religious Critic in American Culture*, 127-28
Death, 4, 37, 39, 138, 143, 154, 210; and the Holocaust, 21-22; mass, 166-68, 174, 185; in news stories, 45-46
"Death of God" movement/theologians, 170
Death of Satan, The (Delbanco), 118n
Declaration of Independence, 32, 71, 76-78, 131
Delbanco, Andrew: *The Death of Satan*, 118n
DeMille, Cecil B., 122, 125
Democracy, 72-73, 132, 135, 137
Democracy in America (Tocqueville), 131
Denny, Reginald O., 153-54, 156-57
Dershowitz, Alan, 145
Desecration, 46, 86n
Desmond, Norma, 122-26, 137-38, 138n
Despair, 21, 26; and American life, 76, 104; and "the death of God," 173; racism and, 165n; in *Sophie's Choice*, 37; in *Sunset Boulevard*, 123; Wiesel and, 205, 208, 210
Devil, 106, 118n
Dewey, John, 12, 17n

DeWitt, John L., 33
Dietrich, Marlene, 99
Disbelief, 132
Discourse about religion. *See* Talk about religion
Disillusionment, 20, 56, 96, 103, 117n, 128
Dissatisfaction, 102
Dissent, 133, 136
Diversity, 2, 14, 50, 92, 159, 161, 169; cultural and racial, 30–32; in experience, 5; religious, 132
Division, 30–31, 44, 142, 166
Divorce, 99
Do Children Need Religion? (Fay), 53–54
Dramaturge, 156
Dreams, 26, 37, 121, 123–26, 137–38, 205, 213, 228, 230; American, 14, 27, 32, 40, 69, 77, 143, 148, 219
Dreams on Fire/Embers of Hope (Castuera), 160–63
Drug addiction, 57, 96, 147
Du, Soon Ja, 164n
Dunne, John R., 34
Durkheim, Émile, 70, 229, 233

Earthquakes, 148–50
Economics, 58, 81–82, 96, 98, 100, 105, 117n, 175, 188, 226; buying power, 235; and human values, 242n; productivity, 235; and religion, 233, 237; Reich's views on, 230–33; Schor's views on, 233–37
Economic security, 117n
Education, 96, 105, 112, 117n
Edwards, Jonathan, 12
Eisenhower, Dwight D., 78
Elders, Jocelyn, 141n
Ellison, Ralph: *Invisible Man,* 29–31, 35
Emerson, Ralph Waldo, 17n
Empty Church, The (Reeves), 120n
England, 100, 185
Environment, 105, 117n
Epic of America, The (Adams), 28
Episcopalians, 93
Equal Employment Opportunity Commission (EEOC), 141n
Equality, 32, 77–78, 135, 194n, 240
Ethics, 59–60, 85, 100, 112, 116n
"Ethnic cleansing," 47, 169, 173, 185, 198
Evaluating, 5, 14, 90, 97

Evil, 223–24; problem of, 173, 189
Executive Order 9066, 33
Expectation, 117n
Experience: American, 168; particularity in, 2–3, 19, 76; plurality within, 2; private/personal and public dimensions of, 5, 8–9, 11, 17; and religion, 4, 76; religious character of, 11; variety of, 2, 4, 9, 137
"Experts," 6, 15, 51, 68, 80, 97

Faces at the Bottom of the Well (Bell), 165n
Faith, 61–64n, 74, 84; biblical, 174
Falwell, Jerry, 141n
Farley, Dick, 149
Farrakhan, Louis, 45
Fay, Martha: *Do Children Need Religion?* 53–54
Fazio, Vic, 141n
Fear and Loathing in Las Vegas (Thompson), 69–70
Final Solution. *See* Holocaust
Fiorenza, Elisabeth Schüssler, 53
Fire, 150–53, 161, 205; as religious symbol, 163–64n
Flag Day, 70, 79–80
Floods: biblical, 222–25; Great Flood of '93, 225–29, 232, 239
Food production, 183
Forgiveness, 63n, 105, 109
Fort McHenry, 129, 137
Franklin, Benjamin, 236–37, 242n
Freedom, 2, 29, 32, 37–38, 95, 112, 129, 131, 147, 205, 219; religion and, 134–35, 137; of religious expression, 129, 131–33; of speech, 86n, 115n; Wiesel's views on, 198, 215
Frost, Robert, 229
Fuhrman, Mark, 145

Gallup, George H., Jr., 68, 93–94; *The Saints among Us,* 83–84, 94, 96, 106–13
Garreau, Joel: *The Nine Nations of America,* 114n
Gates, Daryl, 153
Gay men and women, 47, 167, 185
Generation X, 55
Genocide, 26, 167, 169; Armenian, 185; in Cambodia, 185; in Rwanda, 185; as state policy, 184

God, 39, 53, 56, 58, 61n, 64n, 77–78,
105–6, 129, 135, 137, 144, 180, 209–
11; acts of, 150; fire as symbol for, 152;
functional status of, 189; gratitude to,
110, Hasidic views of, 211–12; of his-
tory, 169, 172–74, 181, 187–88; and
the Holocaust, 199; as Holy Nothing-
ness, 172–73; judgment of, 223; protest
against, 212; silence of, 200; as *Sophia*
(Wisdom), 65n; word of, 222
Golay, Michael: *Where America Stands*,
1996, 113–19nn
Golden Rule, 51, 104
Goldhagen, Daniel, 193n
Goldman, Kim, 146
Goldman, Ronald, 144, 146, 148
Good Life and Its Discontents, The
(Samuelson), 117n
Good Samaritan, 111
Grace, 39, 238–39
Graham, Billy, 144
Great Depression, 142
Greene, Bob, 79
Greer, Roosevelt, 144
Guilt, 104
Guns, 66n, 100
Gutierrez, Luis, 79

Hackney, Sheldon, 139n
Hadaway, Kirk, 119n
Halverson, Richard C., 145
Hamilton, William, 170, 192n
Hamlet (Shakespeare), 126
Hampton, Christopher, 123
Hanley, Barbara, 45–49, 60n
Happiness, 103, 115n, 117n
Harlans, Latasha, 164n
Hasidism, 211–12, 214–15
Hate, 36, 166, 201, 204, 214–15
Heaven, 64n, 105
Heaven's Gate cult, 45, 66n
Hedonism, 50
Hegel, Georg Wilhelm Friedrich, 180
Hell, 105–6, 199
Helstock, Yehezkel, 215
Helstock, Yehiel-Meir Halevy, 214–15
Heritage Foundation, 74
Heroes, 94, 98, 112
Herrnstein, Richard J., 186; *The Bell
Curve*, 186, 194n

Hershiser, Orel, 1, 7–11, 16–17, 18n
Heschel, Susannah, 53
Hewitt, Hugh, 57
Highlands Institute for American Reli-
gious Thought (HIART), 127–28,
130
Hindus, 57, 168
Hiroshima, 34
History, 4, 77, 126, 128, 134, 156, 160,
175, 189, 230; Jewish, 173; as slaughter
bench, 180
Hitler, Adolf, 167, 173, 206; resistance
against, 177
Holidays: American, 58, 70; religious, 64n
Holliday, George, 153
Holocaust, 26–28, 67n, 166–68, 195; and
advance of civilization, 175; and the
American Dream, 32–33, 200–202; and
Christian-Jewish relations, 130; definition of, 167; meanings of the word,
167; opinion polls about, 197–98, 215n;
other names for, 167; questions raised
by, 205–6; as theme in Rich's poetry,
21–22; in thought of Rubenstein, 168–
81, 184–85, 189; in thought of Wiesel,
197–212, 214–15
Homelessness, 30, 147
hooks, bell, 53
Hoover, Herbert, 129
Hoover, Stewart M., 45–49, 60n, 61n
Hope, 137, 157, 160, 208, 213, 219, 228–
29; for American life, 15; and despair,
210; personal dimensions of, 103; public
dimensions of, 73; as theme in *Sunset
Boulevard*, 123
Howe, Julia Ward, 75, 87n
Hughes, Langston, 35–36
Humanities, 126–27

Identity, 8–9, 22, 28, 59, 167–68; Ameri-
can, 13, 30, 91–93, 202; Jewish, 45, 174,
179; religious, 54; shared, 14
Identity politics, 31
Immigration, 23, 34, 67n, 182–83
Index of Leading Cultural Indicators, The
(Bennett), 74–75
Indifference, 104, 132, 197–98, 204, 209,
213
Individualism, 95, 173
"In God We Trust," 192n

Institute for Christian and Jewish Studies (ICJS), 129-30
Integrity, 101
Interdependence, 3, 11, 32, 40, 103, 110, 121, 142, 204, 209, 213; Sereny's views on, 27-28
Internet, 61n, 64n, 66n, 233; pornography on, 115n
Interpretation, 3, 17, 28, 126-31
Into That Darkness (Sereny), 27-28, 40
Invisibility, 31, 36
Invisible Man (Ellison), 29-31, 35
Ireland, Patricia, 79
Ireland: famine in, 185
Isaac, 209
Isaiah, 201, 222
Islam, 45, 47
Israel, Maggid of Kozhenitz, 211
Israelis, 168
Ito, Lance A., 145

Jackson, Jesse, 227
Jackson, Robert H., 42n
Jacobs, Steven, 161
James, Henry, 31
James, William, 12, 17n; *The Varieties of Religious Experience*, 111
Japan, 33, 100
Jefferson, Thomas, 178
Jehovah's Witnesses, 167
Jen, Gish: *Typical American*, 92
Jennings, Peter, 50, 61n
Jessup, David, 160
Jesus, 62n, 111, 176, 188, 222
Jesus Christ Superstar (Webber), 122
Jews, 22, 26, 33, 45, 93, 107, 167, 172-73, 176; abandonment of, 34, 204; charged with deicide, 176; demonization of, 176
Job, 174, 209
Jobe, Frank, 1, 7, 17
John Paul II: *Crossing the Threshold of Hope*, 50
Johnson, Elizabeth, 65n; *She Who Is*, 50
Jones, Timothy: *The Saints among Us*, 83-84, 94, 96, 106-13
Jordan, Michael, 94-95
Joseph and the Amazing Technicolor Dreamcoat (Webber), 122
Judaism, 187. *See also* Hasidism; Jews; Traditions
Judeo-Roman War, 176

Jungian psychology, 52
Justice, 3, 17-18n, 20, 28, 32, 71-72, 75, 85, 140n, 155, 173, 181, 233; as biblical theme, 209-10; and O. J. Simpson trials, 146-47; and Pledge of Allegiance, 77

Karlin, Joyce A., 164n
Kaskaskia Island, 226-27, 241n
Kemmis, Daniel, 77, 88n
Keneally, Thomas: *Schindler's List*, 126
Kennedy, John F., 228-29
Key, Francis Scott, 129, 192n
Kim, Peter: *The Day Americans Told the Truth*, 90, 94-113, 113-19nn; *The Second American Revolution*, 95-96
King, Rodney, 142, 144, 152-55, 160, 162-63, 164n, 166
Knowledge, 123-26
Koon, Stacey C., 152, 154
Korematsu v. United States, 41n
Koresh, David, 46
Kosmin, Barry, 56-57, 119n

Lachman, Seymour, 56-57, 119n
Land, 76-77
Lange, Tom, 145
Language, 4, 76-78, 93, 155-56, 197, 207-8
Laughter, 85-86, 211
Laumann, Edward O., 99
Law, 58, 134; equal protection under, 33
Lazarus, Emma, 34
Lee, Howard, 149
Leisure time, 233-37; decline of, 233-35, 242n; and shopping, 235
Lerner, Michael, 164n
Les Miserables (play), 37
Levi-Yitzhak of Berditchev, 211
Lewy, Guenter, 241n
Liberty, 3, 17-18n, 29, 40, 71-72, 85, 181; and Pledge of Allegiance, 77; religious, 46, 135-36
Life (magazine), 62-63n
Limbaugh, Rush, 141n
Lincoln, Abraham, 29, 112, 192n
Listening, 15, 94, 103, 128, 150, 155-57, 160, 195
Literature, 126
Loneliness, 84, 93, 95, 126, 161
Lorde, Audre, 53

Los Angeles, Calif., 23–24, 122–23, 142–166, 182
Los Angeles Times, 7–9, 16, 47, 149, 151, 154, 163n
Love, 20, 36–37, 39, 173
Loyalty, 19, 21, 26, 32, 36, 51, 68, 82, 96, 121, 123, 147, 191, 232, 237, 240; focus of, 75–76; nature of, 3–4; and promises, 71–72; and religion, 59; and things that matter most, 14
Lying, 101, 104

Machacek, David W., 66n
Maclean, Norman: *A River Runs Through It,* 238–40
Madonna, 75, 94–95
Maier, Hans, 178–79. *See also* Améry, Jean
Majdanek, 199
Manzanar, 33
Maps/mapping, 20–22, 40, 72, 94–95, 102, 107, 169, 232
Markey, Patrick, 238
Marler, Penny Long, 119n
Mars, 47
Martinez, Al, 151, 163n
Marx, Karl, 109
Maryland, 131
Masumoto, David Mas, 88n
Materialism, 93, 235
McFague, Sallie, 53
Meaning, 1, 3, 15, 84, 93, 191; and economic consumption, 236, 242n; religious, 171–72; search for, 50–52, 212–15
Meisler, Stanley, 182
Memorialization, 67n
Memory, 15, 22, 31, 58, 67n, 73, 121, 168, 170, 182, 200, 205
Menahem-Mendl of Kotzk, 211–12
Mending the world, 202–5, 212
Methods, 12–13; in public opinion polls, 48, 97–98, 107–9, 113–14nn, 119n
Mfume, Kweisi, 88n
Miles, Margaret R., 66–67n
Miller, Katie, 158
Million Man March, 45
Mine Eyes Have Seen the Glory (Balmer), 57
Minnich, Richard, 151
Mississippi River, 226–29, 238

Missouri River, 226–29, 238
Modernization, 185
Mohammed, 188
Momaday, N. Scott, 76–77, 88n
Money, 185, 236–37; time as, 237
Monotheism, 187–88
Moore, Thomas, 52–53; *Care of the Soul,* 52
Moral authority, 94–95
Moral consensus, 95
Moral crisis, 56, 74, 96
Morality, 59–60, 85, 158, 180, 208; religion's affect on, 133, 229
Moral Majority, 45
Mormons, 93
Moses, 144, 188, 209, 221
Moyers, Bill, 57
Muktananda of Ganeshpuri, 166, 190
Multiculturalism, 30
Murals, 22, 40, 95, 137, 169, 232
Murder, 99–100, 104, 144–48, 212
Murray, Cecil L. "Chip," 161
Murray, Charles, 186; *The Bell Curve,* 186, 194n
Muslims, 56, 93, 107, 168
Mysticism, 172
Myths, 1, 128

Nagasaki, 34
Nahman of Bratzlav, 211
Narratives, 1, 14, 16–17, 18n, 31, 128
National Anthem ("The Star-Spangled Banner"), 71, 88n, 129
National Association for the Advancement of Colored People (NAACP), 79–80, 88n
National conversation, 139n
National decline, 102–4
Nationalism, 184, 206
National Survey of Religious Identification (NSRI), 56–57
Nation of Islam, 45
Naturalization, 67n
Nazi Germany, 22, 26, 34, 43n, 167, 173, 197–98, 204, 215; as genocidal state, 176–77, 201; occupation of Austria, 179
Needs, 17, 26, 44, 72, 93, 105, 112; particularity of, 9, 22; public expression of, 9; qualities of, 13–14; religious, 87n, 126, 148, 169, 177, 200, 205, 230,

240; and self-interest, 76. *See also*
Private/public distinction; Selfhood
Neumann, Jim, 150–51
Neutrality, 204, 209
New beginnings, 32, 40, 88n, 219, 230
Newspapers, 45–50; circulation, 60n;
readership, 48
Newsweek (magazine), 50, 55, 60n, 61n,
63n, 74, 79, 118n, 163n; poll about O. J.
Simpson criminal trial, 163n
Newton, John, 75, 87n
New Yorker, 29–30
New York Times, 46, 64n, 92
Nichols, Nick, 149–50
Niebuhr, Gustav, 46
Night (Wiesel), 197, 200, 202–3, 206,
216n
Nihilism, 50, 164n
Nine Nations of America, The (Garreau),
114n
Noah, 223–27, 229–30, 239
Norris, Kathleen, 88n
Nuremberg Laws, 179

Oath, The (Wiesel), 212–13
Office of Special Investigations, 34
Oklahoma City bombing, 47
Olympic Games (Atlanta, 1996), 47
"On the Pulse of Morning" (Angelou),
219, 229–30; as expression of religion
in public, 230
Openness, 15, 195, 206, 209, 240
Opinion polls, 34, 41n, 48–49, 60n, 61–
64n, 66n, 81, 90–113, 113–20nn, 121,
133; about the Holocaust, 197–98, 215n
Opportunity, 28–29
Optimism, 32, 75, 101, 109, 117n, 160, 180
Overworked American, The (Schor), 233–37

Page, William Tyler, 87n
Pagels, Elaine, 53
Palestinians, 168
Paradox, 102–3
Parents, 54
Parker, Lance Jerome, 154
Parochialism, 11
Patriotism, 102
Patterson, James: *The Day Americans Told
the Truth,* 90, 94–113, 113–19nn; *The
Second American Revolution,* 95–96

Paul, Saint, 188
Peace, 147, 162, 225
Pearl Jam, 75
Pearson, Linnea Juanita, 161
Peirce, Charles Sanders, 17n
Personal vs. national well-being, 102–3
Pessimism, 117n, 128, 190
Phantom of the Opera, The (Webber), 122
Philanthropy, 102, 109, 116–17n
Philosophy, 25–26, 58, 126, 205; Ameri-
can, 12, 17n
Picou, Ben, 227
Plaschke, Bill, 8, 16–17
Plato, 26
Pledge of Allegiance, 69–72, 76–78
Pluralism, 55, 83, 128, 130; religious, 84,
87n, 93, 130–31, 160–63
Poetry, 20–22, 36, 155–57, 229–30
Poland, 167, 214–15. *See also* Auschwitz;
Holocaust
Police brutality, 153
Politics, 58, 83, 118–19n, 134, 175; of
conversion, 164n
Population: American, 40n, 56, 91–92,
108, 114n; elimination, 175, 184–85;
plight of world's children, 193n; surplus,
175, 181–90, 231; world, 181
Pornography, 115n
Posey, Bill, 232
Poverty, 102, 117n, 133, 181–82, 188, 194n
Powell, Laurence M., 152–54
Prayer, 8–9, 62–63n, 144–45, 147–48, 199,
227; in schools, 63n, 132
Private/public distinction, 4, 18, 21, 44,
115n, 138, 169, 171, 177, 200, 213, 230,
240; in Hershisher's career, 8–9; and
the Pledge of Allegiance, 71–72; and
prayer, 147; and self-interest, 76; and
society, 75; and talk about religion, 5–6,
14, 22, 51; and the soul, 52–53. *See also*
Needs; Selfhood
Progress, 175, 187, 190
Promise Keepers, 47
Prosperity, 56, 162, 225
Protest, 26, 199, 210–12, 227
Providence, 187, 190
Public intellectuals, 128
Public interest, 5, 75
Pulp Fiction (film), 57
Purposes, 1, 128

Quay, James, 40n
Questions, 54, 147, 152, 154–55, 163, 224, 227, 237–41, 242n; and the American Dream, 178; and economics, 237; and the Holocaust, 32–33; about perspectives, 22–23, 26–27, 40; and racism, 36; about religion, 13–15, 112, 150, 166; in *Sunset Boulevard*, 126, 138; Wiesel and, 200, 205–7

Rabbit at Rest (Updike), 37–39
Rabbit Is Rich (Updike), 37–39
Rabbit Redux (Updike), 37–38
Rabbit Run (Updike), 37–38
Raccoon River, 228
Race Matters (West), 164–65n
Racism, 18n, 43n, 102, 159, 206; and the American Dream, 82; antisemitic/Nazi, 167, 176, 184, 201; Ellison and, 30, 35; intelligence and, 186; permanence of, in U.S., 165n; Rodney King and, 153; and O. J. Simpson trials, 146–47
Radelfinger, Martin, 45–49, 60n
Ratanassra, Havanpola, 162
Razaf, Andy, 43n
Reagan, Ronald, 38
Reality, 1–2, 172, 178
Redfield, James: *The Celestine Prophecy*, 50
Redford, Robert, 238
Reeves, Thomas C.: *The Empty Church*, 120n
Refugees, 182
Regret, 103
Reich, Robert B., 237, 239; "vestigial thinking," 230–32; *The Work of Nations*, 230–33
Relativism, 128
Religion: against itself, 195, 206, 212; attendance at religious observances, 57, 62n, 84, 87n, 106, 119n, 202; biblical, 172; books about, 50–57; children and, 47, 53–54; critics of, 59; defining themes of, 123; definition of, 1, 4; destructive aspects of, 133, 166, 240; dissonance and, 189; evaluation of, 59, 133, 135; as force for good, 133; importance of, 131, 134, 233, 240; indifference toward, 132; institutional, 62n; "mainstreaming" of news about, 49; morality and,

57; in movies, 57, 66–67n; in music, 57–58, 60; national holidays and, 58; Native American, 93; New Age, 54, 93; newspaper and magazine coverage of, 45–50, 61–64n; nontraditional expressions of, 5, 10; nonverbal expressions of, 4; philanthropy and, 61–62n, 109, 116–17n; politics and, 118–19n; public expressions of, 5–6, 9–10, 134, 166, 181, 189–90, 227, 229, 240; in public life, 10, 44; questions about, 199; as remedy for nation's problems, 119n; revival of, 186; as social and public activity, 135; as source of energy, 111; study of, 126; as therapeutic device, 117n; triage and, 187–88; trivialization of, 132, 134; women and, 53, 65n, 107
Religious Critic in American Culture, The (Dean), 127–28
Religious critics, 128
Religious harassment, 141n
Remnick, David, 29–30
Republic, 72–73, 77
Responsibility, 129; civic, 110; God's, 203–4; humanity's, 203–4; moral, 102, 232–33
Reverence, 74
Rhetoric, 58
Rich, Adrienne, 19–23; *An Atlas of the Difficult World*, 20–22
Riegner, Gerhart, 21
Right and wrong, 94–95, 135
Rights, 181; civil, 133, 154; functional status of, 178, 180; human, 29, 166, 175–81; individual, 34, 178; natural, 178–80; and public expressions of religion, 181; unalienable, 178–80
Riordan, Richard, 144
Riots, 143, 152–63
Rituals, 1, 128, 196
River Jordan, 222
River Runs Through It, A (Maclean), 238–40; theme of help in, 239
Rivers, 221–22, 225, 229–30, 237, 240. *See also individual names*
Roberts, Sam: *Who We Are*, 92–93
Robinson, John, 242n
Role models, 94
Rollyson, Carl: *Where America Stands, 1996*, 113–19nn

Roma (Gypsies), 167
Roman Catholics, 93, 131
Roof, Wade Clark, 54–55
Roosevelt, Franklin D., 33
Roosevelt, Theodore, 86–87n, 192n
Rosove, John L., 161
Ross, Betsy, 70
Roth, Lyn, 7
Roth, Sarah, 202–4
Rousett, David, 203
Royce, Josiah, 12, 17n
Rubenstein, Richard L., 168–76, 178–95;
    After Auschwitz, 169–75, 184, 190–91,
    191–92nn; *The Age of Triage*, 184–90;
    The Cunning of History, 175, 178, 184;
    on Holocaust as holy war, 193n; the-
    ology of, 170–75; views about human
    rights, 178; views about surplus people,
    184–85
Ruether, Rosemary Radford, 53
Russell, Letty, 53
Ryan, Allan S., Jr., 34–35

Sages and Dreamers (Wiesel), 214–15
Saintliness, 111–12
Saints, 107–13; "supersaints," 108
Saints among Us, The (Gallup and Jones),
    83–84, 94, 96, 106–13
Samuelson, Robert J.: *The Good Life and
    Its Discontents*, 117n
Sandburg, Carl, 78–79, 85–86
Sanders, Scott Russell, 88n
Satan, 106, 118n
Schindler's List (film and novel), 57, 126,
    168
Schor, Juliet B., 239; *The Overworked
    American*, 233–37
Schuller, Robert, 146
Schulte, Eduard, 21
Schwartz, Murray, 126
Science, 47, 64n, 135
Scoggin, Danny, 149
Scoggin, Jean, 149–50
Search for Meaning, The (Berman), 50–52
Searching, 11, 14, 19, 50–52
Second American Revolution, The (Patter-
    son and Kim), 95–96
Segregation, 133; of Jews, 177
Seib, Al, 149
Self-contradiction, 103
Self-evident truths, 178, 201

Selfhood, 17, 26, 44, 93, 105, 112, 126,
    200, 240; Angelou's views on, 230;
    individualism and, 173; and Nazism,
    177; public dimensions of, 21, 71–
    72; qualities of, 13–14; religion and,
    169; and self-interest, 76; stories and,
    138. *See also* Needs; Private/public
    distinction
Self-interest, 75–76, 232
Selfishness, 76, 96, 102, 117n, 228
Sellars, Peter, 157–58
Senses of the sacred, 3, 13, 26, 68, 157;
    American, 3–4, 61n
Sense(s) of the whole, 1–5, 13, 68, 96, 171;
    American, 17n, 82; the sacred in it, 1,
    3–5, 31–32, 36, 51, 76, 82, 90, 121, 123,
    128, 181, 237, 240; search for, 90
Separation of church and state, 12, 64n,
    132, 134, 136, 139n, 192n
Serbia, 168
Sereny, Gitta: *Into That Darkness*, 27–28,
    40
Sermons, 47, 160–63
Service, 90, 96, 110, 140n
Sex, 59, 99
Sexual abuse, 100
Shakespeare, William: *Hamlet*, 126
Shame, 104
Shapiro, Robert, 145
Sharing, 19, 90, 148, 159, 205, 209, 219,
    240; and American stories, 121; of in-
    terpretations, 126–31; and meaning,
    212–13; and talk about religion, 10–11,
    13–16, 127
She Who Is (Johnson), 50
Shoah. See Holocaust
Silence, 123, 156, 172, 179, 224; the need
    to break, 44; religion and, 4; and talk
    about religion, 82; as theme in *The
    Oath*, 213; "things unspoken," 168–69,
    191; Wiesel and, 197, 200
Simon Wiesenthal Center, 168
Simpson, Nicole Brown, 144, 146, 148
Simpson, O. J., 144–48; "trial of the
    century," 145
Sin, 47, 104, 106, 171
Slavery, 91, 133
Small groups, 126–31, 139n
Smith, Anna Deavere: *Twilight: Los
    Angeles, 1992*, 155–62, 164n
Smith, Samuel, 75, 87–88n

Snyder, Tom, 79–80, 83
Sobibor, 27
Social Darwinism, 194n
Sociology, 175
Sollod, Robert N., 84–85
Sophie's Choice (Styron), 32–33, 36–37
Soul, 52–53
Southern Baptists, 93
Spain, 100
Speth, James Gustav, 181
Spielberg, Steven: *Schindler's List,* 57, 126, 168
Spiritual crisis, 138n
Spiritual culture, 1, 5, 128
Sports, 9–10, 49
Springsteen, Bruce, 228
Stalin, Joseph, 185
Stangl, Franz, 27
"Star-Spangled Banner, The." *See* National Anthem
Statue of Liberty, 34
Stegner, Wallace, 225
Stories, 13, 19, 46–47, 111, 121–26, 128, 142, 155–63, 209, 240; American, 225–29; biblical, 220–25, 239; Exodus, 144, 221; flood, 222–29; Genesis, 222–25; of help, 150, 156–57; John the Baptist and Salome, 124; Joseph, 214; Noah, 223–27, 239; Samson and Delilah, 122, 124–25
Styron, William: *Sophie's Choice,* 32–33, 36–37
Suicide, 21, 37, 45, 100, 180, 213
Sumner, William Graham, 194n
Sunset Boulevard (Webber), 121–27, 131, 137–38, 138n
Supreme Court decisions, 12, 33, 42n
Swanson, Gloria, 138n

Talk about religion: absence of, 82, 84–85; in America, 1, 5–6, 10–12, 14, 27, 40, 44, 49, 58, 68–69, 121, 239–40; deepening, 219–40; defined, 4–5; difficulty of, 97; divisive, 141n; evaluation of, 5, 19, 166, 191; and freedom, 240; Holocaust and, 168, 199–201; how to, 195–215; humanities and, 127; importance of, 74, 76, 82, 90, 96–97, 112–13, 120n, 155–56, 159–60, 163, 213, 219, 233, 240, 242n; inadequacy of, 14; as "the last taboo," 51; paradox about, 6, 44; prayer

and, 147–48; private, 5, 14; in public, 9–10, 44, 68; public, 5, 10, 14–15; quality of, in America, 14, 44–45, 49, 51–52, 68–69; quantity of, in America, 14, 44, 49, 58, 68–69; social nature of, 5; and stories of help, 150; unavoidability of, 46, 59; unexpected, 5–10, 13, 44, 47, 58; varieties of, 10–12, 49; wrong kinds of, 14, 166, 171, 176, 187–88
Taxes, 105
Tears, 161, 202, 215
Technology, 175–77, 185, 231–33
Television, 50, 57, 100, 146, 153, 196; CNBC, 79–82; program rating system, 114–15n; talks shows, 196–200; V-chip, 115n
Ten Commandments, 106
Theater, 155
Theology: Christian, 204; of covenant and election, 187–88; and dissonance, 189; flood, 227; radical, 170; relevance of, 171
Theories, 1, 128
Things that matter most, 2–4, 15, 51, 90, 121, 128, 147, 155, 157, 195, 237, 240
Third Reich. *See* Nazi Germany
Thomas, Cal, 79
Thompson, Hunter S.: *Fear and Loathing in Las Vegas,* 69–70
Thoreau, Henry David, 17n
Thum, Nancy, 7
Time (magazine), 50, 63–64n, 79, 170
Tocqueville, Alexis de, 131–33; *Democracy in America,* 131
Torture, 179–80
Traditions, 1, 54, 128, 182, 205, 219, 232; American, 17–18n, 72, 76; Christian, 204; Jewish, 21, 173, 190, 211–12; religious, 84, 161, 171, 191, 230
Treblinka, 26–27, 34, 199, 201
Triage, 184–89
Trust, 90, 169; loss of, 101, 104, 129, 179, 240
Tule Lake, 33–34
Turenne, Veronique de, 64–65n
Twentysomethings, 55
Twilight: Los Angeles, 1992 (Smith), 155–62, 164n; as public expression of religion, 157
2-Live Crew, 75
Typical American (Jen), 92

Uelmen, Gerald F., 145
Understanding, 11, 13, 44, 90, 159, 200, 205–8, 240
Unforgiven (film), 57
Unitarians, 56–57
United Nations Development Program (UNDP), 181
United Nations Fund for Population Activities, 182
Unity, 70–71, 77, 90–91, 139n, 159
Unsettling of America, The (Berry), 77
Updike, John, 37–40, 72; *Rabbit at Rest*, 37–39; *Rabbit Is Rich*, 37–39; *Rabbit Redux*, 37–38; *Rabbit Run*, 37–38
U.S. census, 23, 91–93, 121
U.S. Census Bureau, 40–41n
U.S. Constitution, 32, 42n, 46, 58, 71–72, 91, 135–36, 161, 229; First Amendment, 132, 136
U.S. Department of Justice, 34, 154
U.S. Holocaust Memorial Museum, 33, 58, 67n, 168, 200–202, 215–16nn
U.S. Immigration and Naturalization Service, 67n
U.S. News and World Report (magazine), 50, 61–62n

Valentino, Rudolf, 124
van Buren, Paul, 170, 192n
Vannatter, Philip, 145
Varieties of Religious Experience, The (James), 111
"Very religious" Americans, 106–7
Vietnam War, 38, 45, 86n, 101, 133
Violence, 3, 57, 96, 100, 104, 166, 223; technicians of, 178
Virtue, 4, 68, 73–75, 85
Volunteerism, 104–5, 140n

Wallace, Amy, 149
Wallace, Jane, 79–80, 83
Waller, Thomas "Fats," 43n
War criminals, 34–35
Washington, George, 70, 91
Washington, D.C., 33, 40, 200–201, 229, 238
Water, 221–22, 225, 228–29, 237
Watergate, 101
Wealth, 98, 181, 188; American, 231; concentration of, 232
Webber, Andrew Lloyd, 121–23; *Jesus Christ Superstar*, 122; *Joseph and the Amazing Technicolor Dreamcoat*, 122; *The Phantom of the Opera*, 122; *Sunset Boulevard*, 121–27, 131, 137–38, 138n
Weber, Max, 175
Wehmeyer, Peggy, 50
Welch, Reginald, 141n
West, Cornel, 158; *Race Matters*, 164–65n
West, Nathanael, 142–43, 153; *The Day of the Locust*, 142–44, 162
"When the Saints Go Marching In," 113, 165n
Where America Stands, 1996 (Golay and Rollyson), 113–19nn
White, Gayle, 220
Whitehead, Alfred North, 17n
Who We Are (Roberts), 92–93
Wiesel, Elie, 195–215, 215–17nn, 221, 223; *The Accident*, 202–5; on despair, 205; on friendship, 212–13; on Hasidism, 211–12; on indifference, 197–98, 204, 209; key themes in thought of, 205–15; on language, 207–8; *Night*, 197, 200, 202–3, 206, 216n; *The Oath*, 212–13; with Oprah Winfrey, 197–200; on questions, 206–7; on remembering, 201; *Sages and Dreamers*, 214–15; views about God, 199
Wilder, Billy: *Sunset Boulevard*, 138n
Williams, Damian, 154
Williams, Willie L., 147
Wilson, Woodrow, 70
Wind, Timothy E., 152
Wind, 151–52
Winfrey, Oprah, 195–200
Woodward, Kenneth L., 62n
Work, 100, 188, 230–37; and American spending, 233–36; significance of, 104; week, 235–36; women and, 236
Work of Nations, The (Reich), 230–33
World War I, 70
World War II, 21–22, 33, 35, 71, 230
Worldwatch Institute, 183
Worship, 57, 84, 119n, 135
Wuthnow, Robert, 62n, 116–18nn, 120n, 139–40n, 242n
Wyman, David S., 34

Yugoslavia, 47, 168, 185

Zyklon B, 177

J O H N   K .   R O T H is the Russell K. Pitzer Professor of Philosophy at Claremont McKenna College. He is the author or editor of more than twenty books, including *The American Religious Experience: The Roots, Trends, and Future of American Theology* (with Frederick Sontag), *American Dreams: Meditations on Life in the United States, A Consuming Fire: Encounters with Elie Wiesel and the Holocaust,* and *Approaches to Auschwitz: The Holocaust and Its Legacy* (with Richard L. Rubenstein). In 1988, he was named U.S. National Professor of the Year by the Council for Advancement and Support of Education (CASE) and the Carnegie Foundation for the Advancement of Teaching.

WITHDRAWN

DATE DUE

GAYLORD			PRINTED IN U.S.A.